William Stirling-Maxwell

Annals of the Artists of Spain - A New Edition Incorporating the Author's Own Notes, Additions and Emendations

Volume the First

William Stirling-Maxwell

Annals of the Artists of Spain - A New Edition Incorporating the Author's Own Notes, Additions and Emendations
Volume the First

ISBN/EAN: 9783337279707

Printed in Europe, USA, Canada, Australia, Japan

Cover: Foto ©ninafisch / pixelio.de

More available books at **www.hansebooks.com**

ANNALS

OF THE

ARTISTS OF SPAIN

BY

SIR WILLIAM STIRLING-MAXWELL
BARONET

A New Edition
INCORPORATING THE AUTHOR'S OWN NOTES
ADDITIONS AND EMENDATIONS

With Portrait and Twenty-four Steel and Mezzotint Engravings
ALSO NUMEROUS ENGRAVINGS ON WOOD

IN FOUR VOLUMES
VOLUME THE FIRST

LONDON
JOHN C. NIMMO
14, KING WILLIAM STREET, STRAND
MDCCCXCI

*Theirs was the skill, rich colour and clear light
To weave in graceful forms by fancy dream'd,
So well that many a shape and figure bright,
Though flat, in sooth, reliev'd and rounded seem'd.
And hands, deluded, vainly strove to clasp
Those airy nothings mocking still their grasp.*

DEDICATION OF THE FIRST EDITION.

To the Reader.

Many Alterations and Additions made by my father, and referred to in the Editor's Preface, have been carefully incorporated in this New Edition of his Works; and the Illustrations now added are chosen from many which he had collected for that purpose.

JOHN STIRLING-MAXWELL.

POLLOK, *Sept.* 1890.

ILLUSTRATIONS

VOLUME THE FIRST.

	PAGE
GENERAL TITLE-PAGE—*Design for an Altar. From a drawing by Alonso Cano, drawn on stone*	i
SIR WILLIAM STIRLING-MAXWELL, BARONET. *From a portrait by George Richmond, R.A., at Keir; engraved on copper by R. B. Parkes*	Frontispiece
VASE OF LILIES. *H. Golzius*	xiv
IRON CROSS *on a Church at Mirando del Ebro*	xxxiv
SEAL OF DON JOHN OF AUSTRIA. *From a paper addressed to " nos bons amis les bourgeois pères et echevins de Beaumont," 23rd April 1578, in the Collection of T. Weigel, Leipzig* . .	xlviii
IRON CROSS *at Toledo*	80
IRON CROSS *on the Belfry of the Convent at Almeria, in the Cork Wood near Gibraltar*	114
A WOMAN'S HAND, *known as* La Mano de la Teta; *supposed to be a fragment of the Statue of the Virgin executed by Torrigiano*	127
ALONSO BERRUGUETE. *From a panel in the Silleria del Coro, formerly in San Benito el Real, at Valladolid, and now (1849) in the Museo there. From the author's own sketch, which he lent to Mr. Thomas Macquoid to make a drawing for the head in the Renaissance Court in the Crystal Palace, Sydenham, 1854* .	160
SIGNATURE OF JUAN DE YCIAR	172
IRON CROSS *on a Stone Pillar at Illescas* . .	199

ILLUSTRATIONS.

	PAGE
DON GASPAR DE GUZMAN, COUNT OF OLIVARES. *Engraved in mezzotint on copper by R. B. Parkes*	249
IRON CROSS AND VANE *on one of the towers of the Lonja at Seville* .	267
DOMENICO THEOTOCOPULI, *known as El Greco. From a picture by himself, now at Keir; engraved on steel by H. Adlard* . . .	328
DAUGHTER OF THEOTOCOPULI, *painted by her father; now at Keir. Engraved in mezzotint on copper by R. B. Parkes* . .	338
IRON CROSS *near the Hospital of St. John Baptist at Toledo*	360

Ornamental Escutcheon, designed by Jean de Laune, and engraved by Etienne de Laune, 1578;—the Arms of Stirling-Maxwell inserted instead of the Artist's Name.

PREFACE TO THE PRESENT EDITION.

HE importance of this work, still the most complete general survey of Spanish art, seemed to warrant its republication; and this appeared fully justified as well by the scarcity and consequent high price of the original edition as by the prominence to which the subject has risen in public estimation.

During the last thirty years of his life, the accomplished author made numerous corrections and alterations in both the text and the notes, besides inserting copious additions; and all these are now carefully incorporated.

With many additions which the author subsequently made to it, the revised, and, in many passages, rewritten, portion relating to Spain's greatest painter, Velazquez, which he published separately in 1856, is here placed in its proper position; effect being also given to a number of incidental modifications affecting other parts of the work.

As the introductory chapter of that publication involved, in both the matter and the form of the introductory chapter of the "Annals," so many changes to which effect could not possibly be given by mere alteration, it is now printed in the Appendix, the original text being reprinted with merely verbal corrections. The comparison will doubtless be interesting to the student, as showing the changes, on some points, that occurred in the author's views between the dates of the two publications.

Since the work was published, many of the pictures referred to have changed hands or location; but by the aid of the most recent catalogues of the important public galleries, and otherwise, the editor has been able to give the present references to nearly all, as well as to amplify many on other points.

In referring to Ford's "Handbook for Spain," the author chiefly used the first edition, of 1845, but as that has been long out of print, and is practically inaccessible, references are now also given to the third edition, of 1855, which was "entirely revised, with great additions," and is recognised as the best edition of that charming guide-book.

PREFACE.

All the editor's additions in the notes are placed within brackets.

The editor desires to acknowledge the great value of the comprehensive and accurate catalogue of the works of Velazquez and Murillo, by Mr. Charles B. Curtis, as well as of the elaborate and appreciative " Diego Velazquez and his Times," of Professor Carl Justi of Bonn, translated by Professor Keane, works which are both invaluable to the student of Spanish art.

Sir John Stirling-Maxwell, Baronet, of Pollok, and Archibald Stirling, Esquire, of Keir, placed in the editor's hands not only the author's corrected and annotated copies of the works, but also his extensive collection of illustrations of Spanish art, from which the additional plates now given are carefully chosen. They also gave the use of all the original steel and wood engravings, as well as of the ornamental initial letters, &c., selected by the author, and permitted the most free reference to be made to everything in the rich and unique store of literature and art at Keir that could be of service in the preparation of this edition of their distinguished father's work.

For this, and for their uniform courtesy and kindness, as well as for the personal trouble and interest which they have taken, both publisher and editor beg to thank them.

ROBERT GUY.

September, 1890.

PREFACE TO FIRST EDITION.

HERE are but two valid excuses for the publication of a book. One is, that the subject is new, or at least, unexhausted; the other, that the writer is so graced and gifted, that the gentle reader may be supposed willing to tread even a beaten path for the sake of the pleasure of his company. Preferring no claim to the latter plea, I hope to be able to show that these "Annals of the Artists of Spain" are entitled to the benefit of the former. They were first conceived in 1843, in the course of a journey through the delightful land of Velazquez and Murillo; and they were in great part composed before the more cultivated languages on this side the Pyrenees possessed any separate work on Spanish art better than the few books of which I shall now give a brief notice.

The earliest English work on the subject, with which

I am acquainted, is "The Lives of Spanish Painters, Sculptors, and Architects, translated from Velasco," 8vo, London, 1739, a meagre abridgment of the biographical part of the Spanish work of Palomino, and at once scarce and worthless.

The next is "Anecdotes of Eminent Painters in Spain, during the Sixteenth and Seventeenth Centuries, with Cursory Remarks on the Present State of the Arts in that Kingdom;" by Richard Cumberland, 2 vols. 12mo, London, 1782; reprinted, in 1787, without revision or correction, but with a supplementary volume, likewise in 12mo, entitled "Catalogue of Paintings in the King of Spain's Palace at Madrid."

The author, well known as a second-rate novelist, dramatist, and poet, was sent to Spain in 1780, by Lord North, on a secret mission, and resided about a year at Madrid, where his agreeable qualities and pretty daughters rendered him very popular in society. But failing to effect the diplomatic purposes for which he was sent, the Government at home, according to his account, refused to repay him the expenses of his journey, and reduced him to the brink of ruin. His anecdotes were, therefore, drawn up under the pressure of necessity, and rather with a view to the publisher's cash than the author's reputation. Palomino was the author from whom he drew most of his flimsy materials; for, although he acknowledges his obligations to the scarce treatise of Pacheco, he culls nothing from it which he did not find in the pages of Palomino. His work has been justly styled by Bourgoing, "une compilation indigeste, peu digne d'être la sœur des Mesdemoiselles Cumberland."[1] Correcting none of Palomino's numerous errors, he blunders largely and intrepidly on his own account. For instance, he tells us first (vol. ii. p. 32), that Velazquez went to Italy with the ambassador, who was going to bring back the Archduchess Mariana, the second Queen of Philip IV., and soon afterwards (p. 36), that her predecessor, Queen Isabella, had died during Velazquez's absence, leaving us to infer that the King, a pedant in etiquette, had negotiated, and perhaps solemnised his second marriage during the life of his first wife. Describing the familiarity and friendship in which Philip II. lived with his painter Sanchez Coello, he says (vol. i. p. 90), that "in those moments when his temper relaxed into complacency," the King "would mount the ladder (the only one he ever climbed without ambition or disgrace) that privately communicated with the painting-room" of the artist. The words of Palomino, whom he followed, are these, "The King was accustomed often to come to the apartment of Sanchez, *por un transito secreto, con ropa delevantar*,[2] by a secret passage, in his *dressing-gown*," an article of apparel which Cumberland, catching at the sound, and impatient of wasting a moment

---

[1] *Nouveau Voyage en Espagne*, 3 tom. 8vo, Paris, 1789, tom. iii. p. 258.
[2] Palomino, fol. Madrid, 1724, tom. iii. p. 260.

in reaching his dictionary, pleasantly converted into a *ladder*. Besides its inaccuracy, his work also labours under another grave disadvantage, that of having been composed without personal acquaintance, on the author's part, with Valencia and Andalusia, and their rich treasuries of local art. The Catalogue of the King of Spain's galleries at Madrid, made at Cumberland's request by the superintendent of the pictures in the royal palace, though meagre and unsatisfactory, is valuable as a record of the condition of one of the finest collections in Europe before it had been thinned by the pillaging Bonaparte and imbecile Bourbon.

The next work on Spanish art, now somewhat rare, is called "The Life of Bartolomé E. Murillo," compiled from the writings of various authors; translated by Edward Davis, Esq., late Captain in the First Regiment of Life Guards, 8vo, London, 1819, pp. ciii. 183. It is a collection of extracts relating to Murillo from the writings of Cumberland, Bourgoing, D'Argenvilla, Palomino, Ponz, Jovellanos, and Cean Bermudez, some of them translated, and some in the original French or Spanish, and strung together with a few pages and notes by the gallant captain himself. The sole merit of the book consists in the version of Cean Bermudez's Letter on the life and works of Murillo, which, though sufficiently ill done, is not quite so unintelligible as the original compositions of the translator.

Fourteen years after the utterances of the ex-life-guardsman, appeared "A Dictionary of Spanish Painters," comprehending simply that part of their biography immediately connected with the arts; from the fourteenth century to the eighteenth; by A. O'Neil, two parts, 1833-4, pp. xi. 280, 308, with four illustrations. This work seems to be an abridgment of Cean Bermudez's excellent dictionary, although the lady author has not seen fit to entrust the reader with the name of any one of her sources of information. I am sorry to be able to praise nothing in the book but the beauty of the paper and printing.

Even this slender praise must be withheld from the next work on the subject, "The History of the Spanish School of Painting," to which is appended an historical sketch of the rise and progress of the art of miniature illumination, by the author of "Travels through Sicily and the Lipari Islands," the "History of the Azores," and the "History of the Various Styles of Architecture," sm. 8vo, London, 1843, pp. ii. 199. From so voluminous a writer some slight knowledge of his business might have been expected. Yet he cites none of his authorities, and from the gross blunders of his own production, I suspect Mrs. O'Neil's book to have been the only one which he consulted. No Frenchman could have mis-spelt Spanish names with more persevering ingenuity than this historian, who likewise rivals Cumberland in inaccuracy, and Davies in dulness and bad English.

These were the only books on Spanish art in our

in reaching his dictionary, pleasantly converted into a *ladder*. Besides its inaccuracy, his work also labours under another grave disadvantage, that of having been composed without personal acquaintance, on the author's part, with Valencia and Andalusia, and their rich treasuries of local art. The Catalogue of the King of Spain's galleries at Madrid, made at Cumberland's request by the superintendent of the pictures in the royal palace, though meagre and unsatisfactory, is valuable as a record of the condition of one of the finest collections in Europe before it had been thinned by the pillaging Bonaparte and imbecile Bourbon.

The next work on Spanish art, now somewhat rare, is called "The Life of Bartolomé E. Murillo," compiled from the writings of various authors; translated by Edward Davis, Esq., late Captain in the First Regiment of Life Guards, 8vo, London, 1819, pp. ciii. 183. It is a collection of extracts relating to Murillo from the writings of Cumberland, Bourgoing, D'Argenvilla, Palomino, Ponz, Jovellanos, and Cean Bermudez, some of them translated, and some in the original French or Spanish, and strung together with a few pages and notes by the gallant captain himself. The sole merit of the book consists in the version of Cean Bermudez's Letter on the life and works of Murillo, which, though sufficiently ill done, is not quite so unintelligible as the original compositions of the translator.

Fourteen years after the utterances of the ex-life-

PREFACE TO FIRST EDITION.

guardsman, appeared "A Dictionary of Spanish Painters," comprehending simply that part of their biography immediately connected with the arts; from the fourteenth century to the eighteenth; by A. O'Neil, two parts, 1833-4, pp. xi. 280, 308, with four illustrations. This work seems to be an abridgment of Cean Bermudez's excellent dictionary, although the lady author has not seen fit to entrust the reader with the name of any one of her sources of information. I am sorry to be able to praise nothing in the book but the beauty of the paper and printing.

Even this slender praise must be withheld from the next work on the subject, "The History of the Spanish School of Painting," to which is appended an historical sketch of the rise and progress of the art of miniature illumination, by the author of "Travels through Sicily and the Lipari Islands," the " History of the Azores," and the "History of the Various Styles of Architecture," sm. 8vo, London, 1843, pp. ii. 199. From so voluminous a writer some slight knowledge of his business might have been expected. Yet he cites none of his authorities, and from the gross blunders of his own production, I suspect Mrs. O'Neil's book to have been the only one which he consulted. No Frenchman could have mis-spelt Spanish names with more persevering ingenuity than this historian, who likewise rivals Cumberland in inaccuracy, and Davies in dulness and bad English.

These were the only books on Spanish art in our

language when I conceived the design of the present work. Up to that time even the journals of our travellers, our rich periodical literature, and the labours of our encyclopædists afforded, so far as my researches have extended, little worthy of note on the subject, except the brief but accurate accounts of some of the Spanish artists in the second volume of "Sketches in Spain during the Years 1829-1832;" by Captain S. S. Cook (now Widdrington), R.N., &c.; 2 vols. 8vo, London, 1834; an excellent article on the Spanish painters, contributed to the *Foreign Quarterly Review*, No. xxvi., May 1834, by Sir Edmund Head; and an admirable life of Velazquez, for which the *Penny Cyclopædia* is indebted to the pen of Mr. Ford. Two-thirds of the following chapters were written, and the greater part of the materials for the remainder was collected before I was informed that another and a better labourer was turning up the almost virgin soil of my literary field. Had I sooner become aware that Sir Edmund Head had undertaken the task, I would gladly have resigned to his abler hands the care of the tillage, and to his well-established reputation, the undivided honours of a new harvest. The "Handbook of the History of the Spanish and French Schools of Painting," sm. 8vo, London, 1848, pp. xiv. 373, is not only the most complete book on the subject, but is worthy both of the author's cultivated artistic taste and literary skill. Sir Edmund's readers will doubtless regret what I, as a later writer on the same

PREFACE TO FIRST EDITION.

subject, must regard as very fortunate for myself, that the plan of his work demanded brevity and condensation, and compelled the artist, who was best qualified to execute a finished picture, to restrict himself to the production of a sketch. As one of his readers, I may take the liberty of suggesting that his above-mentioned article in the *Foreign Quarterly Review* might be interwoven with advantage into the next edition of his "Handbook."

From a list of English works treating of Spanish art, it would be absurd to omit "The Handbook for Travellers in Spain and Readers at Home," by Richard Ford, post 8vo, London 1845, pp. x. 1064; second edition, 1847, pp. lxii. 645. It would be equally absurd to attempt to say anything new in praise of a book which, put forth with the humblest of all titles and in the least inviting of forms, immediately became one of the most popular books in our language. A cyclopædia of learning on all matters pertaining to the Peninsula, the "Handbook" deserves my gratitude, not only as the most delightful of travelling companions, but as the principal pioneer of my researches in the artistic history of Spain. Although the second edition contains much new and valuable matter, I have chiefly referred to the first, by which indeed Mr. Ford desires to be judged. Yielding to the mistaken wish of his publisher that the volume should be rendered cheaper and more portable, "many are the wild Iberian flowers," says the author in his second edition (p. lvi.), "which have been rooted out, and

more are the old stones of antiquity which have been
removed." These "stones" and "flowers" all readers
of the original work will regret, and they will be little
disposed to approve the self-sacrifice of the writer at the
Albemarle Street shrine. The charming "Gatherings in
Spain," fcap. 8vo, 1846, have certainly preserved some
of the loppings of the "Handbook." But let us hope that
Mr. Ford will some day give us a complete edition of
his unrivalled writings on Spain, worthy of himself and
his subject, and embellished with some of his original
drawings, which prove his pencil to possess no less grace
and vigour than his pen. To these Annals he has kindly
contributed a sketch of the Capuchin convent at Seville,
(p. 1038). to which, I am sorry to say, the woodcutter has
done great injustice. I am also indebted to him for the
use of his rich and rare Spanish prints, drawings, and
library, and for much general advice and assistance,
without which my work would have been disfigured
with far more than its present numerous imperfections.

French literature has done even less for the history of
Spanish art than our own. "The Irish are a very Catholic
people, and by no means malignant in their manners,"
says the Canon Fernandez Navarrete,[1] "yet, of the whole
multitude of them who have come over to Spain, not
one has ever applied himself to the arts, nor to the toils

---

[1] *Conservacion de Monarquias y discursos politicos*, por el Licenciado Pedro Fernandez Navarrete, Canonigo de la Iglesia de Santiago, &c., fol., Madrid, 1626, p. 57.

of husbandry, nor to any occupation but begging." As those Milesian islanders of 1626 had the gift of eschewing useful labour, so Frenchmen, with a few illustrious exceptions, have a peculiar power of not appreciating or understanding foreign genius. In evidence of this their accounts of Spanish art may be cited.

The earliest with which I am acquainted is the *Histoire abregée des plus fameux Peintres, Sculpteurs, et Architectes Espagnols, traduit de l'Espagnol de Palomino Velasco;* sm. 8vo, Paris, 1749, pp. iv. 39, in which the blunders of the old Spaniard have been multiplied by his translator.

Then comes the *Dictionnaire des Peintres Espagnols, par F. Quilliet,* 8vo, Paris, 1816, pp. xxxvii. 407. M. Quilliet resided for many years in Spain, and was keeper of the Royal Gallery of the Escorial during the reign of the intrusive King Joseph; but writing in Paris under the Restoration, he dedicates his Dictionary, in dulcet tones of legitimist loyalty, to the Duke of Berri. *Haz buena farina y no toques bocina,* "Make good flour without blowing a trumpet," says a Castilian proverb much disregarded by M. Quilliet, who heralds his meagre performance with a preface full of flourish and pretension. Confessing that he has taken Cean Bermudez for his guide, he assures us that he himself had consulted all the authorities of that writer. "Je revis tout ce qu' avait vu Cean," he says, and he gives a list of the Spanish books and MSS. cited by the indefatigable Spaniard

But his work affords no evidence of such researches, and I fear that he must endure the imputation of a literary dishonesty, more contemptible than uncommon, of parading as authorities books of which he has never read a line, or perhaps even seen the backs on a library shelf. If he really consulted the curious MSS. of Diaz del Valle, Jusepe Martinez, and the Alfaros, why does he not say where he found them, a fact which ought always to be stated when MSS. are quoted, and in this case of the greater consequence, because the libraries, indicated by Cean Bermudez as possessing these documents, may well be supposed to have been dispersed during the eventful space of time from 1800 to 1816. But whether M. Quilliet did or did not consult the MSS. and rare books with which he claims such intimate acquaintance, it is certain that he has not preserved a single fact of importance which has not already been given to the world by Cean Bermudez, while he has omitted many which that able writer had collected to his hand. The scraps of new information, few and far between, which may be detected by a careful reader in his pages, are rendered of no value at all, because we are not in a condition to judge of their authenticity. For example, at the end of the story of Antonio Pereda and the sham dueña painted by him on a screen to satisfy the fashionable requirements of his lady wife, we are told that that picture was sold for a high price at the artist's death. M. Quilliet did not find this information in Palomino, nor in Cean Bermudez, for neither of them mention the sale; and it is rather too much to expect us to take the unsupported evidence of a French book of 1816 with regard to the prices of a Madrid auction in 1669 or 1670. But for his pretension to original research, I should have briefly dismissed M. Quilliet as a dull and careless translator of Cean Bermudez, a character in which he appeared for the second time, when he induced the Roman Academy of St. Luke to print a work of his entitled *Les Arts Italiens en Espagne, ou histoire des artistes Italiens qui contribuèrent à embellir les Castilles;* fol., Rome, 1824, and published in the same form and at the same date in Italian.

The next French work on the subject is *Vie complète des Peintres Espagnols, et Histoire de la Peinture Espagnole,* par Et. Huard (de l'île Bourbon), *Première Partie;* 8vo, Paris, 1839, pp. 212; *Seconde et dernière Partie,* 1841, pp. 272; with three paltry illustrations, one of which is the portrait, not of Velazquez or Murillo, but of M. Huard. This production was begun, it appears, as a sort of handbook for the Spanish gallery of the Louvre, and panegyric on Baron Taylor, who amassed that colossal collection of bad and spurious pictures. Whatever its pages contain of truth has obviously been taken from M. Quilliet, whose dictionary, and the Louvre catalogues, were probably the only books that M. Huard took the trouble to look into. Borrowing his lives of Spanish painters from M. Quilliet, as Goldsmith's scribbler translated Homer out of Pope, M. Huard has likewise traduced the rival whom he robbed. He condemns the Dictionary as a cold, colourless, and incomplete work, and boasts of his own researches in libraries and cabinets of engravings (p. ii.), prudently, however, omitting to name any collection to which he was indebted, or any author whom he had consulted, except M. Quilliet. But more than this, he has signalised himself by an offence of which I am happy to say our worst English writers on the subject are blameless. To such of his lives as appeared most wanting, in M. Quilliet's pages, in warmth and colour, he has added those agreeable qualities by freely supplying incidents from his own imagination. In the early part of the life of Ribera, for instance, he entertains us by narrating how, being turned out of the school of Ribalta for want of money to pay the customary fee, the young artist wandered about Valencia, sketching in the streets, and how on the evening of the second day he lay down to die in the ruins of a chapel. "Il se mourait donc d'inanition," proceeds this intrepid novelist (p. 6), "quand passa près de lui une jeune femme qui entendit les plaintes que la faim arrachait au pauvre artiste; elle lui donna, d'une main tremblante, non cette aumône du riche mais ce partage du malheureux ; Ribéra eut la force de se lever, il n'était plus seul sur la terre, il avait trouvé une amie et avec elle le bonheur." In short, "cette ange que Dieu avoit envoyée pour le consoler," became his mistress, and lived with him on the funds which he obtained by sign-painting, until she "devait retourner dans sa demeure céleste," and he found means of going to Italy. Not content with thus giving the Valencian a mistress, M. Huard also furnishes him with a grandfather, one Antoine Ribera (p. 11), of whose existence Palomino, Dominici, and Cean Bermudez were profoundly ignorant. If M. Huard has been so fortunate as to discover in some dusty MS. or forgotten book, anecdotes or names which have escaped those writers, why does he not let the world know where the discovery was made; if he is fond of inditing romance, why should he circumscribe his circle of readers, and engender doubts in their minds as to his own sanity, by calling his fictions complete lives of the Spanish painters? His inventions, for such I conclude everything in his book that I have not seen elsewhere to be, are marked by a singular ignorance of the most commonplace things of Spain. Thus, he informs us that Francisco de Solis painted for a certain convent at Madrid a figure of the Virgin, young and beautiful, standing on a dragon with red eyes and flame-vomiting jaws, "afin de produire une de ces oppositions vulgaires qui ne manquent jamais leur effet" (p. 21), as if the symbol of the Evil One, which the etiquette of Spanish painting required to be introduced into that subject, had been a mere tasteless whim of the painter. Having thus displayed his ignorance of Spain and the Bible, he proceeds to narrate with great gravity how all the fine ladies and Phrynes of Madrid rushed to be pourtrayed as Virgins of the Conception, and in some cases compelled Solis to paint their favourite "*bow-wow* (*toutou favori*) cat, or parrot," under the crescent, in place of "Mary's impetuous dragon;" and he crowns the monstrous fable by informing us that Solis was, therefore, called the Painter of Conceptions; the sole foundation of the story being that Solis did paint a picture of the Conception at Madrid, and that the title applied to him was sometimes given to Murillo at Seville. Of course this writer exercises his national privilege of mis-spelling Spanish names and misplacing Spanish titles; of romancing about Estremadura, Toledo, Borgona, and Vargara, and of inventing incidents for the life of Don Guevara, as journalists of France pen paragraphs on Lord Henry Brougham or Sir Peel, and dramatic critics parade their acquaintance with Shakespeare by discoursing of him with playful affection as "le vieux Williams." Even of Italian he takes care to show his ignorance by explaining that the Valencian companions of Ribera called him *Il Espagnoleto*, "en faisant allusion à la facilité prodigieuse avec laquelle il dessinait et composait" (p. 6); as if calling M. Huard "the little Frenchman" would convey any adequate idea of the "prodigious facility" with which he has obscured a fine subject with stupid and impudent fictions.

M. Louis Viardot is the only other French writer on Spanish art whose works deserve notice. Well known as an essayist on the picture galleries of Europe, he has given us, in *Les Musées d'Espagne, d'Angleterre, et de*

Belgique, sm. 8vo, Paris, 1843, pp. x. 382, lively and agreeable sketches of some of the chief Spanish masters. Setting aside the author's "intuitive inspirations," they are light and readable, and, if they do not possess the merit, they are at least not disfigured by an affectation, of learning. M. Viardot is also author of the notices of Spanish painters which form the letterpress to the French collection of engravings known as *La Galerie Aguado*, published in Paris in 1837.

Of the German works which I have consulted, by far the best is Fiorillo's *Geschichte der Mahlerey in Spanien*, pp. x. 470, besides the index, forming vol. iv. of the *Geschichte der zeichnenden Kunst von ihrer Wiederaufalebung bis auf die neuesten Zeiten*, 6 band. 8vo, Göttingen, 1798-1808. It appears to be a careful abstract of Cean Bermudez's Dictionary, and it contains (pp. 464-470) a useful list of Spanish and other books on the subject. In Dr. Kugler's dry and unsatisfactory *Handbuch der Kunstgeschichte*, 8vo, Stuttgart, 1842, pp. xxiv. 917, the five pages devoted to the masters of Spain are, like most of his other pages, a mere catalogue of names. But even so much as this is not to be found in any Italian work with which I am acquainted.

The Spanish authors who have been my chief guides are, first, Cean Bermudez, and after him, Palomino, Ponz, Pacheco, Carducho, and Butron. These writers being also painters, I have given so full an account of them and their literary works in their proper places in the following chapters, that it is unnecessary to discuss their merits here. So also in the case of my other authorities; for I have likewise made it a rule to acknowledge my literary debts, whenever and wherever contracted, so explicitly that my readers, unlike those of M. Huard, may at once, if it please them, verify my accuracy or detect my mistakes.

I trust that I have now established my original proposition, that a new book on Spanish art was a desideratum in our literature when my work was begun. I think I have also shown that at that time any accurate or extended knowledge of the subject was to be obtained only from Spanish authors who are not commonly found on the shelves of private libraries in England, and still more rarely in the hands of English readers. Even now I venture to hope that these Annals may in some measure serve purposes as yet unattempted by an English pen. Besides narrating the lives of the painters, I have given an account of the more remarkable sculptors, goldsmiths, and engravers of Spain. I have likewise endeavoured to afford some view of the national and social peculiarities of condition in which Spanish artists flourished, and which coloured their lives, and directed, or at least strongly influenced, their genius. In pursuance of this object, I have occasionally ventured into the field of history, especially in reviewing the characters of the princes of the Spanish house of Austria, of all royal houses the foremost in the protection and

PREFACE TO FIRST EDITION.

promotion of the fine arts. Of the anecdotes of the more remarkable artists, which Pacheco and Palomino narrated, and Cumberland despised, I have rejected but few, holding that every relic of the personal history of a man of genius has a certain value, and being disposed to regard even the slightest with that sort of interest with which Sir David Wilkie detected some of the hairs of Vandyck's pencil in the portrait of a Cardinal in a palace at Genoa.[1] I have also dilated, more than English writers on art have generally thought fit to do, on the legends of the most remarkable saints whose names do not appear in the New Testament, remembering that I am addressing readers who, though versed in the loves and labours of Jupiter and Hercules, are by no means familiar with the bucolical achievements of St. Isidro or the nautical skill of St. Raymond, and may perhaps have never even heard the names of the holy Eulalia of Merida, or Justa and Rufina, the sainted patronesses of Seville.

The chronological system of arrangement which I have chosen, will, I trust, secure to my work the advantages of continuous narrative and yet permit of occasional digressions. In order, however, to combine these advantages with the convenience of a dictionary, I have provided an ample table of contents and index, by means of which the reader will be able to turn at

---

[1] Cunningham's *Life of Wilkie*, vol. ii. p. 450.

once to the precise passage in the biography of any artist that he may happen to be in seach of, to the titles of books quoted, and to the explanation of any words which may require it.

The Catalogues, which I have compiled, of the pictures of Velazquez and Murillo now existing in the principal national and royal galleries, and in some of the best private collections, may perhaps one day be curious and valuable records. While the sheets were passing through the press, one royal collector lost, and another abdicated, his crown ; and it is impossible to foresee the effects of the French revolution of 1848 on the dynasties and galleries of Europe. These Catalogues include, I am aware, many doubtful, and some certainly spurious, pictures ; but they also contain all the finest specimens of those great masters. I have carefully noted as far as possible the engravings which have been executed from them ; and to avoid repetition, whenever a picture has been described in the "Annals," the reader is referred to the passage.

Of the illustrations to the following chapters, I may venture to say that I am not aware of the existence of any engraved portraits of El Greco, Joanes, V. Carducho, and Zurbaran ; of any views of the interior of the Hospital-church of Charity, the Capuchin convent and Murillo's house at Seville ; of any engraving from Murillo's "Guardian Angel," or from a drawing by Alonso Cano, except those which are now offered to the public.

Several monograms of artists are likewise reproduced, which have escaped Orlandi, Bartsch, Brulliot, and other dilligent collectors.

While I have thus ventured to point out the particulars in which I trust these " Annals" may be found to possess some value, I would not have it supposed that I am blind to their numerous defects. The workman who compares the conception with the result of his labour knows full well how wide is the distance which separates the thing hoped for and intended from the thing actually accomplished. It is rare, indeed, for the literary artist "to see of the travail of his soul, and be satisfied;" to find that complacent feeling justified by the concurrent satisfaction of the reader is scarcely more rare. In reviewing my work, I have detected many faults of arrangement, which are now irremediable, and many omissions which I have been obliged to remedy by a chapter of additions and corrections, a chapter in defence of which I have nothing to say, except that it has enabled me to give my readers the benefit of gleanings from certain books which have been published since my own went to press. Worse than all, in observing with dismay the unexpected array of figures with which my final pages are numbered, I begin to fear that I have myself sinned in the sort which I have rebuked in others, and that, groaning under the prolixity of Castilian writers, I have given my English readers just cause to grumble under mine. *Quien en caça, o en guerra, o en amores se mete, no sale quando quiere*, says the Castilian proverb; "he who goes hunting, campaigning, or wooing, cannot leave off at his own pleasure." So literary adventure, partaking somewhat of the nature of each of these pursuits, resembles them also in leading those who engage in it far beyond their first intended limits. If I have sometimes overtasked my readers' powers of endurance, my hope is that I have at least opened the way to "fresh fields and pastures new," which a more skilful guide may one day render as pleasant to others as they have been to me.

38 Clarges Street,
April 13*th*, 1848.

PREFACE

TO

"VELAZQUEZ AND HIS WORKS."

HE following pages were designed to contain the life of Velazquez, as narrated in the "Annals of the Artists of Spain" (8vo, London, 1848), with such additions as its re-publication in a separate form seemed to require, and as later travel and reading have enabled me to supply. In the execution of this design, however, the work has been nearly re-written. I hope that it may not have been increased in bulk without being also somewhat improved in quality.

The catalogue of prints is founded on a list of those in my own collection, and in the still larger collection of my friend, Mr. Charles Morse, to whom I am indebted for much kind aid in the compilation. To this list I have added the names of all the prints that I could see, or hear of, elsewhere; and if it be not a complete catalogue, it is at least the first that has yet been attempted of the prints after the great master of Castile.

The only materials for the personal history of Velazquez are to be found in the account of his early life in the work of his father-in-law, Pacheco, printed in 1649; and in the biographies of Spanish artists, published by Palomino, in 1724, and by Cean Bermudez, in 1800. Except the brief glimpse of him afforded in the verses of Boschini (see infra, p. 762), I know of no other source of information. Cumberland, in compiling his "Anecdotes of Painting in Spain" (2 vols. 12mo, London, 1782), appears to have followed Palomino alone; while later writers have generally been contented to take their facts from the laborious and accurate Cean Bermudez. In the preface to my "Annals of the Artists of Spain," I have so fully discussed the merits of the principal writers, Spanish, English, French, and German, on the biography of Spanish artists, that I do not think it necessary now to repeat my remarks.

But since the "Annals" appeared, a new biography of Velazquez has been put forth at Paris. It forms two *livraisons* of a work called *Histoire des Peintres de toutes les Écoles*, now in course of manufacture by M. Charles Blanc, under the direction of M. Armengaud, and apparently got up for the sake of the woodcuts, which, although generally taken from well-known engraved subjects, are often admirably executed. Of the notice of Velazquez, extending to sixteen quarto pages, it is sufficient to say that it is still more inexact than the worthless books of MM. Quilliet and Huard, from which it has been compiled. On the first page is a woodcut portrait, which is called the portrait of Velazquez, because Baron Taylor was pleased, on his own authority, so to designate a picture which he purchased in Spain for the late King Louis Philippe. An old copy of the well-known portrait in the palace of the *Uffizi* at Florence, which hung in the same room at the Louvre, might have enabled him to avoid or correct the blunder, which M. Blanc also might have escaped had he taken the trouble to consult the ordinary print portraits of Velazquez. The carelessness which is thus displayed on his first page follows M. Blanc through his whole work; and I know few books so little capable of affording either instruction or amusement.

LONDON, *February* 25, 1855.

CHAPTER I.

INTRODUCTION.

	PAGE
Political importance of Spain, during the sixteenth and seventeenth centuries, coeval with her greatness in art	1
Ferdinand and Isabella	3
Charles V.	3
Philip II.	4
Philip III.	4
Philip IV.	4
Charles II.	5
House of Bourbon	5
Spanish sculpture	5
Spanish architecture	7
Spanish painting compared with Spanish literature	8
School of Castile	9
School of Estremadura	10
School of Andalusia	10
School of Valencia	10
Aragon and Catalonia, &c.	10
Grave character of Spanish painting	11
Spanish painters contrasted with Italian	12
Murillo	13
Influence of the Inquisition	14
Pictorial improprieties punished	14
Influence of the national character	15
The Church the chief patron of art	16
The Catholic painter an important servant of the Church	17
Remark of Don J. de Butron	17
Painting popular with the multitude	18
Devotion of some Spanish painters	19
Joanes	19
Vargas	19
Clerical artists	19
Factor	20
Borras	20
Leon and Fuente del Saz	20
Cotan	20
Berenguer	20
Ferrado	20
Cespedes	20
Rocllas	21
Cano	21
Rizi	21
Espadaña	21
Mascareñas	21
Juncosa	21
Maria de Valdes	21
Laws of religious painting	21
Fr. J. I. de Ayala	22
Knotty points discussed	22
Nude figures forbidden	23

CONTENTS.

	PAGE
Story of the effects of an altar-piece	23
Miraculous images	25
Joanes commanded to paint the Virgin	25
Becerra aided by her in a carving	26
She sits to S. Cotan	26
Miracles performed by an unfinished picture of the Virgin	26
The Virgin of Nieva, and the Virgin of Monserrate	27
Micael carves a healing image and dies	27
Favour shown to artists by saints	29
Legend of the Painter-Friar, the Devil, and the Virgin	30
Legend of Our Lady, the Devil, and the Painter	32
Court painters in Spain, in general decorous in their choice of subjects	35
Spanish princes not fond of pictorial improprieties	35
General character of Spanish painting	38
Painters of the religious orders: Murillo, Espinosa, Carducho, Zurbaran, Roelas	38
Models of drapery excellent, and always at hand	38
Colouring—School of Castile	39
El Mudo	39
El Greco	39
Female heads	39
Tristan	39
Southern schools; Andalusia and Valencia	39
Painters of Seville fond of subjects of still life; their "bodegones"	40
Valencian flower-painters	40
Spanish painters distinguished in portraiture	40
Joanes	41
Velazquez and Murillo not inferior as portrait-painters to Titian and Vandyck	41

	PAGE
Female portraits not common in Spain	41
Spanish jealousy the cause	41
Sir K. Digby's adventure	41
Husbands and wives	42
Habits of female life	43
Portraits of Spanish ladies rare	43
Female costume	43
Tasteless dress	43
Absurd modes of dressing hair	44
Court dresses	44
Universal and extravagant use of rouge	45
Ladies of Vittoria	46
Rouged statues	46
Portraits of royal personages	47
Excellence of Court portrait-painters	47
The characters of the Austrian princes to be read in their portraits	48
Charles V. and his family	48
A. S. Coello	48
Philip II., his queen and children	48
Pantoja de la Cruz	48
Philip III. and his family	49
Pantoja	49
Philip IV.	49
Rubens	49
Velazquez	49
Queens and brothers of Philip IV.	50
His children	50
Charles II. and Queen Louisa	50
Carreño	50
Landscape painting little cultivated	50
Landscape painters not generally born amongst fine scenery	51
Painters of landscape abound in the north	52
Best painters of Italian scenery foreigners	52
Few foreign painters of landscape in Spain	54
The greater painters of Spain in general natives	54

CONTENTS.

	PAGE		PAGE
Spanish art long unknown to the rest of Europe	54	Valencia: Cathedral	72
Name of Murillo early known in England	55	Colegio del Corp. Chr. Academia de S. Carlos	72
Spanish painters known in France in eighteenth century	56	Public collections of Spain might be improved by exchanging with each other their superfluous pictures	72
Dictum of the Abbé Dubos	56	Foreign collections of Spanish pictures	73
Exportation of pictures during the War of Independence in Spain	57	Paris: Louvre	73
Daring picture-dealers	58	St. Petersburg: The Hermitage	75
Plundering French commanders	58	Munich: Pinakothek	75
King Joseph pilfers with judgment	58	Vienna: Belvedere Palace	76
Effects of French rapine and English commerce	59	Berlin	76
		Dresden	77
No public galleries in Europe so rich in Spanish pictures as those of Spain	59	Brunswick, Cassel, and Frankfort	77
		Antwerp, Brussels, Amsterdam	77
Madrid Real Museo	59	The Hague	77
Madrid Real Academia de S. Fernando	62	Stockholm	78
		Copenhagen	78
Museo Nacional	63	Frederiksborg	78
Toledo: Cathedral	64	London: National Gallery	78
Valladolid: Museo	65	Dulwich College	79
Zaragoza and Barcelona	66	Italy	79
Cordoba	66	Florence	79
Cadiz	67	Milan	79
Seville: Museo	67	Parma	79
Seville:, Chapel of the University	70	Bologna	79
Chapel of the Hospital de la Caridad	70	Venice	79
		Rome	79
Seville: Cathedral	70	Turin	80
Valencia: Museo	70	Naples	80

CHAPTER II.

NOTICES OF EARLY ART TO THE END OF THE REIGN OF FERDINAND AND ISABELLA THE CATHOLIC, 1516.

Earlier works of painting and sculpture	81	Alonso VIII	83
Cathedrals, abbeys, and palaces of the Middle Ages	82	Cathedrals of Cuença and Leon	83
		St. Ferdinand III	83
Cathedral of Santiago	82	Cathedral of Burgos	83
El Maestro Mateo	82	Cathedral of Toledo—built by El Maestro Pedro Perez	83
Cathedral of Tarragona	82	Portrait of St. Ferdinand at Seville	83

VOL. I.   *d*

CONTENTS.

	PAGE
Alonso X. el Sabio	84
Pedro de Pamplona, painter of illuminations	84
Sancho IV. el Bravo	85
Rodrigo Esteban, painter	85
Pedro I. el Cruel	85
Alcazar of Seville	85
Early painters in Aragon and Catalonia	85
Torrente, 1323	86
Fort	86
Cesilles, 1382	86
Juan I.	87
Starnina of Florence	87
Chartreuse of Paular	88
Monastery of Guadalupe	88
Cathedral of Oviedo	88
Henry III.	88
Cathedral of Huesca, 1400	89
Cathedral of Seville, 1401	89
Juan II.	90
Dello of Florence	91
Dello's epitaph	92
J. Alfon	92
Rogel the Fleming	92
Oratory	92
El Maestro Jorge Ingles	93
Toledo	93
Dolfin, the first stainer of glass	93
The Rodriguez, sculptors	94
Egas	94
School of Andalusia—J. S. de Castro	94
Legend of San Christobal	94
Gonzalo Diaz	96
Moorish decorations imitated by Christian artists	96
Artists in gold and silver at Valladolid and Valencia	97
The Castelnous	97
Fr. J. de Segovia, of Guadalupe: his salt-cellar	97
Progress of taste and refinement	98
Fall of Granada; its effect on Christian art	99
Isabella la Católica; her taste and zeal for the arts	99
Her architectural works at Segovia, Seville, Miraflores, Santiago, Madrid, Toledo	100
Ferdinand el Catolico	100
Effects of his conquest of Naples	101
He builds a convent at Zaragoza	101
The Morlanes, sculptors	101
The Siloes, of Burgos, sculptors and architects	102
Cathedral of Granada	102
Painting	102
A. Rincon	102
His portraits of the Catholic sovereigns	103
Copies at Madrid	103
Ferdinand	104
Isabella	104
Paintings by Rincon at Toledo	105
Altar-piece by Rincon at Robleda de Chavila	105
F. Rincon	106
F. Florez	106
P. Berruguete	106
Santos Cruz	107
J. de Borgoña	107
Paintings in the Sala Capitular del Invierno in the Cathedral of Toledo	107
Fresco in the Capilla Muzarabe	108
Frescoes in the library	109
Portraits of Archbishops of Toledo in chapter-room	109
Mendoza	109
Cisneros	109
Croy	110
School of Andalusia	110
J. Nuñez	110
Aleman introduces stained glass at Seville	111
A. Fernandez	111
Diego de la Barrera	111
Valencia	111
Neapoli and Aregio	112
Munificence of the Church	112
Archbishop Mendoza of Toledo	112
Cardinal Ximenes	113

Vigarny	113
Bishop Ramirez of Salamanca	113
J. A. de Toledo	114
Archbishop Deza	114
Proof of the progress of art under Ferdinand and Isabella	114

CHAPTER III.

REIGN OF THE EMPEROR CHARLES V.—1516-1556.

Brilliant age of Charles V.	115
Close and increasing connection of Spain with Italy	116
Charles V. as a patron of art	116
His fine taste	117
His visit to the Cathedral of Cordoba	117
His regard for Titian	118
Anecdotes of the Emperor and the painter	118
His architectural works	119
Palaces at Madrid	119
The Pardo	119
Granada	119
Toledo	120
His love of painting	120
His pictures at San Yuste	121
Spanish artists in Italy	122
Pedro Francione	122
Giovanni di Spagna	122
Spanish patrons	122
Marquess del Guasto	122
Marquess of Villafranca	123
Pedro de Prado	123
Juan de Toledo	123
Bishop of Salamanca	123
Miguel Florentin	123
Antonio Florentin	124
Pietro Torrigiano	124
Examination of the popular story of Torrigiano	126
"Mano de la teta"	126
Terra cotta statue of St. Jerome	128
Fresco painting brought to Spain by Julio and Alessandro	130
Titian—effect of his works in Spain	131
His portraits of Charles V.	131
Story of his visit to Spain examined	133
Inconclusive evidence for it	133
Good evidence against it	134
Flemish painters	135
Jerome Bos	135
Works of Bos at Madrid	137
Works at Valencia	138
J. C. Vermeyen	138
Pedro Campaña	139
His "Descent from the Cross"	139
His various works at Seville	140
F. Frutet, 1548	141
Hernando Sturmio	143
Legend of Sta. Rufina and Sta. Justa	143
Felipe de Vigarny	145
Vigarny's influence on Spanish art	146
Spanish painted sculpture	147
Colour not admissible in statuary	151
Damian Forment	152
Retablo in Cathedral of Huesca	152
Pedro Machuca	155
The origin and progress of plateresque architecture	156
Diego de Sagredo's "Medidas del Romano"	157
Alonso Berruguete	159
Works in various cities of Spain	163
Salamanca	163
Toledo	163
Palencia	163
Monument of Cardinal Tavera at Toledo	164
Genius and influence of Berruguete	165
Diego de Navas, sculptor	166
Gaspar de Tordesillas	167

xliv   CONTENTS.

	PAGE		PAGE
Xamete	168	Don Felipe de Guevara	181
Fernando Gallegos	168	Painters of illuminations	182
Juan de Villoldo	169	Antonio de Holanda	183
Francisco Comontes	170	Diego de Arroya	183
D. Correa	170	Francisco de Holanda	183
Juan de Yciar	171	Visit to Charles V. at Barcelona	184
His "Arte de Escribir"	172	Travels in Italy and France	187
His "Nuevo Estilo de Screvir Cartas"	174	Drawings	189
		Return to Portugal	189
Tomas Pelegret	176	Writings on art	192
Cuevas	176	His dialogues	192
Ezpeleta	177	Remarks ascribed to Michael Angelo	193
Hernando Yañez 1531	177		
Pedro Rubiales	178	Artists in gold and silver	194
Patrons of art	179	Henrique d'Arphe	195
The Church	179	Antonio d'Arphe	197
Chapter of Seville	179	Juan Ruiz	197
Archbishop Tavera of Toledo	180	A., F., and C. Becerril	198
Francisco de Cobos	180	Goldsmiths permitted to wear silk	198

CHAPTER IV.

REIGN OF PHILIP II.—1556-1598

	PAGE		PAGE
Philip II., his love of the arts	201	Juan Bautista de Toledo	214
His urbanity and kindness to artists	201	Juan de Herrera	215
		Architectural merits of the Escorial	217
Titian	202	Opinion of Francisco de los Santos, and of Cumberland	217
Anthony More	202		
His taste less general than his father's	202	Exterior	217
		Interior	219
Favourite pursuits	203	Patio de los Evangelistos	219
Painting	204	Church	219
Architecture	204	Capilla del Altar Mayor	220
Architectural undertakings	206	Materials and decorations of the Escorial brought from all parts of the world	220
Convent palace of San Lorenzo del Escorial	206		
Philip's anxiety for its completion	207	Artists employed in the decorations of the Escorial	221
Remarkable events of Philip's life connected with the Escorial	208		
		Giacomo Trezzo	221
The Escorial compared with other great buildings	210	Benvenuto Cellini	222
		Josef Frecha	222
Works on the Escorial	211	Clemente Virago	223
Purposes for which it was built	212	Foreign painters in the King's service	223
Architects of the Escorial	214		

CONTENTS.

	PAGE
Italians	224
Titian	224
His "Cena"	224
"Antiope"	224
Portraits	224
Portraits of Philip II.	224
Sofonisba Anguisciola	225
Picture by Sofonisba Angnisciola	226
Journey to Spain	227
Marriages	228
Sayings of Vandyck	230
Works	230
Portraits	230
Sofonisba Gentilesca	231
Castello el Bergamasco	232
Nicolao Granelo	233
Francisco de Viana	234
Romulo Cincinato	234
"El zancajo" at Cuença	236
Patricio Caxes	236
Antonio and Vincenzo Campi	237
Antonio Campi's work on Cremona	239
Luca Cambiaso	239
Death of his wife, and its effects	242
Industry	243
Invitation to Spain	243
Works at the Escorial	244
Disappointment, sickness, death	246
Works at the Escorial	246
Character	247
Merits as an artist	247
O. Cambiaso	248
Lazaro Tavarone	248
Castello el Genoese	248
Federigo Zuccaro	249
Travels	250
Journey to Spain	251
Works at the Escorial	251
Criticism of Philip II.	252
Condemned frescoes	253
Remark of Philip II.	254
Bartolomeo Carducho	254
Works at the Escorial	255
Good-natured criticism	256
His "Cena"	256
Antonio Rizi	257
Pellegrino Tibaldi	257
Invitation to Spain	258
Frescoes in the library	260
Bernardino del Agua	261
Flemish artists	261
Anthony More	261
In England	262
In Spain	263
Michael Coxie	265
Antonio Pupiler	266
Ulric Staenheyl	267

CHAPTER V.

REIGN OF PHILIP II.—1556-1598—(*continued*).

	PAGE
Artists of Castile	269
Luis Morales	269
Visits the Escorial	270
Last interview with the King	271
Self-taught genius	272
Subjects and style	273
Careful finish	276
Scholars	276
Morales the younger	276
Juan Labrador	277
Alonso Sanchez Coello	277
Favour with Philip II.	278
Royal and noble friend	279
Anecdote of Philip II.	280
Praise of Lope de Vega	280
Portrait of Alonso Sanchez Coello	281
Isabella Sanchez Coello	281
Alonso Sanchez Coello's portraits	281
Infant Don Carlos	282
Infanta Isabel Clara Eugenia	283
Queen Isabel de la Paz	284
Antonio Perez	284

CONTENTS.

	PAGE
Paints triumphal arches with Diego de Urbina	285
Religious pictures	285
Portrait of St. Ignatius Loyola	286
Scholars	286
Cristobal Lopez	287
Juan de Urbina	287
Giovanni Narduck, or Fray Juan de la Miseria	287
Gaspar Becerra	289
Works in Italy	289
Dr. Juan de Valverde, and his book, illustrated by Gaspar Becerra	290
Return to Spain	291
Goes to court	291
Religious works	292
Carves for the Queen the figure of Nra. Señora de la Soledad	293
Works in various cities	296
Granada	296
Valladolid, &c.	296
Burgos	296
Segovia	296
Astorga	297
Merits as a painter	298
As a sculptor	299
Scholars	299
Miguel Barroso	299
Rio Bernuis	299
Francisco Lopez	300
Gerónimo Vazquez	300
Miguel Ribas	300
Miguel Martinez	300
Juan Ruiz de Castañeda	300
Juan Fernandez Navarrete	300
Fray Vicente de Santo Domingo	301
El Mudo in Italy	301
Works at the Escorial	302
Picture of "Abraham" in the "Recibimiento"	304
Altar-pieces for the church	305
Sickness and death	306
Testament	306
His quickness and intelligence	308
Offers to copy Titian's "Cena"	308
Style and merits	309
Portraits	309
Portrait of El Mudo	309
Verses of Lope de Vega	310
Luis de Carbajal	311
Portrait of Archbishop Carranza de Miranda	312
Blas del Prado	313
Sent to the Court of Morocco	314
Works now existing at Madrid	315
Portrait of Fray Alonso de Villegas	316
Juan Pantoja de la Cruz	316
Paints Philip III. and his family in two sacred compositions	319
Style and works	320
Portrait of an eagle	321
Other court artists	322
Teodosio Mingot and Gerónimo Cabrera	322
Diego de Urbina	322
Antonio Segura	322
Rodrigo de Holanda	323
Juan Gomez	323
E. Jordan	323
Painters of illuminations	324
Fray Andres de Leon	324
Fray Julian Fuente del Saz	324
Fray Martin de Palencia	324
Embroiderers	325
Fray Lorenzo de Monserrate	325
Diego Rutiner	325
Castilian artists employed by the Church	325
Nicolas de Vergara, the elder	325
Nicolas de Vergara, the younger, and Juan de Vergara	326
Luis de Velasco	326
Isaac de Helle	327
Domenico Theotocopuli, "El Greco"	328
Works at Toledo	328
"El Despojo de las Vestiduras del Señor"	329
Paints "St Maurice" for the Escorial	330
Produces a disagreeable picture, which displeases the King	331

CONTENTS.

	PAGE
Toledo, "El Entierro del Conde de Orgaz" in the church of Santo Tomé	332
Portraits	335
Inscription beneath El Greco's "Entierro del Conde de Orgaz"	336
At Toledo	337
Illescas	337
Madrid	337
Paris	338
Naples	339
Style of painting	339
Works of sculpture and architecture	341
His industry	342
Visited by Pacheco	342
Scholars	342
Sonnet by Gongora	343
Alonso de Herrera	344
Juan Francisco, and Estefano Perola	344
Fray Martin Galindez	345
Josef Martinez	346
Gregorio Martinez	347
Juan de Aneda	347
Juan de Cea	347
Artists of Catalonia	347
Pedro Pablo, Pedro Serafin "el Griego"	347
Pedro Guitart	348
Isaac Hermes	348
Fray Luis Pascual Gaudin	348
Sculptors of Castile	349
Juan de Juni	349
Name	350
Works at Valladolid	351
Altar in church of "Nuestra Señora de la Antigua"	351
"Mater Dolorosa"	352
St. Anthony of Padua, and St. Francis of Asisi	353
Adoration of Magi	353
Works in the Cathedral of Osma	354
At Rioseco	354
Fresco paintings	355
Segovia	355
Santoyo	355
Valladolid	355
Entombment	355
Family	356
Style and merits	356
Rafael de Leon	358
Pedro Arbulo Marguvete	359
Miguel de Ancheta	360

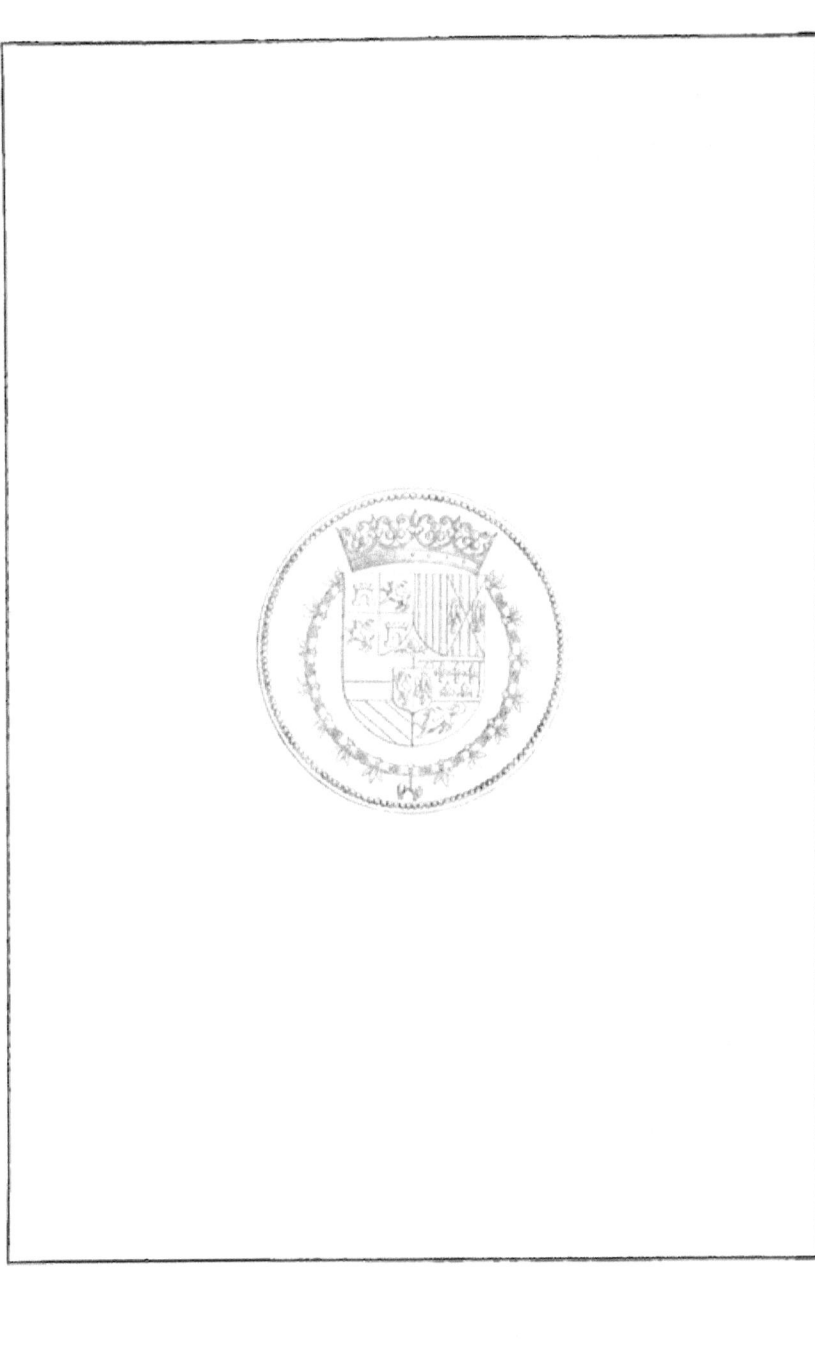

ANNALS
OF
THE ARTISTS OF SPAIN.

CHAPTER I.

INTRODUCTION.

AMONG the most remarkable features in the history of Spain are the rapid growth and decay of her power. She first began to rank among the great kingdoms in the reign of Ferdinand and Isabella. Their great-grandson, Philip II., was the acknowledged leader and protector of Catholic Europe. Under Charles II., great-grandson of the second Philip, Castile had

CHAP. I.

Political importance of Spain during the sixteenth and seventeenth centuries,

CHAP. I.

coeval with
her great-
ness in Art.

ceased to produce statesmen and soldiers, and Peru to furnish ducats, at least to the royal treasury. The monarchy was as feeble as the monarch; its star had run its course in little more than six generations, rising at the end of the fifteenth, and setting at the end of the seventeenth century.

This era was likewise the great period of literature and art in Spain. Growing up with her political greatness, they added lustre to her prosperity, and a grace and charm to her decline. During the middle ages, her taste and imagination had been embodied in the unrivalled multitude of ballads, sung by unknown bards, part of which the Castilian Romanceros still preserve, and in the magnificent cathedrals reared by nameless architects in her Christian cities; the songs and the shrines being equally tinged with the colouring of northern piety and oriental fancy. Poetry, the eldest and most docile of the fine arts, was the first of the sisterhood to be affected by the revival of ancient learning. Spanish writers had borrowed somewhat of refinement and correctness from the Latin and Italian, long ere architecture in Spain had yielded submission to Greek and Roman rules, and ere painting and sculpture had produced aught but uncouth caricatures of the human form. Juan de Mena had written his graceful love songs, Santillana had even wandered from the gay science into the strange field

INTRODUCTION.

of criticism, and Hernan Castillo was probably preparing the first cancionero for the press of Valencia, before the pencil of Rincon had obtained for him the cross of Santiago from the hands of Ferdinand and Isabella.

The reign of "the Catholic Sovereigns" is memorable for the discovery not merely of a new continent, but also of vast regions of intellectual enterprise. History, the drama, and painting, were revived in Spain in the same stirring age that sought and found new empires beyond the great ocean. Pulgar, the father of Castilian history, Cota, the earliest forerunner of Calderon, Rincon, the first native painter in the Peninsula who deserved the name, were the contemporaries of Columbus, and, with the great navigator, mingled in the courtly throngs of the presence chamber of Isabella. The progress of refinement during the first half of the sixteenth century was perhaps more rapid in Spain than in any other country. The iron soldier of Castile, the Roman of his age, became the intellectual vassal of the elegant Italians whom he conquered:

> "Græcia capta ferum victorem cepit, et artes
> Intulit agresti Latio."[1]

Under the Emperor Charles V., the Iberian Peninsula, the fairest province of ancient Rome, grew

---
[1] Horat., *Ep.* II. i. 156.

into the fairest colony of modern art. The classical Boscan and Garcilasso, and the many-gifted Mendoza, left behind them monuments of literature which might bear comparison with those of Italy, Berruguete and Vigarny, schools of painting and sculpture that Florence might have been proud to own. The odes of Fray Luis de Leon were excelled in strength and grace by none ever recited at the court of Ferrara; and pastoral Estremadura could boast a painter—Morales of Badajoz—not unworthy to cope with Sebastian del Piombo on his own lofty ground.

During the reigns of the three Philips, literature and art kept an even pace in their rapid and triumphant march. When Juan de Toledo laid the foundations of the Escorial, Cervantes was writing his early poems and romances in the schools of Madrid. The versatile Theotocopuli was designing his various churches in and around Toledo, and embellishing them with paintings and sculptures, whilst Lope de Vega was dashing off his thousand dramas for the diversion of the court. Mariana composed in the cloister his great history of Spain, whilst Sanchez Coello, the courtier and man of fashion, was illustrating the story of his own times by his fine portraits of royal and noble personages. In the reign of Philip III., Velazquez and Murillo were born, and the great novel of Cervantes first saw the light. Solis and Villegas, Moreto and the

INTRODUCTION.

brothers Leonardo de Argensola, famous in history, poetry, and the drama, were contemporaries of Ribera, Cano, and Zurbaran, and with them shared the favour and patronage of the tasteful Philip IV. When Velazquez received the cross of Santiago, Calderon was amongst the knights who greeted the new companion of that ancient order. In the evil days of Charles II., Spain and her literature and her arts drooped and declined together. Painting strove the hardest against fate, and was the last to succumb. Murillo and Valdés, Mazo and Carreño, and their scholars nobly maintained the honour of a long line of painters, till the total eclipse of Spain in the War of the Succession. With the House of Bourbon came in foreign fashions, and foreign standards of taste. Henceforth Crebillon and Voltaire became the models of Castilian writing; Vanloo and Mengs, of Spanish painting. From the effects of this disastrous imitation, painting, at least, has never recovered.

If Spain holds a high place in the roll of nations illustrious in art, it owes it to her painters; her sculptors have never obtained, nor indeed have often deserved, much notice beyond the limits of the Peninsula. Amongst them, however, were several men of fine genius. Alonso Berruguete, the disciple of Michael Angelo, was a great sculptor; Juni and Hernandez modelled with singular feeling and grace;

and had Montañes and Cano flourished beneath the shadow of the Vatican, they would have been formidable rivals to Bernini and Algardi. Flanders can show no carvings more delicate and masterly than those which still enrich the venerable choirs of many of the Peninsula churches, with stalls, embowered in foliage—almost as light as that which trembled on the living tree—where fruits cluster and birds perch, in endless variety, or those arabesque panels and pillars, where children rise from the cups of lily blossoms, and strange monsters twine themselves in a network of garlands, or the niches, filled with exquisite figures, or the fretted pinnacles, crowned with a thousand various finials, and towering above each other in graceful confusion. But in his high religious statuary—the Virgin of the chapel, or the tutelar saint of the abbey—the Spanish sculptor was too often unhappy in his choice of materials. Neglecting the pure marble and abiding bronze, the time-honoured and fitting vehicles of his thought, he wrought either in metals too precious to escape the chances of war and the rapacity of bankrupt power, or in wood and clay, offering little resistance to the tooth of time, and but too much temptation to the foreign trooper, weary and hungry with his march, and seeking wherewithal to kindle his fire and make the camp-kettle boil. The use of colour—universally adopted in the larger statues and groups—was also injurious to Spanish sculpture; bringing the art, so far as it addressed the taste of vulgar monks and country clowns, within the reach of every hewer of wood who possessed a paint-pot; and causing the works of even the man of genius, at first sight, rather to startle than to please, by their similitude to real flesh and blood.

The early religious architects of Spain were great masters in art. Their magnificent cathedrals—too often mere portions of giant plans—were worthy of a people who possessed so many noble remains of older times, who inherited from the Roman the bridge of Alcantara and the aqueduct of Segovia, and who had won from the Saracen the Mosque of Cordoba and the Alhambra of Granada. But the architects of the Renaissance were a feebler folk, lovers of the ornate, rather than the grand. Machuca, Toledo, and Herrera, indeed, left examples of a pure and admirable style; but they found few followers. Ecclesiastical buildings, while they increased in numbers, grew likewise in ugliness; and the monastic system bore equally hard on the financial resources and the architectural taste of the country. Amongst the churches and convents erected since the end of the sixteenth century, there are few that are not either plain to bareness, or loaded with tawdry decoration; and rare, indeed, it is to meet with that graceful propriety of design, which lends its chief charm to Italian architecture, and is often to be found in the monastery of the Apennine woodlands, as well as in the princely palace on the Corso.

In age, the Spanish school of painting ranks third amongst the national schools of Europe, after the German, and before the French; in artistic importance, second only to the Italian. But Spanish painting, like Spanish literature, has a glory proper and peculiar to itself. It is true that no Spaniard can claim to rank with those great Italian painters, whom their most illustrious followers have regarded with a reverence that forbade rivalry. Spain has no Rafael—no Correggio—nor has she a Dante or a Shakespeare; yet her noble Castilian tongue possesses the single book of which the humour—so strictly national, and yet so true and universal—has become native to all Europe. And Spain has produced the painters whose works unite high excellence of conception and execution, with an absolute adherence to nature, and are thus best fitted to please the most critical as well as the most uneducated eyes. If the visible and material efforts of the pencil may be compared with the airy flights of thought, Velazquez and Murillo may be said to appeal, like Cervantes, to the feelings and perceptions of all men; and, like him, they will be understood and enjoyed where the loftiest strains of

Shakespeare, and the ideal creations of Rafael, would find no sympathy, because addressed to a kindred and responsive imagination belonging only to minds of a higher order. The crazy gentleman of La Mancha and his squire will always be more popular with the many than the wondrous Prince of Denmark. And those who turn away, perplexed and disappointed, from the "Spasimo" or the "Transfiguration," would probably gaze with ever fresh delight on the living and moving captains and spearmen of Velazquez, or on Murillo's thirsty multitudes flocking to the rock that gushed in Horeb.

The venerable city of Toledo was the cradle of Spanish painting: there the school of Castile was founded in the first half of the fifteenth century, and flourished chiefly under the fostering care of munificent prelates and chapters till the close of the reign of Charles V. Villoldo, Blas del Prado, El Greco, Tristan, and others, maintained the reputation of Toledo till the days of Philip IV. Under Philip II., Madrid, the seat of government, became the resort of many good Flemish and Italian artists, and of those native painters, such as El Mudo and Sanchez Coello, who enjoyed, or hoped for, the royal favour. Valladolid, a city more famous for its goldsmiths and sculptors than for its painters, was the chief residence of Philip III.; Madrid, however, continued to prosper as a school of art, and finally

School of Castile.

became, in the brilliant times of Philip IV. and Velazquez, the metropolis of Castilian painting as well as of the monarchy.

School of Estremadura. Of the school of Estremadura, if school it can be called, Morales is the sole glory and representative; and, if his history were better known, it would probably be found that, although he lived and laboured at Badajoz, he belonged to the school of Castile.

School of Andalusia. The great school of Andalusia was founded by Sanchez de Castro, at Seville, about 1454, and flourished till the troubles of the War of Succession. The beautiful Terra Bætica has ever been prolific of genius. The country of Lucan, and Seneca, and Trajan, of Averroes, and Azzarkal, likewise brought forth Vargas, Velazquez, and Murillo. Seville was always the principal seat of Andalusian painting, but some able masters resided also in other cities, as Cespedes at Cordoba, Castillo at Cadiz, and Cano and Moya at Granada.

School of Valencia. The Valencian school sprang into eminence under Vicente Joanes about the middle of the sixteenth century, and sank into mediocrity at the death of the younger Espinosa in 1680.

Aragon and Catalonia, &c. The northern provinces and the Balearic Isles were not prolific, yet not altogether destitute, of artists. Till the end of the eighteenth century, Zaragoza possessed a respectable school of painting, of which Josef Martinez[1] may be considered the chief; and Barcelona is justly proud of Viladomat,[2] who maintained the honour of the Spanish pencil in the corrupt age of Philip V.

Spanish art, like Spanish nature, is in the highest degree national and peculiar. Its three principal schools of painting differ in style from each other, but they all agree in the great features which distinguish them from the other schools of Europe. The same deeply religious tone is common to all. In Spain alone can painting be said to have drawn all its inspiration from Christian fountains, and, like the architecture of the middle ages, to be an exponent of a people's faith. Its first professors, indeed, acquired their skill by the study of Italian models and by communion with Italian minds. But the skill which at Florence and Venice would have been employed chiefly to adorn palace-halls with the adventures of pious Æneas, or ladies' bowers with passages from the Art of Love, was at Toledo, Seville, and Valencia usually dedicated to the service of God and the Church. Spanish painters are very rarely to be found in the regions of history or classical mythology. Sion hill delights them more than the Aonian mount, and Siloa's brook than ancient Tiber or the laurel-shaded

---

[1] Infra, chap. x.   [2] Infra, chap. xvi.

INTRODUCTION.

CHAP. I.

Orontes. Their pastoral scenes are laid, not in the vales of Arcady, but in the fields of Judea, where Ruth gleaned after the reapers of Boaz, and where Bethlehem shepherds watched their flocks on the night of the nativity. In their landscapes it is a musing hermit, or, perhaps, a company of monks, that moves through the forest solitude, or reposes by the brink of the torrent: not there

> "Gratia cum Nymphis geminisque sororibus audet
> Ducere nuda choros." [1]

Their fancy loves best to deal with the legendary history of the Virgin, and the life and passion of the Redeemer, with the glorious company of Apostles, the goodly fellowship of Prophets, and the noble army of Martyrs and Saints; and they tread this sacred ground with habitual solemnity and decorum.

Spanish Painters contrasted with Italian.

The great religious painters of Spain rarely descended to secular subjects. Not so the Italians. Rafael could pass from the creation of his heavenly Madonnas to round the youthful contours of a Psyche, or elaborate the charms of a Galatea; Correggio, from the Magdalene repenting in the desert, to Antiope surprised in the forest. Vicente Joanes of Valencia would have held such transition to be

---

[1] Horat., *Carm.* Lib. iv., 8. v. 5, 6.

a sin, little short of sacrilege, and worthy of the severest penance. Titian's "Last Supper," and his "Assumption of the Virgin," are doubtless amongst the noblest of religious compositions. But his fancy ranged more freely over profane than sacred ground; his Maries are fair and comely, but they sometimes want the life and warmth that breathe in his Graces and his Floras, in whom he delighted to reproduce his auburn-haired mistress, who figures in one of his most charming allegories [1] with his name inscribed on her bosom. The Queen of Love herself was his favourite subject; she it was that most fully drew forth all

> "The wondrous skill and sweet wit of the man." [2]

Far different were the themes on which Murillo put forth his highest powers. After the "Mystery of the Immaculate Conception," he repeated, probably more frequently than any other subject, the "Charity of St. Thomas of Villanueva;" and it was his finest picture of that good prelate, inimitable for simplicity and grandeur, that he was wont to call emphatically "his own." [3]

---

[1] "The Offering to the Goddess of Fecundity." *Catalogo del Real Museo de Madrid* por Madrazo [1843], No. 852 [edition 1889, No. 451]. Two beautiful young women, of whom the lady in question is one, bow before a marble statue, in a forest glade; around them gambol a multitude of children of the true Titian race.
[2] Spenser.   [3] Infra, chap. xii.

INTRODUCTION.

CHAP. I.

Influence of the Inquisition.

The sobriety and purity of imagination which distinguished the Spanish painters, is mainly to be attributed to the restraining influence of the Inquisition. Palomino [1] quotes a decree of that tribunal, forbidding the making or exposing of immodest paintings and sculptures, on pain of excommunication, a fine of fifteen hundred ducats, and a year's exile. The Holy Office also appointed inspectors, whose duty it was to see that no works of that kind were exposed to view in churches and other public places. Pacheco, the painter and historian of art, held this post at Seville, and Palomino himself at Madrid. To treat a sacred subject in an indecorous or unorthodox manner was an offence held to merit personal punishment.

Pictorial improprieties punished.

Pacheco tells us that he knew a painter at Cordoba, imprisoned for introducing into a picture of the Crucifixion, the Blessed Virgin in an embroidered petticoat and fardingale, and St. John in trunk hose; and he styles the incarceration, "a justly deserved chastisement." [2] But the rules of the Inquisition cannot have been observed to the letter, otherwise so many of the Loves and Graces of Italian painting would not have been left hanging, almost to our days, on the walls of the Escorial.

Another cause of the severity and decency of

---

[1] Pal., tom. ii., p. 138.
[2] Pacheco, *Arte de la Pintura*, p. 456.

Spanish art is to be found in the character of the Spanish people. The proverbial gravity — which distinguishes the Spaniard, like his cloak—which appears in his manner of address, and in the common phrases of his speech, is but an index of his earnest and thoughtful nature. The Faith of the Cross, nourished with the blood of Moor and Christian, nowhere struck its roots so deep, or spread them so wide, as in Spain. Pious enthusiasm pervaded all orders of men; the noble and learned as well as the vulgar. The wisdom of antiquity could not sap the creed of Alcalá or Salamanca, nor the style of Plato or Cicero seduce their scholars into any leaning to the religion of Greece or Rome. Whilst Alexander Borgia—a Spaniard indeed by birth, but Italianised by education—polluted the Vatican with filthy sensuality, whilst the elegant epicurean, Pope Leo, banqueted gaily with infidel wits, or hunted and hawked in the woods and plains around Viterbo—the mitre of Toledo was worn by the Franciscan Ximenes, once a hermit in the caves of the rocks, who had not doffed the hair-shirt in assuming the purple, nor in his high estate feared to peril his life for the Faith. In the nineteenth century, of which superstition is not the characteristic, a duchess, returning from a ball, and meeting the Host at midnight in the streets of Madrid, resigned her coach to the priests attendant on its

CHAP. I.

Influence of the National Character.

CHAP. I.

Majesty[1] the Wafer, and found her way home on foot.[2] After all the revolutions and convulsions of Spain, where episcopal crosses have been coined into dollars to pay for the bayonetting of friars militant on the hills of Biscay, and the Primacy has become a smaller ecclesiastical prize than our Sodor and Man; it is still in Spain—constant, when seeming most false,—religious, when seeming careless of all creeds—that the pious Catholic looks hopefully to see the Faith of Rome rise, refreshed, regenerate, and irresistible.[3]

The Church the chief patron of Art.

Nurtured in so devout a land, it was but natural that Spanish art should show itself devout. The painter was early secured to the service of religion. His first inspiration was drawn from the pictured walls of the churches or cloisters of his native place, where he had knelt a wondering child beside his mother, where he had loitered or begged when a

---

[1] "Su Magestad" is the style and title both of Isabel II. and the consecrated bread of the altar.

[2] *L'Espagne sous Ferdinand VII.*, par le Marquis de Custine, 4 tom., 12mo. Bruxelles, 1838, tom. i. p. 224. The Duchess of Alba, it must be confessed, turned off her coachman for not getting out of the way. Queen Christina herself has been known to leave her carriage and kneel in the street as the Host went by.

[3] See the able article on Spain in the *Dublin Review*, No. XXXVI., Art. iv., containing an interesting sketch of the present state of the Spanish Church, which, though drawn by the too favourable hand of an enthusiastic partisan, displays that knowledge of the subject in which some zealous Protestant travellers, who have lately written books about it, are so lamentably deficient, and the absence of which few of their Protestant readers ever seem to detect.

INTRODUCTION.

boy: to their embellishment his earliest efforts were
dedicated, out of gratitude, perhaps, to the kindly
Carmelite or Cordelier, who had taught him to read,
or fed him with bread and soup on the days of dole;
or who had first noted the impulse of his boyish
fancy, and guided "his desperate charcoal round
the convent walls." As his skill improved, he
would receive orders from neighbouring convents,
and some gracious prior would introduce him to the
notice of the bishop or the tasteful grandee of the
province. The fairest creations of his matured
genius then went to enrich the cathedral or the
royal abbey, or found their way into the gallery of
the sovereign to bloom in the gardens of Flemish
and Italian art. Throughout his whole career the
Church was his best and surest patron. Nor was he
the least important or popular of her ministers. His
art was not merely decorative and delightful, but it
was exercised to instruct the young and the ignorant, that is, the great body of worshippers, in
the scenes of the Gospel history, and in the awful
or touching legends of the saints, whom they
were taught from the cradle to revere. "For the
learned and the lettered," says Don Juan de Butron,
a writer on art in the reign of Philip IV., "written
knowledge may suffice; but for the ignorant, what
master is like painting? They may read their
duty in a picture, although they cannot search for

Marginal notes: CHAP. I. — The Catholic painter an important servant of the Church. — Remark of Don J. de Butron.

it in books."[1] The painter became, therefore, in some sort, a preacher, and his works were standing homilies, more attractive, and perhaps more intelligible, than those usually delivered from the pulpit. The quiet pathos, the expressive silence of the picture, might fix the eye that would drop to sleep beneath the glozing of the Jesuit, and melt hearts that would remain untouched by all the thunders of the Dominican.

Painting popular with the multitude.

We Protestants, to whom religious knowledge comes through another and a better channel, are scarcely capable of appreciating the full importance of the Spanish artist's functions. The Great Bible, chained in the days of King Edward VI. to the parish lectern, silenced for us the eloquence of the altar-piece. But to the simple Catholic of Spain the music of his choir and the pictures of his ancient shrines stood in the place of the theological dogmas which whetted and vexed the intellect of the Protestant peasant of the north. He discoursed of them with as much delight, and perhaps, with as much moral advantage; and he clung to them with as much affectionate reverence. In the great Peninsular war, when the nuns of Loeches—tempted by the gold of an English picture-dealer—had agreed to strip their walls of the six magnificent compositions

---

[1] *Discursos Apologéticos.* 4to, Madrid, 1626, p. 36.

by Rubens, the gift of Olivares to their sisterhood, the country people rose in defence of the heirloom of the village. It was necessary to obtain the assistance of a more powerful spoiler, a French general of brigade, whom the purchaser bribed with two of the disputed pictures, in order that the fitting decorations of a Castilian church might cumber the gallery of an English noble.[1]

The Spanish painter well understood the dignity of his task, and not seldom applied himself to it with a zealous fervour worthy of the holiest friar. Like Fra Angelico at the dawn of Italian painting, Vicente Joanes was wont to prepare himself for a new work by means of prayer and fasting, and the holy Eucharist. The life of Luis de Vargas was as pure as his style; he was accustomed to discipline his body with the scourge, and, like Charles V., he kept by his bedside a coffin, in which he would lie down to meditate on death.

The Spanish clergy have furnished at various times some considerable names to the records of art. The priest sometimes aspired to exhort his flock, the friar to address his brotherhood, in a picture instead of a sermon. There were few religious houses but had possessed, at one time or another, an inmate

---

[1] Buchanan's *Memoirs of Painting, with a History of the Importation of Pictures, by the great Masters, into England.* London, 1824. 2 vols. 8vo. Vol. ii. p. 222.

with some skill or ambition as an artist, who had left a rich chalice or pix in the sacristy, or a picture or carving in the chapel, as the literary brother had bequeathed to the library where he pored and pondered, his MS. tomes,—his curious chronicle, or interminable legend. The fine genius of the deaf and dumb boy of Logroño—afterwards famous throughout Europe as "The Dumb Painter" (*El Mudo*)—was discovered and first directed by a father of the Jeronymite monastery at Estrella. Nicolas Factor, a Franciscan of Valencia, is as well known as a painter of merit, as a "beato," or saint of the second order. Nicolas Borras, of Gandia, during a residence of twenty-five years, filled the church and cloisters of the Jeronymites with a multitude of pictures, of which the best would do no discredit to his great master Joanes. Fray Andres de Leon and Fray Julian Fuente del Saz, monks of the Escorial, exercised their delicate and diligent pencils in illuminating the choir books (*libros de coro*) of their church. The Carthusians of Paular, and Granada, could boast that Sanchez Cotan, one of the ablest of the scholars of Blas del Prado, wore their robe and dwelt within their walls. Ramon Berenguer, at Scala Dei in Catalonia, and Cristobal Ferrado, in the noble Chartreuse of Seville, likewise beguiled, by painting, the hours of solitude and silence imposed by the rule of St. Bruno. Cespedes, the painter-

INTRODUCTION.

poet, was a canon of Cordoba; Juan de Roelas enjoyed a prebendal stall at Olivarez, and Alonso Cano one at Granada. Juan Rizi was an excellent painter; and so good a Benedictine that he rose to be an Abbot, and was at last promoted to an Italian mitre. Espadaña, Inquisitor of Valencia, when the labours of the Holy Office were over, was wont to lay aside his torture-dealing pen for the palette and brush of the amateur; repeating perhaps in the studio the martyrdoms inflicted in the dungeon. Bishop Mascareñas of Segovia also amused his leisure with the pencil; and in the Cathedral of Tarragona, Doctor Josef Juncosa figured both as a popular preacher, and as one of the best and busiest of Catalonian painters. Nor was artistic skill confined to the male religious; for Doña Maria de Valdes, a Cistercian nun, and daughter of Valdes-Leal, Murillo's rival, painted clever portraits in the convent of San Clemente at Seville.

Painting being of so much importance to the Church, a great deal of learning and research was devoted to the investigation of rules for representing sacred subjects and personages. The question was handled in every treatise of art. That considerable portion of Pacheco's book which relates to the subject, is said to have been furnished by his friends of the Jesuits' college at Seville. But the most complete code of Sacro-pictorial law is, perhaps, that of

Fray Juan Interian de Ayala, which was not, however, promulgated till the race of painters for whose guidance it was designed, was nearly extinct. Fray Juan was a doctor and professor of Salamanca, and one of the compilers of the Dictionary of the Spanish Academy; his book, which was in Latin, was entitled "Pictor Christianus Eruditus, sive de erroribus qui passim admittuntur circa pingendas atque effingendas Sacras Imagines."—Matriti, in fol. 1730. A translation into Castilian, by Dr. Luis de Duran, appeared at Madrid in 2 vols. 4to in 1782. The work is, as might be expected, a fine specimen of pompous and prosy trifling. For example— several pages[1] are devoted to the castigation of those unorthodox painters, who draw the Cross of Calvary like a T instead of in the ordinary Latin form;—the question, whether in pictures of the Maries at the sepulchre on the morning of the Resurrection, two angels or only one should be seated on the stone which was rolled away, is anxiously debated,[2] and the artist is finally directed to make his works square with all the Gospels, by adopting both accounts alternately;—and the right of the devil to his horns and tail undergoes a strict examination,[3] of which the result is that the first are fairly fixed

---

[1] Duran's Translation. *El Pintor Christiano y Erudito*, tom. i. p. 431.
[2] Ibid., i. p. 469.   [3] Ibid., i. p. 173.

on his head on the authority of a vision of Santa Teresa, and the second is allowed as being a probable, if not exactly proven, appendage of the fallen angel.

All the writers on this curious subject strongly reprobate any unnecessary display of the nude figure. Ayala censures[1] those artists who expose the feet of their Madonnas—which Spanish women are always so chary of displaying—almost as severely as he does the indecent limner whom he records[2] to have painted for a certain church a holy Virgin suffering martyrdom on a St. Andrew's cross, in the state in which the good Lady Godiva rode through Coventry. Pacheco[3] illustrates his argument against immodest altar-pieces by a singular anecdote of their distressing effects. He had it, he says, from a grave and pious bishop, himself the hero of his tale. The picture was a "Last Judgment," by Martin de Vos, once in the church of the Augustines, now in the Museum[4] at Seville, and is, like other works of the master, a composition of considerable power and merit, but disfigured by ill-placed episodes of broad caricature. The grouping is effective, and

---

[1] Duran's Translation. *El Pintor Christiano y Erudito*, tom. i. p. 25.
[2] Ibid., i. p. 27.
[3] *Arte de la Pintura*, p. 201.
[4] The picture is on panel, six or seven feet square, and is signed "F. Merthen de Vos, 1570." It is (1845) in the small oratory of the transept of the church, now the principal hall of the Museum, where Montañes' fine Crucifix is placed.

many of the principal figures are nobly drawn, and full of various interest and character. But beyond them in the distance the eye is offended by a grotesque devil, who quells certain of the damned that attempt to break their prescribed bounds, by means of vigorous blows of his trident, and administers to one of the more refractory a hearty kick with his cloven hoof, aimed in the most vulgarly insulting direction. Amongst a group of naked women in the foreground, one magnificent specimen of the Lais order, conspicuous for her fair flowing locks and full voluptuous form, is being dragged off by a hideous demon, terminating in a fish, and grinning with horrid glee. It was doubtless on this figure—" a woman remarkable," says Pacheco, " for the beauty and disorder of her person "—that the eye of the bishop chanced to rest, when he was one day saying mass, as a simple friar, before the painting. His quick southern imagination being thus suddenly and strongly excited, the poor man fell into a state of mental discomposure such as he had never before known. " Rather than undergo the same spiritual conflict a second time," said the good prelate, who had made the voyage to America, " I would face a hurricane in the Gulf of Bermuda. Even at the distance of many years, I cannot think of that picture without dread." St. Francis Borja was made of sterner stuff. His son-in-law, the Count of

Leonia, in order to test the perfection of his holy phlegm, placed on an altar at which he was to say mass, a portrait of his dead Duchess, Leonora de Castro, painted as St. Catherine. Thereupon the saint's companion asked what picture that was? "Doña Leonora," said he. He then informed him that it caused no more "alteracion" in his soul than if he had not seen it; only, he commended her to God. "Tell the Count," he added, "to keep it in his house, and bring it here no more, though he has dressed up Leonora as St. Catherine."[1]

The pious enthusiasm of Spanish artists not unfrequently led them to believe, like Fra Angelico, that their fancy was quickened, and their hands strengthened by inspiration from on high. The idea was readily adopted by priestly craft and popular superstition. To the studios of Toledo and Valencia, if their occupants are to be trusted, angels' visits were neither few nor far between. Works not seldom issued thence, little inferior in powers of performing miracles and enriching shrines, to veritable portraits from the easel of St. Luke or the holy kerchief of St. Veronica. Of this kind was a celebrated "Virgin," painted by Joanes at the express command of the holy original, who revealed herself to Fray Martin Alberto, of the order of Jesus, and

---

[1] P. de Ribadineira, *Vida del Pad. F. de Borja*; 4to, Madrid, 1592.

INTRODUCTION.

CHAP. I.

Becerra aided by her in a carving.

She sits to S. Cotar.

Miracles performed by an unfinished picture of the Virgin.

even gave directions about the dress in which she chose to appear.[1] Twice had Gaspar Becerra been baffled in carving an image of the Virgin to the mind of Queen Isabel of Valois; he owed his success at last to a visit paid him by the blessed Mary, who roused him in the night watches, and enjoined him to go to work on a fire-log, which was presently fashioned into one of the most famous idols of Spain. The same divine personage actually honoured Sanchez Cotan with a sitting for her portrait,[2] of which the miracles were innumerable as St. Apollonia's teeth—effectual against toothache—whereof an officer appointed for that purpose at our Reformation—if we may credit Fuller—collected in England enough to fill a tun.[3] The miracles of an image sometimes began when it was still under the pencil or chisel. In a certain church, says Lope de Vega,[4] a painter, mounted on a lofty scaffolding, was painting, on the wall, Our Lady and the Infant Jesus. The platform under his feet, suddenly giving way, fell with a prodigious crash; but not so the painter, for he piously invoked the aid of the Virgin in his picture, and she, promptly putting forth, from the wall, her one finished arm, held him suspended in mid-air till the monks brought a ladder of escape.

---

[1] Palomino, iii. p. 395. [2] Palomino, iii. p. 433.
[3] Fuller's *Church History*, folio. London, 1655. B. vi. p. 331.
[4] El Peregrino en su patria, Lib. i., *Obras;* tom. v., p. 66.

The hand which had thus stood forth in prominent relief, then relapsed once more into the picture. "A thing," ejaculates the pilgrim into whose mouth Lope puts the tale, "worthy of wonder and tears, that the Virgin should leave holding her son, to uphold a sinner who, falling, might peradventure have been damned!"[1] Another Madonna, of great fame in Castile, Our Lady of Nieva, restored to life a painter who was almost dashed to pieces by a fall through a scaffolding, when painting the dome of her chapel.[2] But if these holy effigies rewarded the faithful and devout artist, they sometimes punished him who addressed himself to their service in a spirit of profane levity. Thus Our Lady of Monserrate struck a painter blind, who was about to retouch her celebrated image, carved by St. Luke and adored in the famous monastery of Monserrate amongst the jagged rocks of Catalonia. He remained sightless for many years, till having evinced sufficient contrition, the Virgin was pleased to restore his vision whilst he was chanting "*Profer lumen cæcis*" with the monks.[3]

To have achieved a wonder-working painting or sculpture, was, however, sometimes a perilous as

---

[1] El Peregrino en su patria, Lib. i., *Obras*; tom. v., p. 97.
[2] Villafañe, *Imágenes Milagrosas*, p. 372.
[3] *Historia de la adoracion y uso de las santas Imagenes*, por el maestro Iayme Prados; 4to, Valencia, 1597; p. 401.

well as a glorious distinction. In the plague of Malaga, in 1649, a certain statue of Christ at the column, carved for the cathedral by Giuseppe Micael, an Italian, performed prodigies of healing, and bade fair to rival that holy Crucifix—sculptured at Jerusalem by Nicodemus, and possessed by the Capuchins of Burgos [1]—which sweated on Fridays, and wrought miracles all the week. While the pestilence was yet raging, the sculptor stood one evening musing near the door of the sanctuary where his work was enshrined, but with so sorrowful a countenance, that a friend, hailing him from afar, according to the usages of plague-stricken society, inquired the cause of his sadness. "Think you," said the artist, "that I have anything more to look for on earth, after seeing and hearing the prodigies and marvels of

---

[1] Madame d'Aulnoy, *Relation du Voyage en Espagne*—3 toms. 12mo, La Haye, 1693—tom. i. p. 122. Marie Catherine Jumelle de Berneville, —niece of Madame des Loges, famous for her wit in the reign of Louis XIII., and wife of the Comte d'Aulnoy, who had nearly lost his head under Louis XIV. on a false charge of treason—was one of the most lively and agreeable lady-writers of the age of Madame de Sévigné. She has left several romances (Contes des Fées, Histoire du Comte de Duglas, &c.) as well as memoirs in which facts are sometimes seasoned with fiction. Her *Voyage en Espagne*, and her *Mémoires de la Cour d'Espagne*, are rare, and deserve reprinting for the vivacity of their style, and their curious pictures of manners. In the Amsterdam edition of the latter—2 toms. 12mo, 1716—there is an indifferent portrait of her, in which she is represented as a tall pleasing woman, attired in the brocade petticoat and looped-up negligée of her time. She died in 1705. There is an English translation of the *Voyage*, entitled *The Ingenious and Diverting Letters of the Lady ——'s Travels into Spain*—London, 1692, 3 vols. 12mo—which is very scarce.

this sovereign image which my unworthy hands have made? It is an old tradition amongst the masters of our craft, that he shall soon die to whom it is given to make a miraculous image." And the good Giuseppe erred not in his presentiment; his chisel's task was done; he was "to return no more, nor see his native country;"[1] and within eight days the dead-cart had carried him to the gorged cemetery of Malaga. His name, if not his life, was preserved by the statue—which was long revered for its Esculapian powers, under the title (profanely usurped) of the "Lord of Health" (*El Señor de la Salud*).

Where no direct visits or angelic sittings were vouchsafed, still the saints looked kindly on artists who did them honour, and would stand by them in seasons of spiritual need. Father Martin de Roa[2] used to tell of a young painter who yielded to the entreaty of a loose-minded lord, that he should paint for him an immodest picture. Dying not long after, he was forthwith cast into purgatory, and not released till his patron had repented him of the picture, destroyed it, and done a proportionate number of good works. The intercession of the saints, whom he had in his lifetime depicted, then opened to the painter the gate of Paradise.

---

[1] *Jer.* xxii. 10.   [2] Pacheco, *Arte de la Pintura*, p. 271.

CHAP. I.
Legend of the Painter-Friar, the Devil and the Virgin.

Don Josef de Valdivielso,[1] one of the chaplains of the gay Cardinal Infant Ferdinand of Austria, cites a yet more remarkable instance of celestial interference on behalf of an artist in trouble. A certain young friar, he says, was famous amongst his order for his skill as a painter; and took peculiar delight in drawing the blessed Virgin and the Devil. To heighten the divine beauty of the one, and to devise new and extravagant forms of ugliness for the other, were the chief recreations of his leisure. Vexed at last by the variety and vigour of his sketches, Beelzebub, to be revenged, assumed the form of a lovely maiden, and, so disguised, crossed the path of the religious, who—being of an amorous complexion—fell at once into the trap. The seeming damsel smiled on her shaven wooer, but though willing to be won, would not surrender her charms at a less price than certain rich reliquaries and jewels in the convent-treasury—a price which the friar, in evil hour, consented to pay. He admitted her at midnight within the convent walls, and leading her to the sacristy, took from its antique cabinets the precious things for which she had asked. Then came the moment of vengeance. Passing in their return through the moonlit cloister—as the sinful

---

[1] See his paper against the tax on Pictures—a subject which does not at first sight seem capable of being much illustrated by such a legend—appended to Carducho's *Diálogos de la Pintura*, p. 184.

friar stole along, embracing the booty with one arm and his false Duessa with the other, the demon-lady—"more like a woman than a demon," as the chaplain slyly remarks—suddenly cried out "Thieves!" with diabolical energy. The snoring monks rushed disordered, each from his cell, and detected their unlucky brother in the act of making off with their plate. Excuse being impossible, they tied the culprit to a column, and leaving him till matins, when his punishment was to be determined, went back to their pillows or their prayers. The Devil, unseen during the confusion, re-appeared when all was quiet, but this time in his most hideous shape. Half dead with cold and terror, the discomfited caricaturist stood shivering at his pillar, while his tormentor made unmercifully merry with him; twitting him with his amorous overtures, mocking his stammered prayers, and irreverently suggesting an appeal for aid to the beauty he so loved to delineate. The penitent wretch at last took the advice thus jeeringly given—when lo! the Mother of Mercy, radiant in heavenly loveliness, descended, loosed his cords, and bade him bind the Evil One to the column in his place—an order which, through her strength, he obeyed with not less alacrity than astonishment. She further ordered him to appear amongst the other monks at matins, and charged herself with the task of restoring the stolen plate to its place. The tables were thus suddenly turned. The friar presented himself amongst his brethren to their no small surprise, and voted with much contrition for his own condemnation—a sentence which was, however, reversed, on the sacristy being examined and its contents miraculously found correct. As for the Devil, who remained fast bound to the pillar, he was soundly flogged, and so fell into the pit he had digged for another. His dupe, on the other hand, gathered new strength from his fall, and became not only a wiser and a better man, but likewise an abler artist; for the experience of that terrible night had supplied all that was wanting to the ideal of his favourite subjects. Thenceforth he followed no more after enticing damsels, but remained like a respectable monk in his cloister, painting the Madonna more serenely beautiful, and the Arch-enemy more curiously appalling than ever.

Legend of Our Lady, the Devil, and the Painter.

Lope de Vega[1] relates a still stranger tale of a painter, miraculously released by Our Lady from toils in which the Evil One had enmeshed him. Like the friar, this layman preferred those mysterious personages to all other themes; with prayer and the Eucharist he prepared himself for a picture of the Virgin: and nightmare itself could suggest

---

[1] El Peregrino; Lib. ii. *Obras;* tom. v., p. 97.

no form of horror with which he had not already invested the Devil. Indignant at these proceedings, the latter at last contrived that his persecutor should fall desperately in love with a soldier's wife, that she should return his passion, and that they should finally elope under cover of night. At the moment of their escape, the fiend set the great bells of the church a-ringing, and mingling in human shape with the crowd that collected in the market-place, he spread the report of the event. The friends of the soldier immediately went in pursuit, and guided by the same malicious intelligence, captured the fugitives and lodged them in separate cells in the city prison. Thither the husband repaired, and there, having sufficiently upbraided his partner for her infidelity, he cut off her long beautiful hair, once his peculiar pride, and left her to her fate, which was certain decapitation. Meanwhile the painter, awaiting the same doom, commended himself to Our Lady, and urged, in mitigation of his sin, the zeal with which his pencil had striven to do honour to her beauty. His prayers were crowned with singular and signal success. Opening the prison doors, the Blessed Mary appeared to the lovers as the angel of their deliverance, and conducted them silently and secretly, the one to his solitary lodging, the other to her vacant place in the marriage-bed. At morn the soldier, when he awoke, was confounded by finding his wife by his side, and eagerly asked if her flight and her shorn curls were then all a dream? "A mere dream," said the prudent spouse, "to which thy fear gives the semblance of reality; for never have I strayed from thy house, or harboured a thought hurtful to our mutual honour." Mistrustful of her words, the man arose and searched for the proofs which he had brought from the prison; but he not only missed "those soft alluring locks" from their hiding-place, but found them growing on his wife's head in all their former beauty and abundance. Still not altogether convinced, he went to consult his friends, by whom he was assured that his dishonour was indeed only too certain and too public. On hearing his story, however, they flocked, in eager amazement, to the prison, to satisfy themselves at least of the incarceration of the painter. But his cell also was empty; and the fortunate Lothario was eventually found in his own studio, in all the candour of innocence, preparing to evince his secret gratitude by a new picture of the protectress of his honour and his life. Thus was the Devil once more foiled, and thus the citizens who had been roused by the bells, the pursuers who had captured the truants, the turnkey who barred the prison, the husband who clipped the tresses, and the gossips who told the tale, were made to believe, "by the merits of Mary Our Lady," that they had dreamed a strange, vivid, and unanimous dream.

These legends may serve as specimens of the stories with which Spanish works on art are plentifully garnished. They prove, at least, the intimate connection of religion and art in Spain, and the good understanding that subsisted between priests and painters. But the grave and decorous taste of the nation influenced the artists whose practice lay chiefly in the Court, no less powerfully than it did those who laboured exclusively for the Church. It cannot be said that the Court of the Catholic Kings of the Spains and the Indies was much more strict in its morals than those of the most Christian sovereigns of France, or our own Defenders of the Faith. Madrid, like Paris and London, never lacked its Bassompierres and Rochesters: the race of Portsmouth and Pompadour flourished at Aranjuez as freely as at Windsor and Versailles; nor was the post held by Ortiz and the Godoys a creation of the Bourbons in Spain. But at the Spanish Court it is certain that fewer indecorums were perpetrated on canvas than at others; and amongst all its painters, not one either gained, like Pietro Liberi of Venice, by his lascivious pictures, or deserved, the name of "Libertino."

The Austrian princes descended of Charles V. were all of them rigid formalists in religion and

CHAP. I.
pictorial improprieties.

etiquette, and seldom encouraged improper freedom of the pencil. Philip II., indeed, in his youth, suffered Titian to paint him indulging in that singular pleasure,—offered two centuries later by the profligate Augustus of Poland, after a drinking bout at Dresden, to his boon companion, Frederick William of Prussia, rejected by that intemperate drill-sergeant with virtuous disgust, and described with much animation by his daughter,[1]—the contemplation of the charms of a Venus, unreservedly abandoned to his gaze, and said to be those of his faithless and haughty mistress, the Princess of Eboli. That lady, it would appear, was nothing loath to display her faultless form, holding the opinion perhaps that—

———"Beauty, without falsehood fair,
Needs nought to clothe it but the air;"[2]

for in 1679 a portrait of her in the same character, attended by Cupids, and probably, like the former, the work of a foreigner, adorned one of the sumptuous chambers of the Castle of Buitrago, the ancient seat of her lord, Ruy Gomez de Silva.[3] Her royal lover, however, soon turned away his eyes from beholding such vanities; and finally became so great a

---

[1] *Mémoires de Frédérique Sophie Wilhelmine de Prusse, Margrave de Bareith*, 2 tomes 8vo, Paris 1811—tom. i. p. 112.
[2] Ben Jonson's *Works*, ix. p. 67.—Gifford's ed. 8vo, 1816.
[3] Mme. d'Aulnoy, *Voyage en Espagne*, tom. ii. p. 43.

purist in these matters of deficient drapery, that on the arrival, at the palace, of Cellini's magnificent Crucifixion, his finest work in marble, a present from the Grand Duke of Tuscany, he would not permit the Infantas of Savoy and Flanders to see it till he had arranged his handkerchief discreetly across the figure, where monkish loyalty long revered it as a relic.[1] In the times of Philip IV., the palmy days of portrait painting and gallantry, not the freest fair ones of the Court—neither Maria Calderona the Spanish Nell Gwynne, nor the beautiful Hippolita d'Alby, nor the fearless Duchesse de Chevreuse, seem ever to have loosed their zones in the studios after the fashion of our Villierses and Stuarts—those

> ———"beauties of Sir Peter Lely,
> Whose drapery hints we may admire them freely."[2]

The Spanish Charles II., who was so opposite in mind and morals to his namesake and contemporary, our Merry Monarch, and to whom nothing of his stern great-grandsire had descended but the gloom and prudery of his old age, permitted some foolish monks of the Escorial to employ the

---

[1] Pacheco, *Arte de la Pintura*, p. 632. Mr. Beckford speaks with rapture of this "revered image of the crucified Saviour, formed of the purest *ivory*, which Cellini seems to have sculptured in moments of devout rapture and inspiration."—(*Italy, with Sketches of Spain and Portugal;* London, 8vo, 1834—vol. ii. p. 320.) It is strange that this admirable and observing writer should have taken a marble figure of the size of life for ivory.

[2] Byron, *Don Juan*, cant. xiii. st. 68.

pencil of Luca Giordano in letting down the robe of Titian's St. Margaret, because she slew her dragon, to their thinking, with a too free exposure of leg.[1]

The general character of Spanish painting, therefore, is solemn and religious; its compositions for the most part dark and grand; and its figures more remarkable for the majesty and variety of draperies than for display of anatomical skill. Spain being the elysium of monks, the various religious orders, "white, black, and grey," were there delineated with unusual force and frequency, as the most careless observer will remark in traversing the Spanish division of any large gallery. Murillo and Espinosa were much employed by the friars who wore the brown frock of St. Francis; Carducho and Zurbaran most affected the Carthusians, whose white robes and hoods they managed with fine skill and effect; Roelas was the peculiar painter of the crafty and sable-stoled followers of Loyola. Subjects of this kind naturally gave to the Spanish pencil a great facility in dealing with drapery, of which the national "capa," or cloak, worn alike by Manchegan shepherd and serenading courtier, likewise afforded admirable studies in every street and highway.

---

[1] Cumberland's *Anecdotes*, v. i. 65.

The school of Castile is generally distinguished by a dark and sober style of colouring, grey backgrounds, and clouded skies. One of its great masters, however, El Mudo, imitated with success the splendour of Titian; while another, El Greco, who also had studied at Venice, played a hundred fantastic tricks with colour, which amazed Toledo, and injured his reputation. The female heads in Castilian paintings, in those of Tristan especially, are generally inferior in dignity and interest to the male; their features are too often coarse, and bear the marks of being taken from models in whose veins the blood of the Goth predominated over that of the Moor.

Moving southward, we enter fairer regions both in nature and art. The tawny brown of the Castiles, and the dismal snuff-coloured cloth (*paño pardo*) that drapes the peasant who tills them, give place to fields green and flowery, and mendicants flaunting in blue and scarlet rags. The gay blossoms of the cactus and oleander mantle the southern roots of the sierra, and blush along the margin of the stream. Vivid mulberry and violet hues brighten the canvases of Valencia, reds and golden yellows enrich those of Seville. The Madonnas and saintly women of the painters of these schools reflect the grace and beauty of the daughters of the south, whose arched brows, lustrous eyes, and delicate features, are inherited from Arabian mothers, and their Moslem lords, the captors of Spain, "who

> ——"ennobled her breed
> And high-mettled the blood of her veins."[1]

Painters of Seville fond of subjects of still life;

The Sevillians were fond of introducing into their pictures objects of still life—such as water-jars and baskets of fruit and vegetables—which they painted with admirable effect. These they had excellent opportunities of studying in the weekly fair (*feria*), where Murillo and many of his ablest compeers were wont, in their early days, to gain a livelihood by selling the rude productions of their pencil, which they would retouch on the spot to suit the taste of their homely customers. Some of their "bodegones"—kitchen pieces, as they are called—where fish and game lie mingled with water-melons, citrons, and the large olives of Andalusia, are works of high technical merit. The Valencian painters of still-life chiefly affected the flowers that bloom so lavishly in that soft delicious clime; and have left flower-pieces not excelled in dewy freshness and luxuriant dyes by the most elaborate efforts of the garden artists of Holland.

their "bodegones."

Valencian flower-painters.

Spanish painters distinguished in portraiture.

In portraiture—the most useful and valuable department of painting, which lightens the labour and

---

[1] Campbell, Lines written at sunset on the battlefield at Hastings.

points the tale of the historian and the biographer, embalms beyond the arts of Egypt, and gives to beauty centuries instead of years of triumph—the Spaniard attained a proud eminence. All the greatest painters of Spain have produced admirable portraits. Joanes has been called the Spanish Rafael, and in this branch of his art, he deserves that proud title. If Velazquez and Murillo have not here equalled the achievements of Titian and Vandyck, it is not that the genius and skill of the Spaniards were less, but that the fields of their famous rivals were finer. The Senate of Venice, and the splendid throngs of the imperial court, the Lomellini and Brignoli of Genoa, and the Herberts and Howards of England, afforded better models of manly beauty, than the degenerating nobility of the court of Philip IV., and the clergy and gentry of Seville.

With the beauty of high-born women—the finest touchstone of skill—they were but seldom brought into professional contact. The great portrait-painters of Spain lived in an age of jealous husbands, who cared not to set off to public admiration the charms of their spouses. Velazquez came to reside at court about the same time that Madrid was visited by Sir Kenelm Digby, who had like to have been slain on the night of his arrival for merely looking at a lady. Returning with two friends from supper at Lord

Bristol's, the adventurous knight relates[1] how they came beneath a balcony where a love-lorn fair one stood touching her lute, and how they loitered there awhile to admire her beauty, and listen to "her soul-ravishing harmony." Their delightful contemplations were soon rudely disturbed by the sound of heavy footsteps, by arms glittering in the moonlight, and the furious onset of "fifteen men in mail, with dark lanterns fixed on their bucklers;" when, had not the lover of Venetia Stanley, who slew the leader, been a tall man at his weapon, the streets of Madrid would have been red with the blood of three bold Britons, who, but a moment before, had been "sucking in the fresh air and pleasing themselves in the coolness of the night;" and the story told, not in the valiant swordsman's own curious Memoirs, but in Bristol's next despatch, or by honest Howell in a quaint letter.

Husbands and wives.

Few grandees were content, like the Prince of Eboli, that their wives should play Venus even to a royal Mars. The Duke of Albuquerque, who, at the door of his own palace, waylaid and horsewhipped Philip IV. and Olivares,[2] feigning ignorance of their persons, as the monarch came to pay a nocturnal visit to the duchess,—was not very likely to call in

---

[1] *Private Memoirs*, written by himself, London, 8vo, 1827, p. 154.
[2] Madame d'Aulnoy, *Relation du Voyage d'Espagne*, 3 vols. 12mo La Haye, 1693—vol. ii. 21, 22.

the court-painter to take her grace's portrait. Ladies lived for the most part in a sort of Oriental seclusion amongst duennas, waiting-women, and dwarfs; often treated by their lords rather as menials than as wives, and not sitting with them at table, but eating apart, squatted on the floor "like Turks or journeymen tailors," as a surprised Frenchman wrote in his travels;[1] and going abroad only to mass, or to take the air in curtained coaches on the Prado. It was not the fashion amongst them to sit for their likenesses, as is proved by the rare occurrence of female portraits—of other than royal personages—in collections of Spanish pictures. Of the sixty-two works of Velazquez, in the royal gallery at Madrid, there are only four of this kind; and of these, two represent children, another an ancient matron, and the fourth his own wife.

Even when permitted to make the portrait of a great lady, in the bloom of youth and beauty, the painter of the seventeenth century had to contend with the difficulties of tasteless and even unsightly

---

[1] See the amusing *Voyage d'Espagne*, 12mo, Cologne, 1667 (of which an English translation was published in London, 1670); and also Mme. d'Aulnoy (*Voyage*, II. p. 108), who once attempted to conform to the national attitude, out of politeness to a young Castilian hostess,—who never doubted but that all the Countesses of "the Faubourg" sat cross-legged on carpets,—but unsuccessfully, for, says she, "les jambes me faisoient un mal horrible; tantôt je m'appuyois sur le coude, tantôt sur le main; enfin je renonçois à dîner." It is satisfactory to know that a gentleman of the party, more familiar with foreign customs, at last brought her a chair.

costume. The fairest forms were thrust into long-waisted corsets, stiff and unyielding as armour of proof, and were disguised in hoops of monstrous circumference,—compared, for size, to roofs of houses [1] —in which all the bending lines of beauty were lost, and the finest and the faultiest figures brought to one conventional shape—that of a drum with a funnel planted in its top. Luxuriant tresses were twisted, plaited, and plastered into such shape that the fair head that bore them resembled the top of a mushroom; or curled and bushed out into an amplitude of frizzle that rivalled the cauliflower wig of an Abbé.[2] An ungainly mode also prevailed of parting the hair at the side instead of the top of the head, thus marring the symmetry and balance of its outline, of which some wretched portraits in the Spanish gallery of the Louvre, impudently ascribed to Velazquez, might be cited as examples sufficiently offensive and deterring.

The dresses worn by the great ladies of the Royal Household on state occasions were admirable for the purposes of disguise and disfigurement. The Duchess of Terranova, the heiress of the Mexican principality of Cortes, mounted on a mule, and riding behind her graceful young mistress, Louisa of Orleans, at that Queen's solemn entry into Madrid,

---

[1] *Voyage d'Espagne*, Cologne, 1667, p. 21.
[2] Madame d'Aulnoy, *Voyage en Espagne*, tom. ii. p. 102.

doubtless looked singularly forbidding; her sombre nunlike widow's weeds, crowned with an enormous hat, being well adapted to display to the worst advantage the pale wrinkled face and small sharp eyes of that "terrible Camarera Mayor," whose "I will," and "I won't," made the Court tremble.[1] The baffled rival, or the scolded maid-of-honour—with any taste in dress—could have wished for no severer punishment to overtake her than a portrait drawn under these circumstances by a plain-speaking pencil. But the truth is, the perception of the proprieties of costume was wanting, and the fashions of the fair Spaniards who lived in an age which offered to their charms the best chance of becoming historical, tended—certainly by no design of the sweet sex—to second the wishes of their jealous lords, and to conceal, rather than to set off their attractions; their black eyes, the finest in the world, their pretty hands, skilled in the "nice conduct" of the speaking fan; and more than all, their feet, so dainty and fairylike, of which a glimpse was one of the last precious favours accorded to a lover's sighs and tears.[2]

But worse than all these absurdities was the abomination of rouge, which tinged not only the

Universal and extravagant use of rouge.

---

[1] Mme. d'Aulnoy, *Mémoires de la Cour d'Espagne*, tom. i. pp. 104-203.
[2] Mme. d'Aulnoy, *Voyage en Espagne*, tom. ii. p. 126.

cheeks, but also foreheads, ears, and chins, and was likewise bestowed on the shoulders and hands. In the reign of Philip IV., great was the consumption of vermilion and white-lead on the morning of a royal bull-feast.[1] The ladies of Vittoria—who, doubtless, affected the newest fashions of Madrid—not a little astonished, by their ruddiness, the French Countess who visited their city in 1679. Writing of the theatre there, Madame d'Aulnoy says,[2] "toutes les dames que je vis dans cette assemblée avoient une si prodigieuse quantité de rouge, qui commence juste sous l'œil, et qui passe du menton aux oreilles et aux épaules, et dans les mains, que je n'ai jamais vû d'écrevisses cuites d'une plus belle couleur." "Scarlet" was an epithet that might be properly applied to other ladies besides her of Babylon—and to be "rosy-fingered" was no longer peculiar to the Morn. Had any Castilian Burns chanted beneath his mistress's window or whispered in her ear that she resembled "a red, red rose," the lattice would have been indignantly shut, or the bard, perhaps, might have had his own ears boxed, for a blockhead and a dealer in truisms and prose. The very nymphs and goddesses that figured amongst the statues on the terrace of the royal palace of Madrid had their marble cheeks and bosoms smeared with car-

---

[1] *Voyage d'Espagne*, Cologne, 1667, p. 87.
[2] Madame d'Aulnoy, *Voyage en Espagne*, tom. i. 57.

mine.¹ This perversion of taste at the toilette not only destroyed the complexions of the court-beauties, but, what is much more distressing to lovers of art,—spoiled the female portraits of Velazquez and Carreño. The second King of Prussia used to amuse his leisure by taking likenesses of his grenadiers; and it is said that when he found his work too highly coloured, he would daub the patient's face with red paint till it assumed the same fiery hue.² The difficulty with the Spanish artists was, not to subdue their tints, but to bring them up to the crimson glow of their well-rouged sitters.

The royal portraits of the Austrian dynasty in Spain afford ample evidence of the fine powers of Spanish portrait-painters. That family—perhaps the plainest—was also the best painted of the royal houses of Europe. The noble features of the Stuart, the regal port of the Bourbon, found rarely and at long intervals a Vandyck or a Philippe de Champagne; even the princely houses of Italy want a series of able and honest chroniclers on canvas, such as those who have transmitted to us the faces of their Spanish contemporaries. The policy of the Catholic kings curbed with a heavy hand the liberty of the press; their taste granted full freedom to the pencil.

---

¹ Madame d'Aulnoy, *Voyage en Espagne*, iii. p. 5.
² Lord Dover's *Life of Frederick II.*, 2 vols. 8vo, London, 1832, vol. i. p. 62.

While history, therefore, has caricatured by turns the good and evil of their characters, painting has told the truth and nothing but the truth of their persons. Days of study in the library will but confirm and fill in the story we find sketched in their portraits, where we see the intellectual force that stamps the brow and mouth of the great Emperor reproduced in the gloomier countenance of his terrible son, visible, though in far fainter reflection, in the features—but little changed in form—of Philip III., gradually fading from the lack-lustre eye and sensual lip of Philip IV., and finally lost in the forlorn idiocy that clouds the pale face of Charles II. It is in the colours of Titian that the person of Charles V. is so well known to the world; and though he was doubtless frequently painted by Spanish artists, no example of a contemporary portrait is to be found in the public galleries of Spain. The mild countenance, however, of his Empress, Isabella of Portugal, has been preserved by the accurate pencil of Alonso Sanchez Coello. Philip II., pourtrayed in his better days by Titian, ere his cold features had lost the freshness of youth, was often painted after he became King, by his favourite Sanchez Coello, who has recorded on several canvases the lines and wrinkles as they gathered on his brow, between the victory of St. Quentin and the loss of the Armada. Pantoja de la Cruz has likewise drawn him, noting with unshrinking fidelity the traces of the disease and melancholy of his ghastly old age. His queens, and his sallow sickly children, and his gallant brother Don Juan, fell, according to their dates, to the pencils of More, Coello, and Pantoja, the latter of whom seems to have been warmed into rivalry with Titian by the sweet smile and superb complexion and figure of the dark-eyed Isabella of Valois. Pantoja was likewise the favourite portrait-painter of Philip III. and Queen Margaret, whom, with their Infants and Infantas, he frequently introduced into sacred compositions, flattering at once their vanity and piety by grouping them, in peasant garb, round the bed of St. Anne or the manger at Bethlehem, in pictures of the Nativities of the Virgin and our Lord. With Philip IV. the desire of multiplying his own image on canvas seems to have amounted to a passion. His long pale face and fiercely curling moustachios are to be found on the walls of almost every great gallery. Rubens painted him nearly as often as he did his own peculiar patrons, the good Archduke and Duchess, Albert and Isabella. Perhaps more hours of the King's life were spent in the studio of Velazquez than in the Council of Castile. That great master has painted him in every possible costume and circumstance—attired for the field, the chase, and the pageant, on foot, on horseback, and kneeling in his oratory. For the beautiful

CHAP. I.
Queens and brothers of Philip IV.

Isabella of Bourbon, Philip's first Queen, he has done all that Vandyck did for her sister, our own Henrietta Maria; for the Infants Carlos and Ferdinand all that was done by that famous Fleming for Prince Rupert and his brother. In his portraits of Mariana of Austria, Isabella's rather pretty successor, he has left to all future great ladies some signal warnings against extravagant modes of dressing the hair and the use of rouge. He has saved from oblivion, by many delightful pictures, the little round head of Prince Balthazar Carlos, whose early death placed him almost beneath the level of history; and the girlish beauty of the Infanta Margaret Maria and her playmates blooms for all time in one of his most remarkable works. In the next reign, in the general dearth of genius, the Court painter, Carreño de Miranda, showed himself a man of talent and skill, not only in his graceful portraits of the lovely Queen Louisa of Orleans, but in the more arduous task of grappling with King Charles the Second's leaden eye and projecting nether jaw, so as to transmit to posterity an image—faithful, and yet not altogether unpleasing—of the last withering branch of the royal stock.

His children.

Charles II. and Queen Louisa.

Carreño.

Landscape painting little cultivated.

Landscape painting was but little cultivated in Spain. The Vega of Granada, beautiful beyond the praise of Arabian song; the delicious "garden" of Valencia, where the azure-tiled domes of countless convents glittered amidst their groves of mulberry, and citron, and palm; the stern plains and sierras of Castile; the broad valley of the Guadalquivir, studded with towered cities and goodly abbeys; the wild glens of the Alpuxarras; the pine forests of Soria, have found no Claude or Salvator to feel and express their beauty and magnificence. Velazquez, in all branches of his art a great master, has painted some noble sketches of scenery, as Murillo also has done, though in a less vigorous style. Mazo, a Castilian, Iriarte a Biscayan, but belonging to the school of Andalusia, and the Sevillian Antolinez, are almost the only Spaniards who made the fields their place of study, or whose doings there deserve much notice.

Italian as well as Spanish art seems to afford evidence that the beauties of nature are not most keenly felt where they are most lavishly bestowed. The scenery of Italy has been studied with greater zeal and better results by foreigners than by her own sons. Salvator Rosa, the best of her native landscape-painters, does not generally dwell on the finest and most attractive features of that glorious land. Three Frenchmen—Gelée, Poussin, and Dughet, whom fate might have detained in Normandy and Lorraine, were the first to do pictorial justice to the sky and atmosphere of Italy—to her classic ruins and tall umbrageous pines, her ancient rivers wind-

Landscape painters not generally born amongst fine scenery.

ing through storied fields, and the soft and sunny shores of her blue Mediterranean.

Painters of landscape abound in the North.

It is not till we leave the regions of noble landscapes, grand architecture, and picturesque population, that we reach the lands most prolific of painters capable of doing justice to these things. While far finer subjects for the pencil lay unheeded around the artists of Spain and Italy, the Fleming and the Hollander committed to canvas every varying aspect of their cloudy skies and leaden seas, and canals creeping wearily through interminable flats of lush pasturage—and studied their mills and their gardens, their brick-built streets and trim white-washed churches, with a zeal worthy of a better cause. The august cathedrals of Seville and Leon, the sumptuous mansions of Valencia, the mosques and palaces of Moorish Spain, want their Steenwyks and their Neefs; the fierce sports of the bull-ring and the wild herds of Utrera and Jarama, their Cuyp and Wouvermans, Sneyders and Potter; the posada, with its gay and motley throngs, has no Jan Steen and Ostade, nor the joyous "dance and sunburnt mirth" of the Andalusian vintage a Teniers or a Rubens.

Best painters of Italian scenery foreigners.

In Italy, the omissions of native artists were supplied by their foreign disciples, whose imagination was readily caught by all that was picturesque and peculiar in its life and scenery. Thither students flocked yearly from the north, full of the curiosity and ardour of youth, and eager to see, to learn, and to labour. They saw at once that the sea and sky of Gaeta and Naples were brighter than those they had known in Guelderland and Brabant; that Venice, with its canals margined with Palladian palaces, was fairer and fitter for the purposes of art than Amsterdam; that the villas of the Medici were not as the rural retreat of Vanderhulk; and that the weeds of the Flavian amphitheatre were better than all the tulips of Haarlem. As mere tyros—and perhaps as heretics—on arriving at Rome or Florence, they were not immediately retained by princes and cardinals, and worn out by intense labours prosecuted on ladders and dizzy scaffoldings; but they were left at liberty to indulge fresh emotions and gather new ideas, to sketch as they listed the hoary ruin or the classic costume, and to study and enjoy the new face with which nature shone and smiled around them. Thus it was that the great French painters of landscape turned, half by accident, out of the beaten roads of art into the path that led them to fame; thus it was that Both and Swanevelt divined the secrets of their craft, and acquired that mastery over the atmosphere of the south which covers their faults as with a shield of gold, and makes their pictures, when met with in a northern gallery, cheer and delight us like a burst of sunshine in an English winter's day.

But it was otherwise in Spain. There stranger artists came—as we shall see—with few exceptions, at the invitation of the great, to display, not to improve their genius, and to perform in fresco or on canvas feats similar to those which had won the applause of Brussels or of Rome; and therefore had no leisure to bestow on scenes and subjects neglected by the native pencil. Cambiaso was too much in love, Zuccaro too conceited, Rubens too busy in politics as well as painting, to glean after El Mudo, Joanes, and Ribalta.

Many of the foreign auxiliaries of Italian art became naturalised in their new country; they were made free of the academies, and after their death, were sometimes claimed as native Italians by their Italian biographers. Amongst the greater painters of Spain, only three foreigners are reckoned,—the Fleming Campaña, the Greek Theotocopuli, and the Florentine Vincenzio Carducci—the latter of whom came to Madrid in his childhood, and lived and died a good Castilian.

The fame of Spanish painters, like the honour of certain crowned heads,[1] long suffered from their

---

[1] The witty Prince de Ligne, in his *Vie du Prince Eugène*, makes his hero thus remark on the politic and cautious Head of his House— "Voilà le Duc de Savoie, pour quelque temps le meilleur Autrichien du

geographical position. Till the present century, little was known, on this side the Pyrenees, of the arts of the Peninsula. Ribera—the "Spagnoletto" and favourite of Naples—whose passion for the horrible was little likely to produce a favourable impression of Spanish taste, was long the sole Spaniard whose name and works were familiar to Europe. At Rome, Vargas, Cespedes, and a few others had acquired some distinction in their day; and Velazquez had left a few portraits in the palaces, and enjoyed a traditionary reputation as a member of the academy of St. Luke. Few Spanish pictures travelled northwards, except the royal portraits sent to imperial kinsfolk at Vienna, and the works now and then carried home from Madrid by tasteful ambassadors. The catalogues of the rich collection of our Charles I. do not contain the name of a single Spanish master. Evelyn[1] indeed tells us, that, at the sale of Lord Melford's effects at Whitehall, in 1693, "Lord Godolphin bought the picture of the Boys, by Morillio, the Spaniard, for eighty guineas," which, he remarks, was "deare enough."[2] Yet Cumber-

CHAP. I.

Name of Murillo early known in England.

monde. Sa conduite, que je ne veux pas justifier, me rappelle celle que les Ducs de Lorraine out tenue autre fois, ainsi que les Ducs de Bavière. La Géographie les empêche d'être honnêtes gens."—*Mélanges Historiques et Littéraires*, 5 tomes, 8vo, Paris, 1829, tom. v. p. 29.

[1] *Memoirs of John Evelyn*, 5 vols. 8vo, London, 1827, v. iii. p. 325.

[2] [A writer in *Fraser's Magazine*, vol. xxxviii. (September 1848), p. 307, says, "About the year 1760, the then Lord Godolphin took a fancy to a colt belonging to a Mr. Leathes, of Herringfleet Hall, in Suffolk, which

land,[1] nearly a century later, while he admits Murillo to be better known in England than any Spanish master except Ribera, "very much doubts if any historical group or composition of his be in English hands." The Bourbon accession and increased intercourse with Spain brought a few good Spanish paintings into France to adorn the galleries of Orleans, Praslin, and Presle, most of which at the Revolution emigrated, like their possessors, to England. Yet the Abbé Dubos, in his Reflections on Poetry and Painting, first published in 1719, cites[2] Spain as one of those unfortunate countries where the climate is unfavourable to art, and remarks that she had produced no painter of the first class, and scarcely two of the second; thus with one stroke of his goosequill erasing from the book of fame Velazquez and Cano, Zurbaran and Murillo. Nevertheless the Abbé was a man of curious reading and research,—for he made the discovery that the poetry

---

resembled his celebrated Arabian, and gave this very picture in exchange for it. The painting is now in Mr. J. F. Leathes' valuable gallery at Herringfleet. The signature, 'Morellio,' which appears on the picture, is in curious accordance with Evelyn's orthography."
Curtis states, *Velazquez and Murillo*, roy. 8vo, New York, 1883, p. 291, that the picture was (in 1883) in the gallery of Hill M. Leathes, Esq., Herringfleet Hall, Lowestoft, Suffolk, and adds that, at the Earl of Godolphin's sale by Christie, June 6, 1803, No. 58 (Spanish Beggar Boys), sold for £257, 15s.—ED.]

[1] *Anecdotes*, ii. p. 101.
[2] *Réflexions Critiques sur la Poësie et sur la Peinture*, sixième édition, 3 tomes, 4to, Paris 1755, tom. ii. p. 148.

of the Dutch was superior in vigour and fire of fancy to their painting;[1] and his Reflections—which formed the last round of the literary ladder whereby he climbed into the Academy—passed unquestioned through many editions, and were praised by Voltaire as the best and most accurate work of the kind in modern literature. Meanwhile the countless treasures of Spanish painting—thus triumphantly libelled—hung neglected in their native convents and palaces, far from the highways of Europe, wasting their beauty on gloomy walls, unstudied, unvisited, forgotten, except by a few tasteful and patient spirits, like Ponz and Bosarte.

But the time of their deliverance drew nigh. The French eagles swooped on the Peninsula, and then was the wall of partition broken down that shut out Spanish art from the admiration of Europe. To swell the catalogue of the Louvre was part of the recognised duty of the French armies; to form a gallery for himself had become the ambition of almost every military noble of the empire. The sale of the Orleans, Calonne, and other great collections, had made the acquisition of works of art fashionable in England, and had revived the spirit of the elder Arundels and Oxfords in the Carlisles and the

---

[1] *Réflexions Critiques sur la Poësie et sur la Peinture*, sixième édition, 3 tomes, 4to, Paris 1755, tom. ii. p. 142.

Daring picture-dealers.

Gowers. With the troops of Moore and Wellesley, British picture-dealers took the field, well armed with guineas.[1] The Peninsula was overrun by dilletanti, who invested galleries with consummate skill, and who captured altar-pieces by brilliant manœuvres, that would have covered them with stars had they been employed against batteries and brigades. Convents and cathedrals—venerable shrines of art—were beset by connoisseurs, provided with squadrons of horse or letters of exchange, and demanding the surrender of the Murillos or Canos within; and priest and prebend, prior or abbot, seldom refused to yield to the menaces of death or to the temptation of dollars. Soult at Seville, and Sebastiani at Granada, collected with unerring taste and unexampled rapacity; and having thus signalised themselves as robbers in war, became no less eminent as picture-dealers in peace. King Joseph himself showed great judgment and presence of mind in his selection of the gems of art which he snatched at the last moment from the gallery of the Bourbons, as he fled from their palace at Madrid. Suchet, Victor, and a few of "the least erected spirits," valued paintings only for the gold and jewels on their frames; but the French captains in general had profited by their morning lounges in the

Plundering French commanders.

King Joseph pilfers with judgment.

---

[1] See Buchanan's *Memoirs of Painting.*

Louvre, and had keen eyes as well for a saleable picture as for a good position.¹

By the well-directed efforts of steel and gold, Murillo and his brethren have now found their way, with infinite advantage to their reputation, to the banks of the Seine and the Iser, the Thames and the Neva. French violence and rapine, inexcusable in themselves, have had some redeeming consequences. The avarice of Joseph and his robber-marshals, by circulating the works of the great Spanish masters, has conferred a boon on the artists of Europe. Nor is the loss to Spain so serious as it may at first appear. Great as was their booty, the plunderers left behind, sorely against their will, treasures more precious than those which they carried away; and the rich remainder is now more highly valued than the whole ever was, and more carefully preserved. A review of the various collections of Spanish paintings now existing in the royal and public galleries of Europe, will show that the painters of Spain can still be studied nowhere so effectually as on their native soil.

The Royal Museum of Madrid far exceeds all others in the variety and splendour of its Spanish pictures. This Museum, where Rafael appears as

---

¹ The *Handbook for Spain* tracks Soult and Co. through the scenes of their sacrilegious robberies with unwearied vigour, and a lash always keen, ready, and richly deserved.—See Seville, Granada,—Valencia—&c.

CHAP. I.

great as at Rome, Rubens as vigorous and versatile as at Antwerp and Munich, Claude as sunny and gladdening as in London and Paris, and into which the palaces of Madrid, Aranjuez, the Prado, San Ildefonso, and the Escorial, have poured their treasures to form the richest gallery in the world, is one of the few honourable monuments of the reign of Ferdinand VII. That royal Vandal has, however, little merit in the affair; he was tired of his hereditary Titians, which he thought injured the effect of his Parisian upholstery, and therefore sent them up to the garrets; the honour is due to his first Queen, Maria Isabel of Braganza, whose taste and public spirit conceived and executed the design.[1] The structure—of brick with granite pillars and coignings—does some credit to the architect, Villanueva; its massive cornices and long colonnades form the chief architectural feature of the avenues of the Prado, famous in history and romance. But, having been originally intended for a scientific institution, it is inferior in internal convenience to some of the new Pinacotheks of Germany, and the long central gallery and its vestibules are the only apartments that possess the advantage of sky-light. These favoured regions are appropriated to the patrician pictures of Italy, while those by Velazquez, Murillo,

---

[1] For a full, accurate, and agreeable account of this gallery see *Handbook*—Madrid.

and their countrymen are crowded into two side rooms and some smaller chambers below stairs, where the windows are few and far between; and some of them have even been thrust into the outer darkness of the corridors. Besides being badly lighted, the Spanish collection is also far less complete than it might easily be made; for you will look in vain for several names of renown, such as Correa, Berruguete, and Tristan[1] in the catalogue of Don Pedro Madrazo (*Catálogo de los Cuadros del Real Museo*, Madrid 1843, 12mo, pp. 435), a work accurate indeed as far as dates and figures go, but in which a few historical notices of the more remarkable articles are greatly to be wished for.[2] But here, and here alone, is Velazquez to be seen in all his glory, as the painter of history, landscape and low life, of courtly portraits and solemn altar-pieces, and here he may be studied in sixty first-rate pictures. Of Murillo there are forty-six excellent specimens; and Joanes, Morales, Cano, and Zurbaran, all contribute a variety of fine works. Many good pictures are also to be found here by artists like Pereda, Collantes, Escalante, and Pareja, whose names have hardly crossed the

---

[1] [Correa and Berruguete are still unrepresented, but there has been added one portrait by Tristan (Catálogo, 1889, No. 1048).—ED.]

[2] [This want has been amply supplied in the new catalogue by Don Pedro de Madrazo, published in 1872, which is descriptive and historical in regard to both artists and pictures. The pictures have, however, been renumbered, and we have added the new numbers to the references here given.—ED.]

CHAP. I.

Madrid
Real Academia de S. Fernando.

seas and mountains that bound the Peninsula. It is much to be regretted that the dangerous and often fatal process of cleaning, of which some of the finest Rafaels were the first victims when in the Louvre, has been carried on here, in what is called the restoring-room, with a vigour very unusual in Spain, and an audacity not exceeded in France. The manly touch of Velazquez, and the delicate vapoury tones of Murillo have, in too many instances, disappeared beneath masses of fresh paint, flat and hard, as if they had been laid on with a pallet-knife or a trowel.

The Royal Academy of St. Ferdinand, founded in 1752 by Ferdinand VI.,[1] possesses a collection of about three hundred paintings, which are placed in a suite of apartments in the vast palace in the Calle de Alcalá, which the Academy shares with the Museum of Natural History. There is no catalogue here,[2] and what is worse, in some of the rooms no light. Here are good specimens of Blas del Prado, Pereda, Cincinato, and Orrente; and here also are the wonderful "St. Isabel of Hungary," and the "Dream of the Roman Patrician," masterpieces of Murillo, stolen from Seville by the French, and dishonestly detained by the Government of the day when sent back from the Louvre.

[1] *Estatutos de la Real Academia de S. Fernando*—8vo, Madrid, 1757, p. 6.
[2] [A catalogue was printed in 1824—see note, infra, chap. xvi.]

INTRODUCTION.

CHAP. I.
Museo Nacional.

The National Museum is a vast collection of pictures of all degrees of merit, formed for the nation out of the spoils of the religious houses, under the auspices of the Regent Espartero. The desecrated monasteries of Spain have been turned to strange uses, and have become barracks, hospitals, museums, manufactories, theatres, bull-rings, or quarries, according to the wants of their respective localities. Thus the great convent of the Trinidad, of which the long brick façade with its tall flanking towers forms a principal object in the Calle de Atocha, and the front enclosure, affording a nestling place for book-stalls, serves as the Paternoster Row of the unliterary capital, has been chosen as the magazine of the artistic property of the nation. The pictures, which stand much in need of weeding, arrangement, and light, fill the upper and lower cloisters or galleries which surround the quadrangle, and also the chapel, refectory, and several other apartments. The museum was opened in 1840; but Spaniards being—as a Castilian foreign secretary once serenely observed to an impatient French minister[1]—men and not birds, five years have not sufficed for the preparation of a catalogue. When published, it is to be hoped it

---

[1] M. de Louville writes thus to Torcy, May 10th, 1701:—"Quand on presse Don Antonio de Ubilla d'expédier les dépêches de six semaines, il répond avec un beau sang froid—'En Espagne les hommes ne sont 'pas des oiseaux.'" See *Correspondence of the Honourable Alexander Stanhope*, edited by Lord Mahon, sm. 8vo, London, 1844, p. 195.

will connect with each of the best pictures the name of the convent whence it was taken. The collection contains a few Italian paintings, and some valuable works of the older Flemings and Germans, by which its monotony is relieved. Velazquez, whose pencil was more employed in the palace than the cloister, is here represented only by two portraits of moderate merit. Cano, Zurbaran, and Murillo, whose connections were more conventual, appear to greater advantage. But the contents of the museum having been contributed chiefly by the monasteries around Madrid and Toledo, the productions of the Castilian school far outnumber those of the others. Vincencio Carducho is the presiding genius of the place: his long series of paintings from the Chartreuse of Paular display a vigour of imagination worthy of Rubens, and cover acres of canvas, which might have astonished, (as perhaps they did) Luca Fa Presto himself. Correa, one of the earliest, and Sebastian Muñoz, one of the last of the great Spanish masters, may likewise be best known and appreciated in this gallery.

Toledo possesses no museum, but its venerable metropolitan church is a treasury and monument of Castilian art. The grand portals and beautiful choir display the fine fancy and manual skill of the elder sculptors and their classical successors, while the chapels and chapter-rooms are rich with the works of Juan de Borgoña, El Greco, and other Toledan painters.

The Museum of Valladolid contains many works of art which enriched the monastic houses of Old Castile and Leon, and which were saved from destruction in the civil war by the energy of Don Pedro Gonzalez, director of the Academy, to whose glory be it recorded! It occupies the ancient College of Santa Cruz, one of the six greater colleges of Spain. Founded, in 1494, by the Grand Cardinal Mendoza, this noble Gothic pile has been gently dealt with by the restorers and destroyers of after-times, and retains much of its pristine magnificence. The ornate façade looking on the Plaza, the simpler garden front, and the rich court within, are well preserved and neatly kept. The pictures here, of the highest historical interest, are those by Rubens, which once belonged to the nuns of Fuen-Saldaña, and were refused by that sisterhood to a grandee, high in the court of Ferdinand VI., who offered to give them a magnificent new altar-piece and double revenues in exchange;[1] and which afterwards figured in the Louvre of Napoleon. Amongst Spanish painters—Carducho, Pereda, and Josef Martinez are

---

[1] Bosarte, *Viaje Artistico*, p. 144. In Conder's *Description of Spain and Portugal*, 12mo, London, v. ii. p. 142, it is said that the offer was made by Charles III., with this difference, that he promised a new convent instead of an altar-piece.

pre-eminent in this museum. But the collection shines rather in sculpture than in painting. The bronze monuments of the Duke of Lerma and his Duchess attest the skill of the Italian Leoni. It is here that the classical Berruguete, and Juan de Juni and Hernandez—whose statues of painted wood rival in life and spirit the marbles of Greece—must be studied; they are the tutelars of the place. This museum enjoys the advantage—rare in Spain—of possessing a catalogue, which is to be found in Julian Pastor's "Compendio Histórico Descriptivo de Valladolid. Ibid. 1843."

In Arragon and Catalonia, where art never flourished, the monasteries were less rich in artistic embellishment, and in the troublous times were handled more severely than in the other provinces of Spain. The Museums of Zaragoza[1] and Barcelona, occupying, as usual, old conventual buildings, have therefore little beyond good intentions to recommend them.

Andalusia, a garden of nature and art, possesses three public museums of painting—at Cordoba, Seville, and Cadiz. The first of these, established in one of the dingiest convents of the dull decaying city of the Caliphs, consists of but a few canvases,

---

[1] There is no museum at Zaragoza, but there are a few pictures in the Academy of San Luis. A museum is projected in a convent church, which was full of firewood (1849).

singularly dirty and degraded. The last occupies part of a new Academy of Design in the Plaza de Mina, and, as its chief ornaments, can show only some doubtful Murillos and second-rate Zurbarans, which do little credit to the taste of opulent Cadiz. The Museum of Seville, however, nobly vindicates the genius of Andalusia. Filled with many of the fine works, once so thickly scattered amongst the rich convents of that beautiful city, it is one of the most characteristic and delightful shrines of art in Europe. The edifice, formerly the Monastery of the Merced, an order whose pious business it was to redeem Christian captives from the Infidel, when as yet there were friars in Seville, and corsairs in Algiers and Sallee,—was first erected in 1249 by St. Ferdinand, and sumptuously rebuilt in the time of Charles V. It stood embosomed in a spacious garden, now a waste of weeds and rubbish, amidst which a tall cypress rises solitary and spectre-like. Part of this garden is about to be built upon, and a part added to the little Plaza del Museo, where the citizens talk of erecting the statue of Murillo. The interior of the building, however, is probably as well kept as in the days of the monks, and is a fine specimen of the wealthy convent of a southern clime. The principal court is of elegant design; its cloisters are supported by light coupled columns of white marble, placed on a basement enriched with

Chap. I.
Cadiz.

Seville: Museo.

bright tiles; a fountain murmurs pleasantly in the centre, around it flowers breathe their fragrance, some strutting peacocks spread their plumes, and two noble weeping willows droop their green and graceful boughs, tempering the sunshine and whispering in the breeze. The sole relics of the banished religious are the Cross of St. John, and the Bars of Catalonia—the arms of their order—emblazoned on the rich ceilings, or carved on the curiously panelled doors, and a bad picture or two, wherein turbaned Turks, sitting arrogant and cross-legged, receive bags of money from white-robed friars—grotesque, but yet touching memorials of these meek soldiers of Christ, and their bloodless beneficent crusades.[1] The holy images and inscriptions that once adorned the walls are gone; Our Lady of Mercy and St. Hermenegild have been supplanted in their niches on the grand and richly decorated staircase by plaster casts of Venus and the Apollino—and the light and lofty church, with gilding and gay frescoes, has been transformed into a hall, of which the walls are clothed with the great compositions of Castillo and Herrera, Zurbaran, Roelas, and Murillo. An upper gallery over the principal cloister is also filled with pictures, as well as some chambers opening

---

[1] For an account of these "Padres de la limosna," see the curious "*Topographia é Historia General de Argel*, por el M. Fray Diego de Haedo, Abad de Fromesta." Folio. Valladolid, 1612.

from it—one of which, badly lighted by a single window, is appropriated to a matchless collection of eighteen of Murillo's finest works. In pictures by artists who lived and laboured at Seville, this museum is richer than any other; here Zurbaran and Murillo appear in their full strength, and Valdés Leal, Meneses, Marquez, and some others less generally known, show themselves to have been men of mark and likelihood. But in specimens of the other schools it is very deficient; even Velazquez, a Sevillian by birth and education, though early removed to Madrid, makes no sign in the gallery of his native place. Little pains seem to have been bestowed in cleaning and restoring the pictures, most of which remain in the dry, dusty, and even tattered state in which they left their native cloisters, and would afford fine scope for the exertions of the gentlemen of the Queen's "restoring room." Those which have been newly framed show the taste of the Director of the institution to be curiously bad; for example, the eighteen pictures by Murillo, mentioned above, have frames painted to imitate a sort of brown marble, and also, it would appear, their own prevailing tones. It is to be hoped that the "very loyal, very noble, and unconquered city of Seville," will find ere long a little money and a little judgment to rectify these things; to open a few sky-lights in the upper rooms, and to publish a catalogue.

Seville: Chapel of the University.

The chapel of the University has likewise been opened as a museum, under the auspices of Don Manuel Lopez Cepero, the learned and ingenious Dean of Seville. Besides the fine monumental bronzes and marbles, rescued from the wreck of convents, it contains some excellent pictures by Roelas. The gorgeous chapel of the Hospital of Charity—though its walls were cruelly bared by Soult—is still rich in masterpieces of Murillo. Several of his fairest creations likewise adorn the chapels and sacristies of the magnificent cathedral, where are also to be found the finest existing works of Esturmio, Vargas, Campaña, and Villegas, the patriarchs of Sevillian painting.

Chapel of the Hospital de la Caridad.

Cathedral.

Valencia: Museo.

Valencia has a museum of between six and seven hundred pictures,[1] almost entirely of its own fine school. Entering the city from the acacia-shaded banks of the Turia, by the gate of St. Joseph, a few steps bring you under the high and massive walls of the ancient convent of the Carmen, of which the chapel, standing forward from the pile, and conspicuous for its florid façade of the Ionic and Corinthian orders, now serves as a parish church. The rest of the building is devoted to the museum, and is divided into two courts, in each of which four tall palms, rising from amidst neglected flowers, lift their

---

[1] *Manual de Forasteros en Valencia*, por J. G.; Valencia, 1841, p. 120.

pillar-like stems and plumy heads to the brilliant sky, assorting well with the Oriental character of the many-domed city of the Cid. Of these courts, one has an open and Gothic-vaulted cloister, wainscotted with gay tiles—now much broken—on which sacred histories are painted and pious quatrains inscribed. The other is surrounded above and below by closed galleries, in which, and in the staircase, are gathered, as into one focus, the chief treasures of native painting, from the various religious houses that studded the rich plains and pleasant valleys between the Segura and the Ebro. Marshal Suchet, who directed the French ravages and rapine in this province, was, happily, curious only in church plate and jewels, and spared the pictures—not being aware, like his better-educated peers, of their marketable value. Hence it is that so many exquisite and elaborate works of Joanes, and powerful compositions of the Ribaltas, have found their way into this museum; and also a positive superfluity of specimens of the diligent Borras, and the unequal Geronimo Espinosa. Still the collection—even as regards Valencian masters—is by no means complete, which may be attributed partly to the ingenuity of the poor monks in saving, or as the lay-appropriators call it, purloining, their favourite pictures at the suppression of their monasteries; and partly to the ignorance or dishonesty of the people employed to form the gallery, who here, as in other provinces, too often garnered the chaff and cast the wheat away. According to the custom of Spanish museums, the light is defective, and a catalogue wanting. The old enduring gilding of many finely-carved frames gives a rich effect to the walls; but the paintings are much overcrowded, and hung with so little care that one or two tall canvases have actually been placed lengthways, as if pictures were bricks, and the one thing needful in their arrangement was to build them into a close compact mass. The keeper of the gallery, however, is an artist, and far better acquainted with the history of art than is common with such officials, especially in Spain.

The great rambling cathedral contains some excellent paintings by Joanes, Ribera, and Orrente; the College of Corpus Christi, the masterpieces of the elder Ribalta; and the Academy of San Carlos, a few good pictures of various schools and climes.

The public collections of Spain would be greatly improved by a little judicious barter with each other. The National Museum of Madrid might, for example, give from its abundance a series of Castilian paintings to that of Valencia, in exchange for some of the endless productions of Borras, Espinosa, and others: while the Sevillians might buy with a portion of their native wealth specimens of the other schools. The Queen of Spain possesses sixty-two pictures by Rubens, fifty-five by Giordano, fifty-three by Teniers, forty-nine by Breughel, twenty-seven by Tintoret, twenty-five by Sneyders, twenty-two by Vandyck, and sixteen by Guido. Of each of these masters her Majesty might easily exchange a specimen with the national collections, in order to complete the Spanish department of her gallery, which would thus be rendered perfect as well as unrivalled.

Leaving the Peninsula and its convent-museums, we shall find elsewhere but few public galleries which possess a sufficient number of Spanish pictures to be called a collection. The ex-King of the French[1] has made a more serious attempt to form one than any other monarch of our times. His "Galerie Espagnole," in the Louvre, purchased in Spain by the active Baron Taylor, consists of four hundred and fourteen pictures; and the "Collection Standish"—bequeathed to his Majesty by an English gentleman—one hundred and forty-five pictures and two hundred and fourteen sketches and drawings by Spanish masters. As regards size, therefore, the Spanish gallery of Louis Philippe falls very little short of that of Isabel II. The catalogues—for the most part accurate and excellent in their historical

---

[1] [Louis Philippe. His collection was sold by auction at Messrs. Christie and Manson's rooms, London, in May 1853.—Ed.]

CHAP. I.

notices—abound in high names; they enumerate fifty-two works of Murillo, twenty-three of Velazquez, twenty-five of Cano, and no less than eighty-two of Zurbaran; and specimens of almost every painter of note from ancient Rincon, who painted Isabella the Catholic, down to modern Goya, who painted Maria Louisa the Unchaste. But it is no less true than lamentable, that the walls of the gallery bitterly belie the promise of the catalogues, and that a very large proportion of the paintings fathered on the finest masters, consists of mere copies or imitations by scholars or admirers, or of baser forgeries—the refuse of the studio and the sale-room. Some grains of pure gold, however, sparkle here and there amongst the dross; for example, "The Adoration of the Shepherds,"[1] and "View of the Escorial," by Velazquez; Murillo's "Christ and St. John on the banks of Jordan;" his "Charity of St. Thomas of Villanueva;"[2] his "Virgin of the Conception;" and portraits of himself and his mother; Zurbaran's "Meditating Monk, holding a skull;"[3] and some of Cano's portraits. A few fine works of Murillo and other Spaniards hang amongst the Italian pictures in the long gallery. The Standish drawings are likewise a rare and interesting collection, well worthy of notice.

---

[1] [Now in the National Gallery, No. 232.—ED.]
[2] [Now in the collection of the Earl of Northbrook.—ED.]
[3] [Now in the National Gallery, No. 230.—ED.]

INTRODUCTION.

Next in extent, and perhaps superior in importance to the Spanish collection of the ex-King of the French,[1] is that of the Emperor of Russia. To St. Petersburg and the vast Hermitage of the Czar, fate has transferred one hundred and ten paintings of the Spanish schools, which once adorned the palace of the Prince of the Peace on the Prado of Madrid. The gifts lavished on the minion of the Queen of Spain are appropriately lodged in the sumptuous halls where Catherine wooed her Orloffs and Potemkins. There, beneath gilded cornices, and amongst columns of Siberian porphyry and vases of malachite, hang many fine and original works of Joanes, Tristan, Cespedes, Mayno, Velazquez, and Murillo—placed without method, and catalogued with little accuracy.[2]

At Munich, in the fine Pinakothek, the most convenient and admirable picture-gallery ever constructed—the schools of Spain are represented by only thirty pictures, which, however, form the collection that ranks third amongst those on this side the Pyrenees. Pantoja, Cano, Zurbaran, and Claudio

---

[1] [Supra, p. 73, note. The Spanish collection in the Hermitage, since the dispersion of the Galerie Espagnole of Louis Philippe, is second to none out of Spain.—ED.]

[2] ["The first edition of the present catalogue of the Hermitage appeared in 1863, the second and corrected edition in 1869; therefore the above charge does not apply to the catalogue now in use."—*An Art Tour to the Northern Capitals of Europe*, by J. Beavington Atkinson, 8vo, London, 1873, p. 204, note.]

CHAP. I.

Vienna: Belvedere Palace.

Coello, are seen to advantage here; and Murillo figures as a painter of low life, in six pieces replete with vigorous humour. The Spanish portion of the Bavarian catalogue is full of errors, and quite unworthy of the rest of that well-arranged volume.[1]

The "royal imperial" (*königliche kaiserliche*) gallery in the noble Belvedere Palace at Vienna, which, from the old relations of Spain and Austria, might be expected to be a mine of Spanish art, possesses only a single portrait by Sanchez Coello, and a few works by Velazquez. But one of these, the "Painter's Family Picture," representing himself, his wife and children, and some servants, is perhaps the single production of his pencil out of Spain, that deserves to rank with his grand compositions at Madrid.[2] This priceless picture hangs in one of the lower, and worst-lighted rooms of the palace.

Berlin.

The chaste and admirably-arranged gallery of

---

[1] [A new official Catalogue was published in 1884, and there is now also the illustrated *Notes on the Principal Pictures in the Old Pinakothek*, by Charles L. Eastlake, F.R.I.B.A., 8vo, London, 1884.]

[2] [Curtis, *Velazquez and Murillo*, p. 16, does not "concur in this opinion, and he confesses that he cannot recognise in the picture either the hand or the family of Velazquez; . . . he is inclined to believe that . . . the artist is Mazo (the son-in-law of Velazquez), and that the scene depicts the family, not of Velazquez, but of his son-in-law, with his *muchos hijos*, or possibly the family of some friend or patron of Mazo." Carlo Justi, *Diego Velazquez and his Times*, translated by Professor A. H. Keane, royal 8vo, London, 1889, p. 425, agrees with Curtis.—ED.]

[3] Curtis (ibid., p. 16) says that it now (1883) hangs "in a well-lighted chamber."

INTRODUCTION.

Berlin has a few fair specimens of Ribera, Zurbaran, and Murillo. Dresden, where the finest efforts of Italian, Flemish, Dutch, and German painting waste their splendour and sweetness in the damp dark chambers of a barn-like building[1]—is poor in the Spanish masters, except Ribera. Murillo's name, indeed, appears in the incorrect catalogue, but it is doubtful whether any of his works are to be found on the walls.[2] Brunswick, Hesse Cassel, and Frankfort, have hardly a Spanish picture to show; nor are Antwerp, Brussels, and Amsterdam much better provided. The Hague, however, has a few specimens, especially in the private gallery of the King of Holland, who possesses some excellent works of El Mudo, Velazquez, and Murillo, and opens his palace as freely as if his fine collection were public property.[3]

---

[1] [A handsome new museum has since been built—opened in 1854—in which the valuable collection is now housed to more advantage, and with greater propriety, and there is now an excellent catalogue—compiled by Herr Julius Hübner—giving ample details of the pictures, of which the edition of 1876 is before me. The pictures of the Spanish school are enumerated and described in pp. 185-93, comprising forty-one items, fourteen of which are from the Louis-Philippe collection, two are marked as of doubtful authenticity, and one as a copy (after an original Murillo in the Pinakothek at Munich), while the artists represented are Morales, Joanes (Macip), Correa, Orrente, Roelas, Carducho, Herrera, Ribera, Ribalta, Pereira, Zurbaran, Espinosa, Cano, Velazquez, Valdés Leal, and Murillo.—ED.]

[2] [The collection now includes a St. Roderick (No. 633), formerly in the Gal. Esp. of Louis Philippe, bought for £210, and also a Virgin and Child (No. 634), both by Murillo. See *Velazquez and Murillo*, by Charles B. Curtis, M.A., royal 8vo, New York, 1883, pp. 266 and 151.—ED.]

[3] [This collection was sold by auction in London, in August 1850.—ED.]

CHAP. I.
Stockholm.

Copenhagen.
Frederiksborg.

London: National Gallery.

Stockholm—where pictures were once so plentiful, or despised, according to Winckelman,[1] that some fine Correggios were used to stop the broken windows of the king's stables—has "Two Beggar Boys," by Murillo, in the third-rate gallery of the royal palace. The Danish collection at Copenhagen has no Spanish pictures; but in the beautiful royal castle of Frederiksborg, near Elsinore—interesting not only as a monument of the powers of Inigo Jones, but also as a rich gallery of historical portraiture—there are some portraits of Philip IV. and his family, which are either original works of Velazquez, or admirable copies by his pupils.

The private collections of England could probably furnish forth a gallery of Spanish pictures second only to that of the Queen of Spain. But into our unhappy national collection, lodged in a building that would disgrace the veriest plasterer, and described in a catalogue that seems to have been drawn up by an auctioneer,[2] Murillo alone of Spanish

---

[1] *Reflections on Painting and Sculpture*, 12mo, Glasgow, 1765, p. 5.

[2] [These reproaches are no longer deserved. The removal of the Royal Academy in 1869 to Burlington House, gave greater space to the National collection, and two large additions have since been built; while the excellent catalogue, revised and brought down to December 1888 by Mr. F. W. Burton, and issued in June 1889, is convenient in form and admirably fulfils all requirements. The Spanish school has been increased by thirteen pictures, including one additional example of Murillo, six of Velazquez, two of Ribera, and one of each of Campaña, Morales, Theotocopuli, and Zurbaran.—ED.]

INTRODUCTION.

painters has as yet effected an entrance.[1] He appears there, however, to advantage in several sacred compositions; but the variety of his style may be better appreciated in his works at Dulwich College, where Velazquez likewise shines with some lustre.

South of the Alps, Spanish art is still less known than in Northern Europe. Ribera is sometimes indeed to be met with in Italian collections, where he is often called a Neapolitan. He and Velazquez are the only Spanish masters whose portraits are to be found in the "Sala dei Pittori" of the Florentine gallery, "degli Uffizi." Amongst the glories of art which hang between the allegorical ceilings and the tables of precious *pietre dure* in the Pitti palace, two Madonnas of moderate pretensions feebly vindicate the fame of Murillo. There is scarce a canvas or a panel touched by a Spanish pencil to be found in the Museum of Brera at Milan, the gallery of the Duke at Parma, the Pinacotheca at Bologna, or the Academy of Fine Arts at Venice—collections rich in native works. At the Vatican, Dutchmen, but no Spaniards, are admitted to the chambers, where Rafael holds his court; and at the Capitol, one good portrait by Velazquez is the sole representative of all the schools of Spain, as another is

---

[1] This was written before the fine Boar-hunt at the Pardo (infra, chap. ix.) had been purchased from the late Lord Cowley.

in the royal collection of Turin.[1] Naples is more fortunate than Rome; Ribera triumphs there not only in the churches but also in the royal Museum "degli Studi," where Murillo and Velazquez likewise appear; but the latter is so slightly known, that his excellent, though—for him—not remarkable portrait of a Cardinal is gravely entered in the catalogue as "*suo capo d'opera*."[2] Joanes, the Ribaltas, Cano, and the rarer Spanish masters, are as utter strangers in Italy as Vanderhelst or Hogarth.

---

[1] [According to the catalogue of *La Galerie Royale de Peinture de Turin*, by J. M. Callery, 12mo, Havre, 1854, the Spanish school is represented by seven pictures—four by Ribera, two by Velazquez, and one by Murillo.—Ed.]

[2] *Les Musées d'Italie*, par Louis Viardot, p. 308. 12mo, Paris, 1842. This agreeable writer, and warm admirer of Spanish art, is an excellent cicerone for all the great galleries of Europe. His *Musées d'Espagne, d'Angleterre et de Belgique*, his *Musées d'Allemagne et de Russie*, 12mo, Paris, 1841, and the above-mentioned volume, should find a place in the carriage or portmanteau of every picture-loving traveller.

CHAPTER II.

NOTICES OF EARLY ART TO THE END OF THE REIGN OF FERDINAND AND ISABELLA THE CATHOLIC, 1516.

HE most venerable specimens of Spanish art which rewarded the diligent researches of Cean Bermudez, were a missal in the royal library at Madrid, adorned with illuminations and rude portraits of ancient kings, chiefly the work of Vigila, a monk of Abelda at the close of the tenth century; and a wooden feretory or ark, covered with plates of gold and ivory carvings, made in 1033 by one Aparicio, by order of King Don Sancho el Mayor, to receive the body of St. Millan, and preserved with its precious contents in the monastery of Yuso.

An historical sketch of Spanish painting would

hardly be complete without some notice of those great religious or royal foundations which cradled its infancy, and were enriched with the trophies of its prime. Of the shadowy middle ages, perhaps the most important relic that exists in Spain, is the Cathedral of Santiago in Galicia, the holiest spot in the Peninsula, and the Loretto of Western Europe. Begun in 1002, and finished in 1128, by the zealous Archbishop, Diego Gelmirez,[1] various towers, and many a gorgeous chapel, were added in after times by royal or mitred benefactors. To one Master Mateo, the architect who, in 1188, built the grand portal—rich with foliaged niches and sculptured saints—Ferdinand II., of Castile, granted a pension of one hundred maravedis [2]—" ex amore omnipotentis Dei, per quem regnant reges, et ob reverentiam sanctissimi apostoli Jacobi patroni nostri piissimi,"[3] —probably the first instance on record of the patronage of art by the munificent house of Castile. The Norman Cathedral of Tarragona, one of the noblest of the temples that look on the Mediterranean, was begun in 1131, by St. Olegarius its Bishop, but re-

---

[1] Llaguno and Cean Bermudez. *Noticias de los Arquitectos y Arquitectura de España*, 4 vols., 8vo, Madrid 1829, tom. i. p. 32, from which the following notices of cathedral and conventual buildings are in general taken.
[2] Now worth about eightpence sterling. The maravedi, however, had anciently a higher actual, as well as relative value.
[3] See the original grant, as quoted by Cean Bermudez.

ceived most of its embellishments at the hands of his successors in the next century.

Alonso VIII. founded, in 1177, the Cathedral of Cuença, which so grandly crowns the rock-built town with its grey Gothic towers, and which within is all glorious with native jasper and marble. The Cathedral of Leon, unrivalled amongst churches in the pointed style for the airy grace of its design, and for its cunning lace-like masonry, was begun by Bishop Manrique de Lara, at the close of the same century.

At Burgos, in 1221, St. Ferdinand, the third of his name, founded on the site of his own palace, the exquisitely ornate Cathedral,[1] which points to heaven with spires more rich and delicate than any that crown the cities of the imperial Rhine. Five years later, the same pious conqueror employed a certain Master Pedro Perez to rebuild the Cathedral of Toledo, the metropolitan church of the monarchy, for four hundred years a nucleus and gathering-place for genius, where artists swarmed and laboured like bees, and where splendid prelates—the Popes of the Peninsula—lavished their princely revenues to make fair and glorious the temple of God entrusted to their care. There is preserved in the convent of San Clemente, at Seville, a portrait of the royal Saint, a work of venerable aspect, "of a dark, dingy

---

[1] It was built by the Bishop Maurice, an Englishman. See *Mariana*, lib. xii. chap. v.

colour, and ornamented with gilding," and reckoned authentic, and coeval with the conquest of Seville. So highly was it prized by the nuns of that royal foundation, that they refused to send it to be copied at the Alcazar, where Ferdinand VII. was residing in 1823, pleading the statutes of their house; and the copy which appears in the series of Kings in the Hall of Ambassadors, was made in the convent.[1] At Osma, in Old Castile, Juan, St. Ferdinand's Chancellor and the Bishop of the Diocese, built, in 1232, the fine Cathedral, of which the beauty has been marred by much modern patchwork, while its city has decayed into a poor village.

Alonso X., or the Learned, whose taste inclined rather to books than buildings, had at least one painter of illuminations in his service; for his Bible, in two volumes, written on vellum, and enriched with barbaric brilliancy by Pedro de Pamplona, exists, or lately existed, in the archives of Seville Cathedral. On the last page the artist inscribed this simple record of himself and his patient labour, his piety, and his humble hope of being remembered in his work:—

HIC LIBER EXPLETVS EST: SIT PER SŒCVLA LŒTVS SCRIPTOR. GRATA DIES SIT SIBI. SITQVE QVIES. SCRIPTOR LAVDATVR SCRIPTO. PETRVSQVE VOCATVR PAMPILONENSIS. EI LAVS SIT. HONORQVE DEI.

---

[1] Cook's *Sketches in Spain*, 2 vols. 8vo, London, 1843. v. ii. p. 181.

In the turbulent times of King Sancho the Brave, who reigned amidst external wars and domestic rebellion, Rodrigo Esteban was painter to that monarch, and was paid for certain works, in 1291–2, one hundred maravedis out of the privy purse, as appears by a MS. book of accounts in the royal library. Of this contemporary of Cimabue, none of the productions, nor any further notices exist. His works, doubtless, bore the same relation to the achievements of the great age of Spanish painting that the venerable verses in which the learned Alonso embodied his alchemical lore bear to the classical poems of Garcilasso.

Pedro the Cruel, or the Just, whose history and character, like that of our Richard III., form a tilting-ground for historians, bestowed great pains on the renovation and embellishment of the Alcazar of Seville, the ancient palace of the Sultan Abderahman. Many of its light marble columns he brought from Valencia, and much of the delicate stucco embroidery was the work of Moors from Granada.

During the fourteenth century, Arragon and Catalonia possessed a few painters, and gave a promise of distinction in that branch of art which they did not afterwards fulfil. In Italy, art had already begun to revive from its mediæval torpor, and the genius of the pencil to breathe somewhat of life and beauty into the forms of virgins and saints, drawn after the venerable models of Byzantium. Spanish churchmen, returning from the Vatican, must have observed, and perhaps may have envied, the new and graceful adornments of Italian altars; and many a merchant of Barcelona had doubtless bowed and marvelled before the frescoes of Giotto and Orcagna in the Campo Santo at Pisa, and beheld with jealous admiration the dawning glory of art at Florence. The taste of the clergy and of wealthy burghers may have been the means of fostering artistic talent in the active and mercantile provinces of the north, of bringing over masters from Italy, or sending Spanish disciples to their schools. At Zaragoza, so early as 1323, died Ramon Torrente, a painter, leaving behind him a scholar named Guillen Fort.[1] Later in the century, Juan Cesilles practised painting at Barcelona, and in 1382 engaged himself to execute, at the price of 330 ducats of Arragon,[2] for the high altar of the church of San Pedro, in the town of Reus, a series of pictures on the history of the Apostles. These early paintings remained in the church till 1557, when they were

---

[1] *Handbook*, 1845, p. 975 [3rd edition, London, 1855, p. 907], where some unpublished MSS. of Cean Bermudez are referred to as an authority.
[2] The ducat of Arragon was probably worth about four shillings and sixpence sterling, and the whole sum somewhat less than £75.

unhappily removed to make way for some newer garniture of the altar.

Juan I. was especially the patron of painting, and entertained in his service the first Italian artist who appeared in Spain, Gherardo Starnina, a disciple of Antonio da Venezia, born at Florence in 1354, and employed to paint, in fresco, the life of St. Antony, the Abbot, in the chapel of the Castilians in Santa Croce. This painter attracted the notice of the Spaniards who visited that city. Their invitations, and a private feud which rendered absence from home advisable, induced him to visit Castile, where he lived for several years. Although even the names of his works there have perished, his epitaph in the church of S. Jacopo sopra Arno assures us that they were "pulcherrima opera." His history bears a favourable testimony to the generosity of Juan, and the refinement of his court; for, "whereas," says Vasari, "he left Florence poor and clownish, he returned thither a rich and courteous gentleman." He died there in 1403, or, according to another account, in 1415. He seems to have been a man of humour and unable to resist a joke, even on serious subjects; for Vasari relates that, being ordered to paint in the chapel of S. Girolamo nel Carmine a picture of that Saint learning his letters, he seized the occasion to introduce a flogging scene, in which the luckless urchin who was horsed (*fanciullo levato a cavallo adosso ad un altro*), writhing under the lash of the pedagogue, took his revenge by biting the ear of the companion whom he bestrode. The series of paintings, however, in which this facetious episode occurred made the name of Starnina famous in Tuscany, and even throughout Italy.[1]

Juan I. founded, in 1388, amongst the lower hills of the Guadarrama chain, the wealthy Chartreuse of Paular with its sumptuous church, which afterwards became famous for its flocks and its paper-mills, its fine pictures, and for several cowled painters of its own. Amidst the wilds of Estremadura he likewise founded, about the same time, the royal monastery of Guadalupe—the seat of a celebrated Virgin—which, with its towers and spires and spacious courts, resembled a town, and was, until the rise of the Escorial, the most splendid of the Jeronymite houses of Spain. In this reign also, the small, but exquisite Cathedral of Oviedo rose on the ruins of a more venerable church, under the auspices of its Bishop, Gutierre de Toledo.

Henry III. rebuilt the Alcazar of Madrid, which had been burnt down in previous civil wars, and which, after it had been enlarged and beautified, and stored with many of the finest productions of

---

[1] Vasari, 2 vols., 4to, Bologna, 1647, tom. i. p. 138.

art, by a long line of kings, suffered the same fate in the reign of the first Bourbon. He also founded the country Palace of the Pardo near Madrid, which became another treasury of paintings, and the scene of another conflagration in the reign of Philip III.

The beginning of the fifteenth century saw the commencement of two noble cathedrals. Of these the first was begun, at Huesca, in 1400, by Juan de Olotzaga, a Biscayan architect, and in a hundred and fifteen years, grew into one of the noblest buildings in Arragon. The second was the Cathedral of Seville, of which the ample revenues and grand decorations were so long to foster and employ the artistic genius of Andalusia, and of which the interior, with its five mighty aisles and awful choir, remains still unrivalled, the triumph of the rich and solemn Gothic architecture. In 1401, the see being vacant, the chapter determined to rebuild the fabric. "Let us build," said these magnificent ecclesiastics, "a church that shall cause us to be taken for madmen by them who shall come after us."[1] The name of the architect, assuredly one of the greatest masters of his art that ever left his mark upon the earth, perished, with his original plans, in 1734, in the fire of the Palace of Madrid, whither they had been

---

[1] "Fagamos una iglesia para que los de porvenir nos tengan por locos." —See Ponz, v. xi. p. 3, and, as usual, the *Handbook*.

removed by order of Philip II.[1] The work went on, with more or less activity, for more than a century and a half, displaying in its many incongruous parts the successive changes of architectural style. To provide the funds needful for so vast an undertaking, the prebendaries and canons for many years gave up the greater part of their incomes,—an instance of devotion and munificence not uncommon in those old and earnest times, when churchmen were content to offer all their worldly goods on the altar of the Church, hoping for no earthly reward, when the wealth and genius of long ages were patiently given to raise one glorious temple, and when the house of God had precedence, in men's regard, of the palace and the prison. And the example has not even yet been wholly forgotten; for, within the last fifteen years, the good Bishop Silos Moreno, of Cadiz—a worthy follower of the Fonsecas and Lorenzanas of old—by his holy zeal and munificence has made his Cathedral, which he found a ruinous shell, one of the most stately and splendid of modern churches.

Juan II., of Castile, was a lover of both poetry and painting, and his long reign was the era of nascent taste and refinement. He had in his service for

---

[1] Cean Bermudez, *Descripcion Artistica de la Catedral de Sevilla*, 8vo, Sevilla, 1804, p. 20.

several years Dello, a Florentine sculptor and painter, noted for the beauty of his miniature paintings, generally on subjects from Ovid—with which it was then the custom to adorn coffers and other furniture—and for his frescoes in the palace of Giovanni de Medicis, and in the Church of S. Maria Novella. Having acquired wealth and an order of knighthood in Castile, that artist returned to Florence, to indulge his vanity by displaying them. The Signory, however, refused to accord to him the privileges of his new rank, until the King of Castile had written them a warm letter in his behalf. His ostentation was likewise punished by the jeers and gibes of his former acquaintance, as he rode through the streets in sumptuous apparel, on a finely caparisoned horse. With a ludicrous forgetfulness of his new dignities, he would reply to their sarcasms by making with both hands "the sign of the fig;"[1]—(*fece con ambe le mane le fiche;*) but wearied out at last by such annoyances, he returned to Spain. There he was again honourably received at court, lived like a great lord, always painting in an apron of brocade (*grembiale de brocato*), and died in 1421, aged forty-nine. He was honourably

---

[1] This quiet and expressive "retort contemptuous" is conveyed—in Spain at least—"by inserting the head of the thumb between the fore and middle fingers, and raising the back of the hand toward the person thus complimented." (*Handbook* [1845], p. 83.) The Italian method is much the same.

buried, says Vasari, without informing us where, beneath this epitaph:

> DELLVS EQVES FLORENTINVS
> PICTVRÆ ARTE PERCELEBRIS,
> REGISQVE HISPANIARVM LIBERALITATE
> ET ORNAMENTIS AMPLISSIMVS,
> H. S. E.
> S. T. T. L.[1]

Vasari says that his drawing was indifferent, but that he was one of the first artists who attempted to display the muscles of the naked figure.[2] None of his works exists in Spain. In the time of Philip II., there was found, in a chest in the Alcazar of Segovia, a roll of old canvas, on which was painted the Moorish rout at Higueruelas by the arms of Juan II. It was for some time taken for a work of Dello by certain connoisseurs, who forgot, or did not know, that he died ten years before that battle was fought.

At Toledo, in 1418, Juan Alfon, an artist of the city, painted the altar-pieces of the old chapels of the Sagrario, and of los Reyes Nuevos.

Rogel, a native of Flanders, was also painter to Juan II., who presented, in 1445, to the Carthusian friars whom he had established in his own palace of Miraflores, near Burgos, a small oratory, painted by that master. The centre compartment contained

---

[1] Vasari, tom. i. p. 168. The epitaph is given in Castilian by Butron; Discurso xv., fol. 118.
[2] Vasari, tom. i, pp. 166-168.

a "Dead Christ," and the doors or wings his "Nativity," and his "Appearing to the Virgin." It was surrounded by a stone border, on which various figures were painted, and the whole was executed with a delicacy and effect very creditable to that early age. Brought from Spain by a Frenchman, it was offered for sale in London, and passed into the private gallery of the King of Holland.[1]

Master Jorge Ingles, possibly an Englishman, likewise flourished as a painter in this reign. The famous literary Marquess of Santillana ordained him by will, in 1455, to paint for his hospital at Buitrago the pictures of the high altar. Those of them which Cean Bermudez saw, though stiff and hard, like all paintings of the time, afforded evidence of considerable ability. Amongst them were portraits of the Marquess and his wife, which the Duke of Infantado, towards the close of the last century, with a regard for the illustrations of his house, unfortunately rare amongst the Spanish nobility, caused to be brought to Madrid to be cleaned. By his orders, that of the Marquess was well engraved by Fernando Selma.

During the whole of the fifteenth century, Toledo took the lead in the fine arts. Dolfin introduced there, in 1418, painting on glass, which was brought

---

[1] Sir Edmund Head's *Handbook of the Spanish and French Schools of Painting*, post 8vo, London, 1848, p. 30. [This collection was sold by auction in London, in August 1850.—ED.]

to great perfection under the patronage of the Church. About the same time, Alonso Rodriguez and his brothers distinguished themselves in sculpture, as may be seen by their spirited, though rude, groups and figures which adorn the great portal of the Cathedral. Egas, a Fleming from Brussels, was one of the leading sculptors employed on the stately florid portal of the Cathedral of Toledo, called the Gate of Lions, which was begun so early as 1466.

At Seville, Juan Sanchez de Castro, the morning star of the school of Andalusia, appeared about the middle of the century. In 1454 he painted for the Cathedral the pictures of the old Gothic altar, in the chapel of San Josef, which, though stiff and languid in design, still preserved their freshness of colour, when Cean Bermudez wrote, three hundred and fifty years afterwards. For the church of San Julian he painted, in fresco, a giant St. Christopher in a buff tunic and red mantle, an embellishment common in Spanish churches, where it is placed near the door, to inculcate humility on those who come to pray. The legend of this saint, as told by an old English poet, may fitly illustrate this early work of one of the oldest Spanish painters:—

"There was a man of stature big, and big withal in mind,
For serve he would, yet one than whom he greater none might find.
He hearing that the Emperor was in the world most great,
Came to his court, was entertained; and, serving him at meat,

It chanced the Devil was named, whereat the Emperor him blest,
When as until he knew the cause, the Pagan would not rest.
But when he heard this lord to fear the Devil, his ghostly foe,
He left his service, and to seek and serve the Devil did go;
Of Heaven, or Hell, God, or the Devil, he erst nor heard, nor cared,
Alone he sought to serve the same that would by none be dared.
He met (who soon is met) the Devil—was entertained—they walk,
Till coming to a cross, the Devil did fearfully it balk.
The servant musing, questioned his master of his fear—
'One Christ,' quoth he, 'with dread I mind, when doth a cross appear.'
'Then serve thyself,' the giant said, 'that Christ to serve I'll seek.'
For him he askt an hermit, who advised him to be meek,
By which, by faith, and work of alms would sought-for Christ be found,
And how and where to practise these, he gave directions sound.
Then he that scorned his service late to greatest potentates,
Even at a common ferry now to carry all awaits.
Thus doing long, as with a child he over once did wade,
Under his load midway he faints, from sinking hardly stayed.
Admiring how, and asking who, was answered of the child,
As on his shoulders Christ he bore, by being humbly mild,
So through humility his soul to Christ was reconciled,
And of his carriage, Christo-fer thenceforth himself was styled.' [1]

Sanchez de Castro's saint of burden has good reason to faint under his load; for besides the Divine Babe, who holds the world in his hand, he has to sustain the weight of two palmers in dresses of the Middle Ages, who cling to his leathern girdle, and so pass the river dry-shod.[2] The signature of the painter is nearly all that remains of his work, for the figure was repainted in 1775 and 1828 by new and heavy

---

[1] Warner, *Albion's England*, book ix. chap. 50.
[2] Cook's *Sketches of Spain*, 2 vols. 8vo, London, 1834, v. ii. p. 182.

hands.¹ In the Convent of Santiponce (now a penitentiary), near Seville, there formerly existed a painting on panel, of the "Annunciation," by Sanchez de Castro, in which the angel was arrayed in pontifical vestments,—garnished with embroideries setting all chronology at defiance, and representing the twelve Apostles and the Resurrection of Our Lord—and the Virgin held in her hand a rosary and a pair of spectacles!² He must have lived to a great age, for he received from the chapter, in 1516, payment for painting and gilding part of the high altar of the Cathedral. A marble slab in the nave of the church of San Roman, marked the sepulchre where he and his family were laid. Gonzalo Diaz was a disciple of Sanchez de Castro.

The internal troubles of the Christian kingdom in the fifteenth century, and the Moorish wars, which followed the union of the crowns of Arragon and Castile, doubtless retarded the progress of the arts in Spain. The taste of their patrons, however, and the skill of their professors, was steadily, though slowly, increasing. The Moorish decorations, their

---

¹ The signature (which has likewise been repainted) is in Gothic character—Jua Sanchz de Castro, Pintor, Ao. de 1484 (as it appeared to me, though Cean Bermudez says 1454), and there is farther to the left—Se renobo, Ao. de 1828.

² This curious old picture is said to have been taken away by Godoy, Prince of Peace, and may possibly still be in existence. See Davies's *Life of Murillo*, 8vo, London, 1819, p. 17, note.

vivid painting and beautiful lace-like stucco-work, which had been long adopted in Christian palaces, began to be executed by uncircumcised artists even before the fall of Granada. Cean Bermudez quotes a contract, dated 1476, by which one Garcia del Barco and another painter became bound to paint with Moorish work (*obra Morisca*) the corridors of the Duke of Alba's castle, at Barco de Avila, for the sum of 56,000 maravedis. The paper is drawn up with a formal explicitness, which implies that such documents were frequently in use.

The goldsmith's craft was advancing towards its future importance and perfection, and church treasuries were beginning to display somewhat of their coming splendour. Valladolid became famous for the skill of its jewellers and artificers in the precious metals. At Valencia, in 1454, Juan de Castelnou executed, for the Cathedral, for the exposition of the Host on great festivals, a silver Custodia, or shrine, of Gothic design, fourteen palms high; and, in 1460, his son and disciple, Jayme, a silver altar and retablo,[1] or architectural altar-piece, forty palms high and twenty-four wide, profusely embellished with bas-reliefs. Fray Juan de Segovia, a Jeronymite monk of Guadalupe, became famous for his exquisite chalices, reliquaries, and crucifixes. One of his

---

[1] The "retablo" comprehends the entire structure of the altar-piece with its decorations.

best works was the silver salt-cellar, in the shape of a lion (*leon*) tearing open a pomegranate (*granada*), afterwards presented by the Prior, with happy and delicate courtesy, to the Catholic Sovereigns, when they visited the shrine of Our Lady of Guadalupe, to give thanks for the surrender of Baza—two years before Granada opened its gates to the army of Castile and Leon.

The famous camp, built, not of cords and canvas, but of stone and lime, on the slopes of Santa Fé, where Ferdinand and Isabella held their state during the leaguer of the Moorish capital, was remarkable, not only for its discipline, and the daring of its knights and nobles, but also for luxury and magnificence such as few northern courts could then have displayed. The Great Captain—who there served his apprenticeship in war and victory—was distinguished by his sumptuous equipments, as well as by his youthful gallantry. The banquets of the Duke of Infantado[1] shone with plate, and his person glittered with jewels, as brilliantly as if he had been holding peaceful revels in his ancestral halls at Guadalajara. But it was not until that chivalrous host had sung its solemn Te Deum—till the Grand Cardinal, arrayed in vestments embroidered by the fair and pious hands of the Queen, had said the first mass within

---

[1] Prescott's *Ferdinand and Isabella*, London, 1839, vol. ii. p. 326, note.

the mosque of the Alhambra, that Spain enjoyed the repose necessary for the growth and perfection of the elegant arts.

The opening of the Damascus of the West could not but increase that taste for luxury and splendour which already inspired its Christian subduers. The stately mosques and fairy palaces, its gardens and gateways, and marble fountains, afforded superb models for their imitation. And they brought to the conquest of the domains of art all the energy acquired in their long struggle with the Infidel. The great Isabella, to whom Castile owed Granada and the Indies—and history the fairest model of a wife, a mother, and a Queen—aided the progress of taste and intellectual culture no less studiously than she laboured for the political prosperity of her kingdom.[1] Her large and active mind early comprehended the national importance of literature and art. She built and endowed churches, and worked chasubles, and dalmatiques, and processional banners for the clergy, while she also gave an impulse to the weightier matters of learning and piety by her munificence and example. Architecture made a great stride in her reign. By an early statute, passed at Toledo, she provided for the erection of large and spacious buildings for public purposes in the chief

---

[1] Prescott's *Ferdinand and Isabella*, London, 1839, vol. ii. p. 297, note.

towns of her dominions. The Alcazar of Segovia, whose tall keep and clustered turrets form a fine feature in views of that ancient city, was a favourite residence of Isabella, and the rich decorations of its halls and corridors, now degraded into a military school, afford evidence of her taste. To her Alcazar at Seville she added the small Gothic chapel, and she enlarged and embellished, at her own expense, the stately Chartreuse of Miraflores.[1] She and her husband built at Santiago the grand Royal Hospice for pilgrims, and they added largely to the great monastery of St. Jerome, once the pride of Madrid.[2] At Toledo, on one of the finest sites in that romantic capital, they erected the convent of San Juan de los Reyes, the most sumptuous edifice of its day, of which, alas! the church, much dilapidated, is all that has survived the invasion of the trans-pyrenean Vandals. Nearly two hundred pairs of rusty manacles, struck from Christian hands at the fall of Granada, still hang between the rich buttresses of the exterior, to commemorate the conquerors who, in their holy war, vowed this convent to St. John, their patron saint.

Ferdinand the Catholic and the Crafty, the Henry VII. of Spain, whom Shakespeare—speaking by the

---

[1] Bosarte, *Viaje Artistico*, Madrid, 8vo, 1804, p. 269.
[2] Prescott's *Ferdinand and Isabella*, 3 vols. 8vo, London, 1840, vol. ii. p. 346.

mouth of his daughter, our gentle Katherine—so justly styles—

> "The wisest prince that there had reign'd by many
> A year before:"[1]

was too parsimonious, and too deeply immersed in state intrigues, to bestow much care on the arts. But his sagacity easily perceived some of the advantages arising from their cultivation, and he approved, if he did not much aid, the magnificent works undertaken by his Queen. By his conquest of Naples, he extended the communications between Italy and his Spanish dominions; and thus, if the fine arts owed but little to his bounty, his ambition opened the road to knowledge and improvement. He gave, however, 10,000 ducats out of the Indian revenues of Castile, towards the completion of the Cathedral of Seville. In his own city of Zaragoza, he built the monastery of Santa Engracia, which had been planned by his father. An excellent sculptor of Biscay, Juan de Morlanes, whose style resembles that of the old German masters, was principally employed in the decorations. He was assisted by his son, Diego, whose fortunes so throve, in the course of years, by the arts, that, when the Jesuits came, in the next reign, to Zaragoza, he gave them,

---

[1] *Henry VIII.*, Act ii. sc. 4, l. 49.

not only a plan for their church, but also a present of 3,000 ducats.

The Siloes, of Burgos, father and son, were likewise excellent sculptors and architects. Gil, the first, is chiefly known for his stately tombs of King Juan II. and the Infant Don Alonso, erected in the Chartreuse of Miraflores, by order of Queen Isabella, in which the most fantastic imagination has found hands to work its wildest will, and alabaster has been moulded like clay, or trained and twined like the green osier, and where the Gothic genius of Spain flashed with dying splendour.[1] Diego, the son, erected, partly from his father's designs, the noble Cathedral of Granada, which remains an example of the influence of Moslem taste on Christian architecture. He died at a great age, possessed of much wealth in houses and lands, slaves, plate, and jewels.

Painting also was improving, though perhaps more slowly than other arts. Antonio Rincon, the first Spanish painter mentioned by Palomino, was likewise the first who left the stiff Gothic style, and attempted to give to his figures something of the graces and proportions of nature. He was born at Guadalajara, in 1446; and is said to have studied in Italy, under Castagno, or Ghirlandajo, apparently

---

[1] Bosarte, *Viaje Artistico*, p. 273. For an account of these wonderful tombs, see also the *Handbook;* and Théophile Gautier's clever and thoroughly French *Voyage en Espagne*, 12mo, Paris, 1845, p. 58.

on no better grounds than the improvement he made in the barbarous style of his age and country. He lived chiefly at Toledo, where he enjoyed the patronage of the Chapter, and also of Ferdinand and Isabella, who made him their painter-in-ordinary, and, about 1500, gave him the Order of Santiago. The portraits of these Sovereigns, painted by him, long hung over the high altar of the Church of San Juan de los Reyes, at Toledo, but disappeared in the wars of the French usurpation—so fatal to the historical relics, as well as to the fortunes of the Peninsula. The Church of San Blas, at Valladolid, likewise possessed similar portraits, which, in the beginning of this century, had been removed to the staircase of the chaplains' house, near San Juan Letran, in that city, where they were suffering from exposure to the open air, when seen by Bosarte, who praises them for the curious exactness of their costumes.[1] If they have escaped the perils of fire and water, they may, perhaps, still be extant in the Museum of Valladolid.

In one of the lower corridors of the royal gallery of Madrid hang two full-length portraits of the Catholic Sovereigns[2] copied from Rincon, and taken perhaps from the Toledo or Valladolid originals.

---

[1] Bosarte, *Viaje Artistico*, p. 125.
[2] *Catálogo de los Cuadros del Real Museo de Madrid*, 1843, Nos. 1646 and 1647. [These do not appear in the new catalogue, 1889.]

With much of Holbein's hardness, they have much of his strength, but not, however, his splendour of colour. Both seem to have been taken when the royal sitters were in the prime of life. Ferdinand has the dignified presence and the fine features clothed with "impenetrable frigidity," ascribed to him in history.[1] His hair, usually described as bright chestnut, here is dark, and, being cut short and combed over his brow, enhances the cunning keenness of his eyes. Over a cuirass he wears a red surcoat and black cloak, and in his hand he holds a paper, apparently of accounts. The Queen's portrait is no less true to history than her lord's. Her bright auburn hair and blue eyes are amongst the points of resemblance between her and our Queen Elizabeth, recalling that Princess, as she appears in an early portrait, by Holbein, at Hampton Court. But in beauty of person, as in grace of character, the Castilian Queen far excels our imperial "vestal throned by the west." Her forehead is high and full, and her eyes—as yet undimmed by weeping for her only son—softly lustrous, as they might have been when she rode victorious into the Alhambra. The finely-formed mouth indicates energy tempered with gentleness; and the whole expression of the head and bearing of the figure are not unworthy

---

[1] Prescott's *Ferdinand and Isabella*, 8vo, London, 1840, vol. iii. pp. 470–478.

of the woman, of whom those who knew her best have recorded, that they had never known or heard of another, "wise, and fair, and good as she."[1] Her dress is a crimson robe trimmed with gold, over which falls a dark mantle. In her hand she holds a little breviary, as fitting and characteristic a companion of the leisure of the pious Queen, as is the financial return in the fingers of her lord.

If any works of Rincon still remain to the Cathedral of Toledo, they will perhaps be discovered, by some future antiquarian, in the richly carved altar-piece of the chapel of Santiago,—where the Lunas repose in their tombs of ivory-like marble—amongst the paintings of which the Nativity and Entombment of our Lord are the best deserving of notice, for the force of their heads, and their accuracy of execution. At the village of Robleda de Chavila, a few miles west of the Escorial, there existed, and probably still exists, an altar, in the church, containing seventeen

---

[1] There is probably no historical lady upon whose person and character so much trustworthy posthumous praise has been bestowed—few women perhaps have ever deserved so much. Gerónimo de Oviedo y Valdez says of the one—"En hermosura puestas delante de S. A. todas las mugeres que yo he visto ninguna vi tan graciosa, ni tanto de ver como su persona."—*Quincuagenas* MS., quoted by Prescott, *Ferdinand and Isabella*, vol. iii. p. 250. Peter Martyr speaks thus of the other, in his letter to the Archbishop of Granada and the Count of Tendilla, written after Isabella's death—"Orbata est terræ facies mirabili ornamento inaudito hactenus. In sexu nam fœmineo et potenti licentiâ nullam memini me legisse quam huic Natura Deusque formaverit, comparari dignam." *Opus Epistolarum.* Ep. cclxxix. folio, Amstel. 1670, p. 159.

pictures on the life of the Virgin, painted entirely by Rincon, which Cean Bermudez praises for their "drawing, beauty, character, expression, and excellent draperies." He died in 1500, leaving a son, Fernando, his scholar, who assisted Juan de Borgoña in various works at Toledo, and whose name appears in the accounts of the College of San Ildefonso at Alcalá, in 1518, when he was paid 500 maravedis for the humble service of polishing (*dando lustre*) the medallion of Cardinal de Cisneros.

Francisco Florez was an excellent painter of illuminations, in the service of Isabella, whose missal, in old stamped morocco, with silver clasps and knobs—with the crown and cipher F.Y.—a fine specimen of ancient binding, delicately embellished by his hand, is still preserved in the Cathedral of Granada.[1]

Pedro Berruguete was a native of Paredes de Nava, and painter to Philip I., or the Handsome, the Flemish husband of the unhappy Infanta Juana, by whom he was ennobled. His earliest known works are supposed to be those which he painted with one

---

[1] Its miniature paintings are, perhaps, hardly equal to the flowered and scrolled borders; the best of them, and the most gracefully designed, is the Crucifixion (the largest in the volume, occurring at p. 312). On the back of the last leaf is this inscription in black-letter, like the rest:— Missale mixtu de mandato serenissima regine hispaniares domine nre Elizabeth explicit: Per me Franciscum flores librarior, Capelle illus trissimi principis dni nri scriptorem. Die no. lune s. de xbiii Mensis julii Anno dni M.CCCC. XCVI (Aug. 6 has been added by a later pen).

Santos Cruz, for the high altar of the Cathedral of Avila. In 1483, he was employed with Rincon, by the Chapter of Toledo, to paint the walls of the old "Sagrario," or chapel where the Host is kept, attached to the Cathedral,[1] for which they were paid 75,000 maravedis. He likewise painted the cloister in 1495, and the vestry in 1497, and received for those works respectively 57,000, and 36,000 maravedis. He married Elvira Gonzalez, a lady of condition, by whom he had several children (one of whom, Alonso, became famous as an artist), and died at Madrid, it is supposed, about 1500. Cean Bermudez considers him entitled to rank, as a painter, with Pietro Perugino.

Juan de Borgoña enjoyed a high reputation at Toledo, and the patronage of its great Archbishop Ximenes de Cisneros. From 1495 to 1499, he was employed, with other artists, in executing, in the cloisters of the Cathedral, a variety of sacred paintings, now unhappily buried beneath the pallid frescoes of Bayeu and Maella. He likewise worked at Alcalá de Henares, for the university. Between 1508 and 1511, he painted, on the walls of the winter chapter-room at Toledo, a series of religious subjects, the designs for which were seen and approved by the

---

[1] The Sagrario is usually the largest of the chapels, and separate from the rest of the fabric. In some Cathedrals—those of Seville and Toledo, for instance—it is used as a parish church.

CHAP. II.

Archbishop. These works are well preserved, and are admirable for their brilliant colouring and tasteful draperies. The "Nativity of the Virgin" is the best: St. Anne lies in a canopied bed, and the Holy Babe is brought to her to be kissed, by a young nurse beautiful as a Madonna of Perugino. The lower end of the finely-proportioned, but badly-lighted room, is occupied by "The Last Judgment," a large and remarkable composition. Immediately beneath the figure of Our Lord, a hideous fiend, in the shape of a boar, roots a fair and reluctant woman out of her grave with his snout, as if she were a truffle, twining his tusks in her long amber locks. To the left, are drawn up in line, a party of the wicked, each figure being the incarnation of a sin of which the name is written on a label above, in Gothic letters, as "Soberbia," "Avaricia," "Luxuria," and the like. On their shoulders sit little malicious imps, in the likeness of monkeys, and round their lower limbs flames climb and curl. The forms of the good and faithful on the right, display far less vigour of fancy.

Fresco in the Capilla Muzarabe.

In 1514, he painted, on a wall of the Muzarabic Chapel, a fresco of the Conquest of Oran, to commemorate the military exploits of the active archbishop—a work historically interesting and curious as a record of costume, but so much inferior to those in the chapter-room, that documentary evidence alone leads us to believe it to be by the same hand. The mitred leader has just debarked from his galley, and mounted his mule: he wears the scarlet robes and hat of a cardinal; and the cross is carried before him by a priest. The mail-clad soldiery rush to the assault, with equal disregard of discipline and perspective, and easily scale the infidel walls, which they are tall enough to see over.

Borgoña likewise painted, in fresco, the walls of the Cathedral library, for which he was paid, in 1519, 100,000 maravedis. He also executed the series of portraits of the Primates of Spain, in the winter chapter-room, down to Cardinal de Fonseca, inclusive. Like the Scottish Kings at Holyrood House, most of the fabulous and early prelates seem to have been taken from a single model; and their complexions, intended perhaps to alternate between ascetic paleness and jovial rubicundity, are too often either blue or bricky. The countenance of the Grand Cardinal de Mendoza, doubtless taken from an authentic portrait, is handsome, and his air high-bred and cheerful; which accords well with his character and the words of his kinsman and chronicler, Pedro de Salazar, who describes him as "majestic in person, and dignified and venerable in presence; his face well-featured, kindly and serene."[1] Cardinal Ximenes

---

[1] *Cronica de el Gran Cardenal*, folio, Toledo, 1625, cap. lxiii., p. 398.

is taken in profile; his features are spare, and his expression earnest and stern. The Flemish Archbishop de Croy has the fair complexion proper to his country, and the high-born look befitting his princely blood. This collection of portraits affords an inexhaustible, and, probably, virgin mine, for the student of ecclesiastical costume; endless and most gorgeous are its specimens of episcopal ornament, of the crozier, the pallium, the pectoral cross, the gloves and the mitre, *aurifrigiata* or *pretiosa*. Juan de Borgoña sometimes gave designs for church plate. His name ceases to appear in the Cathedral records in 1533, when, it is supposed, he died.

Seville, and the school of Sanchez de Castro, meanwhile produced Juan Nuñez, whose best work was executed for the Cathedral, and represented the Virgin supporting the dead body of Our Lord, with St. Michael and St. Vincent Martyr at her side, and an ecclesiastic kneeling in prayer beneath. Notwithstanding the Gothic stiffness of Christ's figure, Cean Bermudez reckoned this picture not inferior to the works of Albert Durer, for beauty and brilliancy of colouring, fine disposition of drapery, and finish of the extremities, and for the delicate minuteness with which the churchman's embroidered robes are painted. Nuñez, however, sometimes fell, like his master, into absurdities; for he left in the same Cathedral, pictures of the archangels Michael and Gabriel, each with a pair of peacock's wings. The art of staining glass was brought to Seville by Cristobal Aleman, who put into the Cathedral, in 1504, a painted window, the first of that glorious series, afterwards completed by the Flemish brothers Arnao, and Carlos of Bruges.

Aleman introduces stained glass at Seville.

Alexo Fernandez, whose master was Gonzalo Diaz, was a painter of considerable taste and skill, and executed for the Convent of San Jerónimo, at Cordoba, several altar-pieces, on subjects taken from the life of Christ and the patron saint, which were held to equal any contemporary production of the Spanish pencil. Called to Seville in 1508, by the Chapter, he was employed with his brother Jorge, a sculptor, and other artists, in painting and gilding the noble retablo, designed, at the close of the previous century, for the High Altar of the Cathedral, by the Flemish architect, Dancart. He remained at Seville till 1525. "Though his saints," says Cean Burmudez, "are still adorned with gilt diadems and glories, they are better drawn than those of Castro and his disciples, and there belongs to them a noble feeling and character, and an accuracy in the imitation of rich stuffs and other accessories, that denote advancing knowledge." Diego de la Barrera was a scholar of Alexo Fernandez.

A. Fernandez.

Diego de la Barrera.

At Valencia, in 1506, Francisco Neapoli and Pablo

Valencia.

de Aregio, supposed to have been disciples of Leonardo da Vinci, painted, with a correctness and grandeur of design almost worthy of that great master, several passages from the life of the Virgin, on twelve panels of the doors which once enclosed the great silver altar of the Cathedral. Of these pictures, Philip IV. said, several ages afterwards, that "the altar was silver, but its doors were gold."[1] "The Adorations of the Shepherds and of the Kings," are perhaps the most striking and effective pieces of the series. The artists received 3,000 golden ducats for the work, which is said to have been presented to the church by Pope Alexander VI., of the Valencian house of Borgia, a man equally remarkable for his taste, his talents, and his vices. Neapoli and Aregio likewise painted in fresco a part of the walls of the Cathedral; but their works fell before the improvements of some mitred Goth towards the end of the seventeenth century.

Isabella was nobly supported in her efforts for the promotion of art by the magnates of the Church. At Toledo, the Cardinal-Archbishop Mendoza, "the glory and shining light of that ancient house, the idol of Spain, the pride of the conclave,"[2] erected at his own

---

[1] Ponz, *Viaje de España*, tom. iv. p. 40.
[2] Writing to the Archbishop of Granada, on the death of this munificent prelate, Peter Martyr uses these words:—"Periit patruus ejus Petrus ille Gonzalus Mendotiæ Domus splendor, et lucida fax; periit quem

charges the Foundling Hospital of Santa Cruz, and at Valladolid a College of the same name ¹—magnificent piles, each of which was ten years in building.²

His famous successor, Ximenes de Cisneros, was still more munificent in his patronage of letters and arts. During the reign of that good Archbishop, the ancient capital of the monarchy became the new metropolis of art, a proud eminence which it long maintained. Leaving the graver cares of Church and State, or the compilation of his famous Polyglot, the great Cardinal of Spain was often seen, measuring-rod in hand, amongst the rising walls of his university at Alcalá de Henares, or overlooking the progress of the new decorations which he lavished on his Cathedral. The noble high altar of marble in that venerable church was erected by his orders, and fixed the reputation of its author, Vigarny, one of the best sculptors of Spain. In the Cathedral archives is still preserved his beautiful missal, in seven folio volumes, profusely embellished with paintings and illuminations by Vasquez, Canderoa, and other artists of merit, whose names that work has rescued from oblivion. At Salamanca, Bishop Diego Ramirez, of Cuença, founded the

---

universa colebat Hispania, quem exteri etiam Principes venerabantur, quem ordo Cardineus Collegam sibi esse gloriabatur."—Epist. clix. *Opus Epistolarum*, folio, Amst. 1670, p. 89.

¹ Supra, p. 65.
² Prescott's *Ferdinand and Isabella*, vol. ii. p. 340.

Colegio Mayor, which bore the name of his see, elegant and gorgeous as a fairy palace, but now a ruin, thanks to the soldiers of Ney. There also two dignitaries of the Church, Juan Alvarez de Toledo (uncle to the great Duke of Alba), and Diego de Deza, built the Dominican Convent of San Esteban, one of the latest and one of the most beautiful Gothic buildings in Spain. Deza, who was a friend of Columbus, afterwards became Archbishop of Seville, where he founded the College of San Tomas.

That the fine arts made a rapid progress during the reign of Ferdinand and Isabella, is sufficiently proved by the fact, that when Charles V., who had no predilection for his Castilian subjects, wished to erect a monument to these great ancestors at Granada, the scene of their glory, the execution of the work was entrusted to a sculptor of Burgos, in preference to a Florentine rival of Michael Angelo.

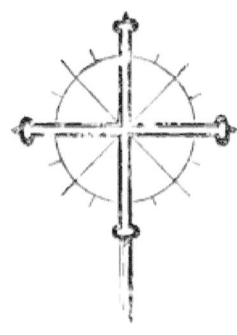

CHAPTER III.

REIGN OF THE EMPEROR CHARLES V.—1516-1556.

"PLUS ULTRA," the superb device of Charles V., was not more significant of his boundless ambition than of the stirring and ardent spirit of his age. The universal mind of Europe was awakening to a fresh activity and unheard-of achievements. The scholar and the artist, as well as the soldier and the statesman, were up and doing. While one cloud of adventurers threw itself on the golden regions of the New World, another, animated with nobler purpose, passed into Italy to learn of the genius of the Old. New languages blossomed into poetry and eloquence. New arts sprang up to adorn and refine civilised life.

The Spanish and Italian peninsulas, to the infinite

CH. III.

Close and increasing connection of Spain with Italy.

advantage of the first, had for some time been brought into close relations with each other. Ferdinand and his Great Captain had made the Crown of the Two Sicilies an appanage of the House of Arragon. "Barcelona the Rich," Malaga, and "Valencia the Fair," were yearly extending their commerce with Genoa and the Italian cities. The union of the vast dominions of Arragon, Castile, Burgundy, and Austria, under the young Emperor, promoted the interchange of interests and ideas among all the countries of Europe. The Italian schools of art began to be filled with a crowd of students, motley as the host revealed to Bradamante on the visioned fields of Romagna.

"Tedesco, Ispano, Greco, Italo e Franco"[1]—

the tasteful and inquiring spirits of all lands came to drink at the ancient fountain-heads of refinement. Long and deep were the draughts of the Spaniard, and the rich effects were found, after many days, in the splendid creations of Castilian and Andalusian genius, till the worn-out dynasty of Austria ceased to hold the Spanish sceptre, and the scholars of Velazquez and Murillo died off at Madrid and Seville.

Charles V. as a patron of art.

With the deep sagacity of his grandsire Ferdinand, Charles V. inherited much of the fine taste

---

[1] *L'Orlando Furioso*, canto iii. st. 55.

of Isabella of Castile. In the midst of wars and
intrigues, which he conducted with all the shrewd-
ness of our Dutch William, in the course of rapid
journeys from Naples to Dover, from the Tagus to
the Danube, that anticipated the fiery dispatch of
Napoleon, he found time to notice and reward many
of the chief artists of foreign countries, as well as
of his own wide dominions. As a patron of art, he
was as well known at Nuremburg and Venice as at
Antwerp and Toledo; and, in the splendid group
of contemporary sovereigns, none went beyond him
in magnificence. Of no prince are recorded more
sayings which show a refined taste and a quick eye.
The burghers of Antwerp religiously preserve his
remark, that the light and soaring spire of their
Cathedral deserved to be put under a glass case.
Florence has not forgotten how he called her the
Queen of the Arno, decked for a perpetual holiday.
The Cordobese historians have chronicled his vain
regrets on visiting the famous mosque of Abderahman, which had become the Cathedral of their city,
for the havoc made in its forest of fairy columns by
the erection of the Christian choir, to which, when
at a distance, he had himself, in an evil hour, consented. The citizens of Cordoba had vainly sought
to arrest the cruel improvements commenced by the
Chapter; and appealed against that Vandalic body
to the Emperor; Charles, however, as yet knowing

little of the Moors and their works, sided with the churchmen, and an ample clearing was forthwith made in the midst of the long continuities of the aisles. But he came, he saw, and he confessed his error; shifting the blame, however, as was natural and not unjust, upon the broad shoulders of the Chapter. "Had I wotted of what ye were doing," said he to the abashed improvers, "you should have laid no finger on this ancient pile. You have built a something, such as is to be found anywhere, and you have destroyed a wonder of the world."[1] The fine speeches which he lavished on Titian are as well known as the more substantial rewards. The painter, happening one day to let fall his brush, the Emperor, who was standing by the easel, picked it up, and gently prevented his apologies by saying that "Titian was worthy to be served by Cæsar." On another occasion, Cæsar having requested Titian to re-touch a picture which hung over the door of the chamber, the artist found that he could not reach it from the floor. The Emperor and some of the courtiers moved a table to his aid, but the height proving insufficient, Charles, without more ado, took the table by one corner, and calling on those gentlemen to assist, fairly hoisted Titian aloft with his own imperial hands, saying, "We must all of us bear up

His regard for Titian. Anecdotes of the Emperor and the painter.

---

[1] Ponz, tom. xvii. p. 2.

this great man, to show that his art is empress of all others." The envy and displeasure with which the men of pomp and ceremonies viewed such familiarities, which appeared to them as so many breaches made in the divinity that did hedge their king and themselves, only gave their master an opportunity to do fresh honour to his favourite, in that celebrated and cutting rebuke, "There are many princes; there is but one Titian." Not less valued, perhaps, by the great painter, than his title, orders, and pensions, was the delicate compliment of the Emperor, when he declared that "no other hand should draw his portrait, since he had thrice received immortality from the pencil of Titian."

In architecture, the field in which princes, from Cheops downwards, have chiefly loved to display their magnificence and eternise their names, Charles left several monuments. At Madrid, he rebuilt the greater part of the Alcazar, which, after being further embellished by his successors, perished by fire in the reign of Philip V. He likewise built anew the hunting seat at the Pardo, near that capital. His unfinished palace at Granada has obtained him both praise and blame. The summer which followed his marriage was passed with his young Empress in the beautiful Alhambra. Neither his admiration [1]

His architectural works.

Palaces at Madrid.

The Pardo.
Granada.

---

[1] Cean Bermudez. *Noticias de los Arquitectos y Arquitectura de España*, tom. i. p. 219.

for its dream-like halls and cool refreshing fountains, nor his unavailing lament for the invaded colonnades of Cordoba, prevented him from razing the winter palace of the Moors, to make way for an edifice out of all keeping with the remainder. Nothing can be said in defence of this outrage, except that Machuca's fragment is a noble specimen of art, and that the Moorish buildings destroyed, were possibly inferior to the rest. To the citadel of Toledo he added, with happier taste, that noble court, of which the shell, "majestic though in ruin," overtops the domes and spires of the ancient city, and looks up the valley of the Tagus to his favourite elm-groves at Aranjuez. The front, the interior arcade, and the staircase are the glory of the architects, Covarubias and Vergara,[1] and are worthy of the imperial builder, and the natural and historic grandeur of the site.

Painting was the art, however, which Charles most delighted to honour, and in which his taste was most cultivated and discriminating. Having learned drawing in his youth, he examined pictures and prints with all the keenness of an artist; and much astonished Æneas Vicus of Parma, by the searching scrutiny that he bestowed on a plate of his own portrait, which that famous engraver had submitted to his eye.[2] In power and ability the first monarch

---

[1] Ponz, i. p. 122.
[2] *Dialogo della Pittura di M. Lodovico Dolce*—12mo, Vinegia, 1557, p. 18.

of his age, it was fitting that he should choose for his peculiar painter the greatest master of his favourite art. But in his Spanish kingdoms it owed little to his care. Perhaps that early distrust of his Castilian subjects, which placed the mitre of Toledo on the head of a Croy, may have influenced him in his predilection for foreign artists. Neither Castile, however, nor his favourite Flanders, could furnish him with a Titian. For such a treasure he was obliged to look "plus ultra," even beyond the limits of his far-stretching empire. Palomino is doubtless carried away by an artist's enthusiasm, when he asserts[1] that Charles regarded the acquisition of a picture by Titian, with as much satisfaction as the conquest of a province. Yet, when he had parted with all his provinces, he retained some of Titian's pictures; when he betook himself to gardening, and watchmaking, and manifold masses at San Yuste, the sole luxury to be found in his simple apartments, with their hangings of sombre brown, was that master's St. Jerome, meditating in a cavern scooped in the cliffs of a green and pleasant valley; a fitting emblem of his own retreat. Before this appropriate picture, or the "Glory" which hung in the convent church, and which, in obedience to his will, was removed, with his body, to the Escorial, he paid his orisons,

His pictures at San Yusto.

---

[1] Palomino, tom. iii. p. 377.

and schooled his mind to forgetfulness of the pomps and vanities of power.¹

During this reign, the fine arts in Spain were steadily advancing towards the meridian splendour which they attained in the next. Spanish professors, as well as Spanish patrons of art, began to be known in Italy. So early as 1504 Alonso Berruguete, as we shall see, had distinguished himself both at Florence and Rome as a painter and sculptor. In 1521, Pedro Francione, a Spaniard, had earned considerable reputation as a painter, at Naples, where some of his works may still be seen in the churches. At the death of Pietro Perugino, in 1524, a Spanish disciple of that painter, known as Giovanni di Spagna, was reckoned the best colourist in his school.² The Spanish viceroys, the grandees who visited their courts, and the magnates of the Iberian Church who attended at the Vatican, were, many of them, admirers and patrons of art. When Rafael died, his favourite pupil and steward, Gian Francesco Penni (*il Fattore*), passed into the service of the famous Marquess del Guasto, Viceroy of Naples, whose grave Castilian countenance has been rendered as familiar to us as that of his master, by the portraits of Titian. To

---

[1] The description of the Monastery of San Yuste, in the *Handbook* [1845, pp. 550–553; 3rd edition, 1855, pp. 496–499], is one of the most admirable passages in those charming volumes.
[2] Vasari, tom. i. p. 411.

that nobleman he sold a fine copy of the "Transfiguration," possibly the same which now adorns the National Museum at Madrid.[1] Under the orders of the Marquess of Villafranca, a later Viceroy of Naples, the Spanish architects, Pedro de Prado and Juan de Toledo, designed and rebuilt many of the finest portions of that noble capital. At Rome, Bishop Bobadilla, of Salamanca, the prelate who superintended the building of the fine Cathedral of that old university city, was amongst the patrons of Benvenuto Cellini. The silver vase executed by him for that bishop will be remembered by that irascible artist's readers as the cause of one of the most amusing scenes of his life.[2]

While Spanish taste and skill thus found improvement in Italy, Italian artists came to seek praise and profit in Spain. Miguel Florentin, as his name imports, a native of Florence, was the best of the early sculptors of Seville. He appeared there early in the

---

[1] This picture, which has been heavily re-painted, differs slightly from the original—the woman who kneels in the foreground, with her back to the spectators, having a mantle of the same pale pink colour as her robe; in the Vatican picture it is blue.

[2] *Vita di Benvenuto Cellini*, 8vo, 1806, tom. i. p. 68. [*The Life of Benvenuto Cellini, newly translated into English* by John Addington Symonds, 3rd ed., 1 vol. demy 8vo, London, 1889, p. 44.—ED.] Benvenuto, who heartily hated all Spaniards, complains that he was treated "*Spagnolescamente*," by which he means scurvily, in the transaction; and says (p. 71) that at their final interview, when the piece of plate was paid for, the bishop spoke to him, "le più pretesche *spagnolissime* parole che imaginar si possa."

century, and executed for the Cathedral, at the expense of the Count of Tendilla, the rich marble monument of that nobleman's brother, the Cardinal-Archbishop Diego de Mendoza; and afterwards (in 1519-22) the stone statues of St. Peter and St. Paul on either side of the Moorish Gate, known as the "Gate of Pardon;" and the spirited bas-relief over the arch, representing "the Money-changers expelled from the Temple by Our Lord." His son, Antonio Florentin, constructed, in 1545-6, for the Cathedral, the grand monument for the exposition of the Host in the Holy Week, annually erected at Easter near the great portal. It was, in its original shape, a tall tapering edifice of three storeys, supported on columns of the three orders, and surmounted by a large cross. Between the columns stood coloured statues of saints, some of them of clay, and others, like the building, of wood, for the most part grandly designed. This monument was altered and injured in 1624, by the addition of a fourth storey of the composite order; but still its effect in the midnight service is superb, when, blazing with church-plate and myriads of waxen tapers, it seems a mountain of light, of which the silver crest is lost in the impenetrable gloom of the vaults above.

Pietro Torrigiano, the roving soldier-sculptor of Florence, came to Spain in 1520, or 1521. Having finished the beautiful tomb of Henry VII.[1] at Westminster,—"a pattern of despair for all posterity to imitate,"[2]—he aspired to construct that of the Catholic Sovereigns at Granada. There, however, he encountered a rival more formidable than any he had met with amongst "the English beasts," as he contemptuously styled his northern patrons; for, although he executed a fine medallion of Charity, in proof of his powers, the work was adjudged, it is said, to Vigarny, of Burgos. He thence went to Seville, where he was more successful, and modelled a Crucifix, a St. Jerome, and several other statues in terra cotta, for the Jeronymite convent of Buenavista. One of these, a Virgin and infant Saviour, so pleased the Duke of Arcos that he ordered a repetition of it for his own palace, and, when the work was delivered, sent the artist away rejoicing with as much copper coin as two men could carry. But on arriving at his own house, and discovering that this weighty recompense amounted to only thirty ducats, Torrigiano in a fit of passion flew back, hammer in hand, and dashed the statue to pieces before the duke's

---

[1] [The tomb stands in Henry the Seventh's chapel, built by that king on the site of the Lady Chapel erected by Henry III.—*Antiquities of St. Peter's Church, Westminster*, 8vo, London, 1711, p. 10. In the *Handbook for Westminster Abbey*, by "Felix Summerly" (Sir Henry Cole, K.C.B.), 12mo, London, 1842, where the tomb is well described, it is stated (p. 88) that it cost fifteen hundred pounds, and took six years to execute.—ED.]

[2] Fuller's *Church History*, folio, London, 1655, p. 255.

face. For this outrage on a sacred image the unhappy sculptor was seized by the Inquisition, condemned as a heretic, and died soon after in its dungeons by voluntary starvation.

Examination of the popular story of Torrigiano.

Such is his story, as told by Vasari,[1] who bears him a pardonable grudge for having broken the nose of Michael Angelo in a boyish fray—a fact attested by the portraits of that great man—when they were fellow-students, in the gardens of Lorenzo the Magnificent. It is repeated with great unction by Cumberland,[2] who sees a sort of poetical justice in the tragical end of the aggressor. Cean Bermudez, on the other hand, treats it as a fable, improbable in itself and discreditable to his country. He admits, indeed, that there is tangible evidence for the tradition of the broken statue, in a beautiful fragment of sculpture—a woman's hand placed on a bit of drapery, supposed to be that of Torrigiano's Virgin

Mano de la teta.

—known as "*la mano de la teta*"—of which plaster casts were common in his time at Seville. Some of these are still used as models in the Sevillian Academy, and may be found in the studios, and from one of them the annexed woodcut is taken. But he asserts that no Crucifix, by the Florentine, was ever known to have existed there; that the meanness of his patron was very unlike the munifi-

---

[1] Tom. ii. p. 58-61.   [2] *Anecdotes*, vol. i. p. 16.

cence of the grandees of that age; that thirty ducats in copper would have been a moderate burden for one man; and that not even the Inquisition would have held it heresy for an artist to destroy his own handiwork.[1] If Torrigiano were imprisoned at all, he concludes that it must have been for demeanour,

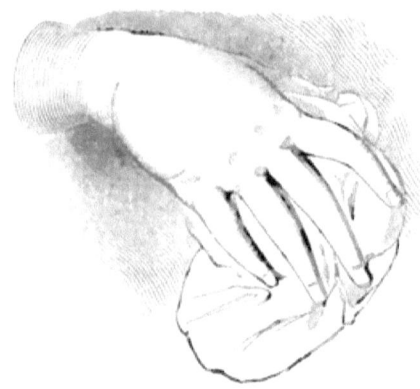

or expressions, not comporting with the duke's dignity—an offence of which he was quite capable, if his character is fairly represented by Cellini, who describes him as a fellow of infinite assurance, with a loud voice, uncouth in his gestures, and more like a bully than a sculptor.[2] On the same side it may

---

[1] Llorente, the historian of the Spanish Inquisition, makes no mention of Torrigiano—a victim he would not have forgotten, had there been any documentary evidence of his seizure.

[2] It is no wonder that Benvenuto had an aversion to Torrigiano, who seems to have been cast in the same mould with himself. The portrait he has left of his countryman is curious and characteristic:—" Era questo

be urged, that the price of a work of art was generally stipulated beforehand—often in writing—many such documents of that time being still in existence, and that it is against historical probability that the pitiful part in the transaction, imputed to the Duke of Arcos, should have been played by the head of the chivalrous house of Ponce de Leon.

Terra cotta statue of St. Jerome.

The story, such as it is, may afford food for thought to the student of art and human nature, as he pauses before Torrigiano's delicate screens, in our own great Abbey, or his St. Jerome, at Seville. That celebrated statue was modelled from the steward of the convent of Buenavista,[1] remarkable in youth for his fine person. It does not appear whether it was coloured, to imitate life, by the sculptor, or afterwards. It was originally placed in a sort of grotto, or cavern, in that convent, which Cean Bermudez twice visited, in company with Goya the painter, who each time spent upwards of an hour in examining it, and pronounced it the finest piece of modern sculpture in Spain, and perhaps in the world. From this appropriate site it has since been removed to

---

uomo da bellissimi forma, audacissimo, aveva più aria di gran soldato che di scultore, massime li suoi mirabilé gesti e la su sonora voce, con una aggrottar di ciglia da spaventare ogni uomo da qual cosa ; ed ogni giorno ragionava delle sue bravure con quelle bestie di quegli Inglesi." *Vita*, tom. i. p. 29. [Symonds' translation, 1889, p. 21.] Vasari also describes Torrigiano as a "proud and choleric" man. The poor sculptor has, however, had enemies only for his historians.

[1] Vasari says, steward to the Botti, Florentine merchants in Spain.

the ancient church of the Merced, now the principal hall of the Seville Museum, where it has been improperly placed on a pedestal, and also suffers dire eclipse from the strong and splendid colouring of the great pictures that enrich the walls. Another, and somewhat whimsical, circumstance further mars its effect, and at first sight leads the visitor to wonder at its fame. The saint is represented of life size, with no drapery but a white cloth thrown round his loins, and kneeling with one knee on a rock. His left hand is raised aloft, and once held a crucifix; his right grasps a stone, with which he is in the act of beating his bosom—a devotional exercise which he daily performed. Unfortunately, however, his attitude—somewhat like that of a man playing at bowls—is such that his object seems to be, not so much to discipline his own body, as to hurl the stone at a statue, in terra cotta, of St. Dominic, by Montañes, at the other end of the transept. That saint, on his part, is supposed to be scourging himself with pious fervour, and his back streams with blood, in proof of the vigour of his strokes; but as only the stump of the instrument remains in his hand, his action, and menacing aspect, favour the idea of defiance, and, in short, he seems to shake his fist at St. Jerome, and dare him to discharge his missile. The effect of two fine works is thus destroyed by their absurd relative position, which provokes the stranger's laughter, diverts his attention from their merits, and proves the directors of the Museum to be either mad wags, who prefer their jokes to their statues, or dull citizens, equally insensible to a statue or a joke. In spite, however, of these disadvantages, the life and spirit of Jerome cannot fail to arrest the eye. His sinewy and attenuated form, his frowning brow and shaggy locks and beard, are modelled in the style of Michael Angelo, and recall the wild energy of his Moses. But Seville must become once more the city of friars and inquisitors, and the Jeronymites must drive out the glass-blowers, and repossess their Doric cloisters of Buenavista, ere we can see, as it ought to be seen, this revered image of their patron saint, which the vicissitude of opinion has dragged from its shadowy shrine to uncover its nakedness in a rival church, turned, by a like fate, into a secular museum.

Fresco painting brought to Spain by Julio and Alessandro.

The art of painting in fresco was brought into Spain early in the reign of the Emperor by Julio and Alessandro, Italian artists, who are supposed to have belonged to the school of Giovanni da Udine. They came to Andalusia about the same time as Torrigiano, being invited by Francisco de los Cobos, the Imperial Secretary, to decorate his mansion at Ubeda. In preparation for the visit of Charles and his bride, they were afterwards employed at the Alhambra, to adorn some of its walls with miniature frescoes in the style of the Vatican, especially those of the Tocador, or dressing-room of the Queen, and the adjacent gallery. In that loveliest of lady's bowers—from whose arched and airy windows many a Moorish sultana, and several Christian queens, have looked down on the stream of the Darro, the laughing Vega, and the sparkling city lying like a bursting pomegranate between its hills at their feet—a few of these paintings may still be seen, though faded and fractured by time, neglect, and relic-loving travellers. They represent battles, ships, and havens, and other fanciful subjects. The artists[1] afterwards established a school in Andalusia, in which were formed some painters of distinction.

The most important service, perhaps, which the taste of the Emperor rendered to painting in Spain, was by bringing into that country many of the finest pictures of Titian. Hence, probably, it was that some of the best of the Castilian painters early showed in their works a leaning to the style of Venice. The portraits alone, of Charles, by Titian, were sufficiently numerous and remarkable to exert a powerful influence on the young artists who were admitted to study in the royal galleries. Never was

Titian—effect of his works in Spain.

His portraits of Charles V.

---

[1] Cumberland (*Anecdotes*, vol. i. p. 22) has adopted an error of Palomino, in ascribing to these masters the frescoes in the Duke of Alba's palace, executed—as we shall have occasion to notice—by the brothers Granelo and Castello, sixty years later.

the person of a great sovereign recorded for all time on canvas by a more brilliant and diligent historian. That masterly hand, which has preserved for us the faces of the princes and captains, the statesmen and scholars of Italy in her greatest age, and of her highborn beauties as they lived, and moved, and had their graceful being—has almost outdone itself in the portraits of the famous Emperor. We can yet behold his pale, but not unpleasing countenance, in his prime of manhood, when the imperial diadem first encircled that full and thoughtful brow amidst the pageants of Bologna. We may see him "turn and wind" his fiery steed

> "with his beaver on;
> His cuisses on his thighs, gallantly armed"

for the field or the tourney; or dressed in his buff coat, with horn at his side, and attended by his favourite hound, as he went to the chase in the mountains of Toledo or the forests of Hungary; or apparelled in satin and cloth of gold for the banquets of Florence or Vienna. And we may scan his features, clouded with care, and wan with the traces of pain, in his older sadder time, when his mind's eye turned from the wearisome state paper, or the glittering board, to the green solitudes of Estremadura, and its ear from brilliant flatteries to the bells and litanies of San Yuste. In such portraits as these, we read more of the man's nature and feelings than in whole pages of Sandoval or Robertson; and from these, Castilian painters learned more of their art than from all the lore of Carducho or Pacheco.

Story of his visit to Spain examined.

It has long been a question, whether Titian visited Spain? His Venetian biographer, Ridolfi,[1] is silent as to the fact; the Spanish writers stoutly maintain it. Palomino asserts that he resided there from 1548 to 1553, apparently on no better ground than the date of his patent as Count Palatine, which he misstates. This instrument, he says, was signed by the Emperor at Barcelona in 1553, a year when it is well known that that monarch was closely confined at Brussels, by gout and his intrigues for the marriage of his son with Mary of England. Nor was he in Spain during any part of the six previous years, which renders it most improbable that Titian, in his old age, then undertook the journey. It required some higher inducement than a vice-regal court could offer, to lure him from the enjoyment of his wealth and honours at home, from the polished society of the Grand Canal, and his pleasant garden by the sea of Venice.

Inconclusive evidence for it.

Cean Bermudez, with more accuracy, assigns to the patent its proper date, 1535, when Charles was at Barcelona, preparing to sail for Tunis. But he maintains that Titian passed the two previous years

---

[1] *Le Maraviglie delle Arte, overo le Vite de gl' illustre Pittori Veneti e dello stato*—4to, Venetia, 1648.

CH. III.

Good evidence against it.

in Spain, alleging, as a proof, his portrait of the Empress Isabella—once at the Palace of the Pardo—which must have been painted in Spain, as she never quitted that country after her marriage, and before 1538, when she died. But it is well known that many of his portraits of great personages were not painted from life; for example, that of the Great Turk, Solyman the Magnificent, who is ranked by Vasari amongst the subjects of his pencil,[1] but whom he is not recorded to have visited in court or camp, and that of the Empress herself, which he finished at Venice in 1544.[2] The best evidence, however, as to the fact is the long series of letters, written by the poet Aretine to Titian and his other friends, and extending from 1530 to 1555, which contains a monthly chronicle of the painter's movements, but no mention of any journey to Spain, or residence there.[3] We may therefore conclude that he never travelled out of Italy, except on occasion of his visits to the Imperial Court at Augsburg and Vienna, in 1548 and 1550. His residence there, and at Bologna

---

[1] Vasari, tom. iii. p. 225.
[2] Northcote's *Life of Titian*, 8vo, London, 1830, vol. ii. 203. This work, though full of interesting matter, is strangely defective in arrangement. Each volume, in fact, contains a separate, and sometimes contradictory life. Thus, in vol. i. 309-10, we are told that Titian went to Spain, and Ridolfi is taken to task for his view of the matter; which, however, is adopted in vol. ii. p. 78, where the Spanish journey is treated as a fable, and the Spanish writers are in turn chastised.
[3] Ibid., vol. ii. 178.

in 1530, may have led the Spaniards into their mistake, as well as the numberless trophies of his genius that graced their royal galleries. The Escorial alone possessed more of his pictures than five years of labour in Spain could have sufficed to produce.

Italians were not the only foreigners whose example improved the artists of Spain. The works of Jerome Bos were so common in the royal collections, and in the convents of Spain, that some writers have supposed that he visited the Peninsula.[1] Of this no proof can be adduced; but his pictures must have been familiar to many of the Spanish painters, and may perhaps have influenced the style of some of them. Nothing is known of this singular artist, except that he was born at Bois-le-duc, about 1450,[2] and painted for the churches and convents of that town and its vicinity. Don Felipe de Guevara, the warm admirer, and perhaps the friend of Bos, praises

Flemish painters.

Jerome Bos.

---

[1] Cean Bermudez says some writers held this opinion, and Don Pedro Madrazo, in his notice of Bos in his *Catalogue of the Queen of Spain's Gallery* [1843] (p. 93), says, "Sábese que pasó gran parte de su vida en España."

[2] Descamps, *La Vie des Peintres Flamands Allemands et Hollandois* (4 tomes 8vo, Paris, 1753-63), tom. i. p. 19. Pilkington (*Dictionary*, 8vo, London, 1829, vol. i. p. 106)—with that indifference to historical fact, unfortunately too common with writers on art, says that Bos was born in 1470, and died in 1530, and that he adopted his peculiar style in consequence of despairing of equalling the great masters whose works he saw at the *Escorial*—a building not founded till thirty-three years after the time when he is supposed to have gone to that world of shadows which he had so often visited in imagination. [The statement is repeated in Allan Cunningham's edition, 1 vol. 8vo, London, 1840, p. 65.—ED.]

his close and exact imitation of nature, the limits of which, he says, he never overstepped, except in representing scenes in hell or purgatory. He bears testimony, however, as well to his fondness for these supernatural subjects as to his high reputation, by remarking that many monstrous compositions of this kind were falsely attributed to him, and that one of his ablest disciples, either out of respect for his master, or for the purpose of the better selling his own works, was in the habit of signing his pictures with the name of "Bosch."[1] The paintings of Bos are, for the most part, executed on panel; his style of drawing is vigorous, though harsh; he coloured well, and sometimes with the brilliancy of his contemporary, Hemling, to whom, however, he was far inferior in sentiment and grace. The strange and grotesque were the favourite fields of his fancy; and there he so delighted to exercise his strong powers of caricature and exaggeration that he might be called the Hogarth of the lower world. He often painted scenes from the Life of St. Anthony, the Egyptian Abbot; and, amongst the tormentors of that sorely-buffeted and hardy eremite, he usually chose to delineate, not those dangerous demons who came in the likeness of blooming maidens, angling with kind looks for his soul, or of jolly topers,

---

[1] Guevara, *Comentarios de la Pintura*, 8vo, Madrid, 1787, p. 41-43.

pledging him in sparkling goblets "when the wine was red and moved itself aright"—but the less pleasing fiends in frightful and bestial shape, whose wicked wont it was to invest the cavern by night, and sting, pinch, and pummel the good man till they left him for dead on the rocky floor. The "Fall of Lucifer and his rebel Angels," and "Adam and Eve expelled from Eden," were also subjects congenial to the taste of Bos, and may be found amongst his pictures in the Royal Gallery of Madrid, most of which were formerly at the Escorial. One of these is a large allegorical piece representing the "Triumphs of Death," and teeming with strange faces and fancies. In the centre, Death, scythe in hand, gallops by on his pale horse, driving reluctant multitudes to his shadowy realms, of which the frontier is marked by a fortification of coffins, manned by a grisly host of skeletons. Behind the Destroyer comes a car—a sort of dead-cart—to pick up the stragglers and the slain. In the foreground a party of revellers are disturbed at their banquet, and a king falls dead, wearing his diadem and purple, thus reading to royal eyes the solemn salutary lesson that

> "The glories of our blood and state,
> Are shadows, not substantial things;
> There is no armour against fate;
> Death lays his icy hand on kings."[1]

---

[1] Shirley, *Ajax and Ulysses*, sc. iii. *Works*, 8vo, London, 1833, vol. vi. p. 396.

CH. III.
Works at Valencia.

When called upon to paint the person of Our blessed Lord, the gloomy genius of Bos selected the most appalling moments of His mortal career. The Museum of Valencia has a series of pictures of this kind, of which the most striking in its horrors is a round panel, once an altar-piece in the Chapel "de los Reyes" of the superb Convent of San Domingo, and signed in Gothic characters "𝕳𝖎𝖊𝖗𝖔𝖓𝖞𝖒𝖚𝖘 𝖇𝖔𝖘𝖈𝖍." Here we behold the countenance of the Redeemer, pale, emaciated, and gory, beneath the crown of thorns; around are grouped the heads of mocking soldiers, gloating over that Divine agony, and grinning hideously like so many incarnate devils.

J. C. Vermeyen.

Juan Cornelio Vermeyen was a Dutch painter, born at Beverwyck about 1500, and invited to Spain, in 1534, by Charles V., whom he accompanied in the expedition to Tunis, of which he preserved some scenes, afterwards transferred to Brussels tapestries. He likewise followed the court to Italy, Germany, and Flanders; and having exercised his art with honour and profit, he died in 1559 at Brussels, and was buried in the Church of St. George, beneath an epitaph of his own writing. The sources whence he drew his early instruction in painting are unknown; but he excelled in several branches; in portraiture, landscape, and in sacred subjects. The Palace of the Pardo was adorned with a number of his pictures;

—eight pieces representing Imperial progresses in Germany, and views of Madrid, Valladolid, Naples, and London, all of which perished in the fire of 1608. Vermeyen was a special favourite of Charles V., who ordered his bust to be executed in marble "for the sake of the gravity and nobleness of his countenance." He was still more remarkable for the length of his beard, which gained him the name of "*el Barbudo,*" or "*Barbalonga,*" and very justly, if it be true, that although the wearer of this superb specimen was a tall man, the Emperor, when in a playful mood, used to amuse himself by treading on it as it trailed on the ground.[1]

Pedro Campaña, a Fleming, was one of the fathers of the school of Seville. He was born, in 1503, at Brussels, where he acquired some knowledge of painting, probably from Vander Weyde, or Van Orley. He then went to Italy, and, passing through Bologna in 1530, was chosen to paint a triumphal arch for the solemn entry of Charles V.—a task which he executed to the admiration of the citizens. After many years spent in study at Rome, he appeared at Seville in, or shortly before, 1548. In that year he painted, for the Church of Santa Cruz, his famous "Descent from the Cross." Though skilfully drawn and rich in colour, this picture is, on the whole, un-

---

[1] Descamps, *Peintres Flamands, &c.*, tom. i. p. 86.

pleasing, from the meagreness of the figures and the antique harshness of its execution. But its name is great in Seville. Pacheco, who borrowed none of its energy, confesses that he did not care to be left alone before it in its dimly-lighted chapel.[1] And though no picture was ever less akin to his own soft and airy style, it was a favourite study of Murillo, who would gaze for hours on its bold strong lines, and was buried, by his own desire, in the chapel where it hung. In spite, however, of its fame and historical interest, it was strangely neglected by that diligent collector, Marshal Soult, in his artistic campaign, and cruelly maltreated by his soldiery, who split the panel on which it was painted into five pieces, and left them to warp and blister in the sunshine in the court of the Alcazar. When the troubles were past, though scarred and seamed beyond the power of varnish, it was tolerably restored by Joaquin Cortes[2] —and it now hangs at the end of the noble Sacristia Mayor of the Cathedral.

Campaña exercised his art at Seville for many years with great success. The statues of the Kings, in the Chapel Royal of the Cathedral, were carved after his designs, which he made in charcoal, receiving for each one a ducat. Many of his works still adorn the churches. The Church of San Isidoro

---

[1] Pacheco, *Arte de la Pintura*, p. 57.
[2] *Handbook for Spain* [1845], p. 255 [3rd edition, 1855, p. 182].

has a "St. Paul the first Hermit," and "St. Anthony the Abbot," remarkable for the force and character of the heads; and that of San Juan de la Palma a fine "Crucifixion." Age improved his style, and it is said that he studied with advantage the works of Vargas when that artist returned from Rome. In his "Purification of the Virgin," in the Chapel of the Mariscal of the Cathedral, we find the harsh stiffness of the "Descent" softened to ease and beauty and an Italian suavity of tone. Rafael himself rarely designed a figure more graceful than the fair-haired damsel descending some steps to the left, who contrasts well with the beggar sprawling beneath—a study from the streets—that, doubtless, did not escape the eye of Murillo. The other smaller devotional pieces in the same altar, and the forcibly painted half-length portraits of the Mariscal Don Pedro Caballero and his family, are likewise works of Campaña. He returned, in his old age, to Brussels, where he died in 1580, and was honoured by having his portrait hung in the Consistory.

Francisco Frutet was a countryman and contemporary of Campaña. Nothing is known of him except that he painted several pictures for convents and churches at Seville, about 1548; and even his very name was lost, till exhumed from some dusty archives by the diligent Cean Bermudez. Several of his works are now in the Sevillian Museum.

Their colouring is Flemish; but in drawing and composition they display a knowledge of the Italian models and a disposition to use them. Thus in the oratory once at the Hospital de las Bubas, in the compartment which represents Our Lord going to Calvary, are introduced several figures from the "Spasimo de Sicilia," by Rafael, and from his "Burning of the Borgo" at the Vatican. The butcher-like figure of Simon the Cyrenian, however, recalls the brawny vulgar forms of Flanders. In the large central picture of the "Crucifixion," Our Lord on the cross is grandly conceived; the rest is indifferent. But of the few existing works of Frutet the best are those once in the convent of the Merced, and [afterwards] in the collection of [the late] Don Julian Williams, British Consul at Seville. They consist of a large centre altar-piece, with figures of life size, representing the Adoration of the Three Kings, remarkable for the variety and high finish of the heads; and four doors or wings, on which are painted the Presentation of Our Lord in the Temple, His Circumcision, a group of Apostles—amongst whom St. Paul stands foremost with his huge sword—and a group of mitred ecclesiastics and priests, excellent pictures, of which the last two are somewhat blemished by the hard execution and monotonous position of the hands.

Hernando Esturmio, or Sturmio of Ziriczea, resided at Seville about the middle of the century. He is supposed to have been a foreigner, and was perhaps a German, whose real name was Sturm. In 1554 he valued for the Chapter certain works of art—as it appears from a document in their archives—and the year following he painted for the Chapel of the Evangelists, of the Cathedral, nine pictures on panel, of which one is signed "*Hernandus Sturmius, Ziriezeensis faciebat*, 1555." The centre compartment represents "St. Gregory saying Mass," the panel above it "the Resurrection of Our Lord," and those at the sides and below "the Four Evangelists and several Saints." The figures are designed with some grace and freedom; the colouring is good, and affords, perhaps, the earliest example of the fine brown tones peculiar to the school of Seville. Of these various holy personages the most pleasing are "Santa Rufina and Santa Justa," patronesses of Seville, whom the "loyal and unconquered" city and its painters delight to honour and to depict. These virgin-martyrs were potters in the gipsy-suburb of Triana in 287, who, being inspired with holy frenzy, broke in pieces the statue of the great Venus of the Sevillians as it was carried along in a solemn procession. For this outrage—on the predecessor in popular veneration of Our Lady "de la Antigua," and themselves—they were scourged with thistles, and sent to walk barefoot in the Sierra Morena, a

Hernando Sturmio.

Legend of Sta. Rufina and Sta. Justa.

discipline through which they continued steadfast in the Christian faith. Being brought back to Seville, Justa was starved to death in a dungeon, while Rufina was exposed in the amphitheatre to a hungry lion, who behaved himself like the gentle beasts of Androcles and Una, "as he her wronged innocence did weet," and left the virgin-victim to be beaten to death by the more savage votaries of Venus. Burgos and an Asturian hermitage dispute with Seville the honour of possessing the bones of these sister-saints.[1] Sturmio has represented them in the usual conventional form; as two blooming maidens, each of whom "with bough of palm a crowned victrice stands,"[2] and who uphold between them the Giralda, or Moorish belfry of the favoured city; on the ground lie some earthen pots, symbols of their lowly calling. Their hands are painted with great care, and their rings, brooches, and ear-rings are remarkable not only for their exquisite finish, but also for their beauty as pieces of jewellery, in which the gems are not less lustrous than Da Vinci's rich ruby on the forehead of Lucrezia Crivelli,—"*La belle Féronnière*" of the Louvre.[3] The tower, in the hands of these pretty potters, also deserves notice,

---

[1] Alfonso de Villegas, *Flos Sanctorum*, folio, Gerona, 1788, p. 631.
[2] Ben Jonson, vol. ix. p. 76.
[3] *Notice des Tableaux exposés dans le Musée Royal*. No. 1091. [Edition 1889, No. 461.]

as being a carefully-executed representation of the Giralda, ere it had received its ornate crown of Christian masonry.

These were the chief foreign auxiliaries of Spanish art in this reign. Amongst the native leaders there were also men whose names have hardly been eclipsed by the glory of after-days. Felipe de Vigarny deserves to be first mentioned, as the reputed successful rival of Torrigiano. He was a native of Burgos, but the year of his birth is not known. His father was a Burgundian, and hence the son is frequently called Felipe de Borgoña. At the beginning of the sixteenth century he had already so distinguished himself in sculpture, that he was called to Toledo by Cardinal Ximenes to superintend the erection of the new high altar in the Cathedral, for which he executed, in 1502, four historical bas-reliefs, and the portraits of the Cardinal and his friend Antonio de Lebrija, the illustrious scholar of Alcalá. He is supposed to have resided there for some years, after which he went to Granada to construct the high altar of the Chapel Royal in the Cathedral. To him are attributed the curious bas-reliefs in painted wood, in that Chapel, representing the "Surrender of the Alhambra," and the "Baptism of the Moslem,"—curious, as authentic records of actual scenes, faces, and costumes, but so rude and uncouth that it seems very doubtful whether they were ever touched by his masterly hand. From Granada he returned to Toledo, but he probably revisited the former city to execute the monument of the Catholic Sovereigns. It is of white marble, and florid in design. On a sarcophagus adorned with scrolls and scutcheons, bas-reliefs, and lovely weeping cherubs, repose the figures of Ferdinand and Isabella, of which the faces are admirably-finished portraits. Much meaner dust lies inurned in more ostentatious sepulchres; but though the Venetian ambassador Navigiero bestowed on it only the contemptuous approval of an Italian, calling it "well enough for Spain."[1] this monument deserves to be ranked amongst the noblest of royal tombs and the most fairly earned of those—

——"incisa notis marmora publicis,
Per quæ spiritus et vita redit bonis
Post mortem ducibus;"[2]

Vigarny's influence on Spanish art.

Till the return of Berruguete from Italy, Vigarny was esteemed the best artist in Spain. He improved the Gothic style of drawing which obtained till his

---

[1] Writing of the Capilla de los Reyes Católicos, in the Cathedral at Granada, he notices "le loro sepulture di marmo, *assai belle per Spagna*"—making no further comment upon them; *Il Viaggio fatto in Spagna et in Francia dal magnifico M. Andrea Navagiero, fu oratore dell' illustrissimo Senato Veneto, alla Cesarea Maesta di Carlo V.*, 12mo, Vinegia, 1563, fol. 23. Some writers hold this monument to have been made at Genoa, but from this remark of the Venetian it would seem to have been the work of a Spaniard.

[2] Horat. *Car.* Lib. IV. viii., 13-15.

time in that country, by giving greater altitude to
the human figure. Before his time the face bore to
the whole body the proportion of one to nine; he
introduced the proportion of one to nine and one-
third. His last works were his carvings and alabaster
sculpture in the choir of Toledo Cathedral, for which
he executed one half of the upper stalls in competition with Berruguete, to whom he was held so nearly
equal that the inscription which records their rivalry
declares that

> CERTAVERUNT TUM ARTIFICUM INGENIA.
> CERTABUNT SEMPER, SPECTATORUM JUDICIA.

Vigarny died at Toledo in 1543, and was buried in
the Cathedral, near the choir.

The name of this first great Castilian sculptor may
naturally lead us to glance at the peculiar style in
which his art was practised in Spain. A large proportion of Spanish ecclesiastical carving was coloured
to imitate life—and this not only in remote convents
and rural churches, but in the polite cities and their
wealthy cathedrals. This painted sculpture, which
holds a middle place between sculpture and painting,
is well deserving of notice, both for the genius it
sometimes displays, and as a national art hardly
known beyond the limits of the Peninsula. The use
of colour in Spanish statuary is of very venerable
antiquity, whether it be considered as a relic of

heathen times or as a practice encouraged or introduced by the Church to aid the illusion with which she strove to invest her worship and move the spirits of the faithful. The close resemblance which exists between the pomps and ceremonies of the ancient and modern superstitions,—those of Egypt and Greece carried to Western Europe by the commerce of Carthage, and that of Papal Rome modified by lingering Paganism,—is a curious chapter in the history of religion.[1] In Spain image-worship reached a height hardly attained in any other part of Christendom, a height probably neither foreseen by its champions, those bold Bishops of Rome, the second and third Gregories, nor predicted by the fiercest Iconoclast who harangued the Council of Byzantium. Besides the most holy effigies, heaven-descended and not made with hands,[2] and of course plentifully endowed with miraculous power—such as the Black Lady of the Pillar at Zaragoza, and the Christ of the Vinestock at Valladolid—there were many sacred images which, even before the hands which fashioned them were cold, began to make the blind see, the lame walk, and friars flourish and grow sleek. To supply these representations of

---

[1] See the admirable Essay on this subject, *Handbook* [1845], pp. 107-114 [3rd edition, 1855, pp. 49-54].
[2] The "εἰκάσματα ἀχειροποίητα" of the Eastern Church—for an account of which see Gibbon, 8vo, London, 1838, chap. xlix. vol. ix. pp. 117-121.

saintly personages, became therefore an important and lucrative part of the business of the studio; and that they should be as life-like as possible, the better to strike the imagination of the vulgar, was the natural desire of their monkish purchasers. St. Bernard, therefore, stood forth to heal, habited, like a brother of the order, in his own white robes; St. Dominic scourged himself in effigy till the red blood flowed from his painted shoulders; and the Virgin, copied from the loveliest models, was presented to her adorers, sweetly smiling, and gloriously apparelled "in clothing of wrought gold." Many of these figures not only presided in their chapels throughout the year, but also, decked with garlands and illuminated by tapers, were carried by Brotherhoods or Guilds instituted in their honour, in the religious processions, once so frequent and splendid, and still favourite holiday shows, in the cities of Spain. For carvings intended for these purposes, clay or terra cotta was sometimes used; but wood was a more convenient and universal material, as being light, cheap, and easily coloured. Cedar, lime, and the indestructible "alerce,"[1] were woods frequently employed, though the preference was generally given to the Sorian pine. The colouring was sometimes laid on canvas, with which the figure was covered, as with a

---

[1] The *Thuya Articulata*. It still grows on the hills of Barbary. Cook's *Sketches in Spain*, vol. i. p. 5.

skin;[1] much care and labour was bestowed on it, and it was usually applied entirely by the hand of the master-artist himself. The effects and gradation of tints were studied as carefully as in paintings on canvas, and distant views and groups were freely introduced in the larger compositions, which were in truth nothing more than pictures in relief, with the principal figures altogether detached from their backgrounds. The imitation of rich stuffs for draperies (*estofar*) was a nice and delicate branch of the art, and was held by writers on the subject to be of no small difficulty and importance.[2] For single figures real draperies were sometimes used, especially for those of Madonnas, of whom many possessed large and magnificent wardrobes, and caskets of jewels worthy of the Queens of the Mogul. In these cases only the head and extremities of the figure were finished, the rest being often left a mere manequin, or block.

In works of this kind, there were several Spanish sculptors who displayed, as we shall see, no inconsiderable ability and taste. But in seeking after effect, by means like these, they undoubtedly mistook the genius of their art. They might have pleaded, perhaps, had they known it, the practice of Athenian artists in the days of Pericles; but although there is evidence to prove that colour was used by

---

[1] Bosarte, *Viaje*, p. 58.   [2] Pacheco, *Arte de la Pintura*, p. 362.

those masters in their statuary, it is by no means certain that illusion was intended.[1] The mantles of variegated marbles with which the Roman sculptors decked the busts of their Cæsars,—of which some specimens doubtless reached Spain; and some full-length statues similarly draped—of which the colossal Apollo, with ample robes of bloomy porphyry, in the Museum of Naples, is perhaps the finest existing example—might be cited as instances of a similar, but more defensible deviation from the simplicity of a pure taste. But it is the business of the sculptor to deal with form alone, to mould the clay into beauty, and to breathe life into the colourless marble, with no other instruments than his modelling-stick or his chisel; as it is the business of the painter to deal with colour, and with his pencil alone to deepen his airy distances, and cause rounded shapes to start gracefully from the flat surface of the canvas. Neither sculpture nor painting can invade the province of the other without loss, and a sacrifice of the dignity of art, for which no illusion, however perfect, can recompense. For, if exact and deceptive imitation of nature be held to be the chief end of art, then are the startling waxen preparations of the anatomical school of Florence higher achievements than the Venus "that enchants the world," in the

CH. III.

Colour not admissible in statuary.

---

[1] See the able article on Spanish art in the *Foreign Quarterly Review*, No. xxvi., pp. 264-5 [by Sir Edmund Head.—ED.].

Tribune, and "the Lord of the unerring bow," the glory of the Vatican; the fairyland (of pasteboard and gaslight) disclosed when the curtain rises on the scenes of a Parisian ballet, than the forest-vales of Poussin, and the stately and sunlit havens of Claude.

Damian Forment, a Valencian by birth, was a sculptor of renown in this reign. He studied in Italy, and is supposed to have formed his style on the works of Donatello. In 1511 he was employed to execute an alabaster altar-piece for the high altar of the Cathedral "of the Pillar," at Zaragoza—a work still existing, and reckoned one of the finest monuments of art in Arragon. It is designed in the florid Gothic style, and is divided into three compartments, or high-canopied niches, of which that in the centre is filled with "the Assumption of the Virgin," and those at the sides with her "Nativity" and "Purification"—all in high relief. Above, around, and beneath these principal groups, are disposed a thousand figures and ornaments of graceful design, and elaborately carved. The artist was employed on this work nearly nine years, and received for his labour 1,200 ducats. In 1520 he began his other great work—the retablo for the high altar of the Cathedral of Huesca, also in alabaster, and in design somewhat like that at Zaragoza. It consists of three principal niches, overhung by canopies of the finest Gothic tracery, and foliage enriched with small saintly figures. The central niche contains the crucifixion of Our Lord, in high relief, the others his progress along the *via dolorosa*, and his deposition from the Cross. Below are a series of smaller niches, in which stand the Saviour, risen and glorified, and His apostles, six on either hand. Lower still, seven compartments are filled with bas-reliefs, representing Our Lord in the last scenes of His life; at the Last Supper, praying in the Garden, betrayed by Judas, scourged, crowned with thorns, led forth to the people, and brought before Pilate. The base is adorned with columns and grotesque figures in the florid plateresque style, which was already superseding the Gothic, and with two exquisitely-wrought medallion profile portraits of the sculptor and his wife. Amongst the historical figures Our Lord crucified is one of the finest, and the executioner dragging Him to Calvary, and the spearman standing beneath the Cross, are admirable for force and expression. Words can give no adequate idea of the infinite variety of fancy and marvellous skill of hand displayed in the ornamental borders—of fruits, flowers, foliage, masks, and heads of men and animals—which surround each piece of sculpture, and the massive yet delicate and airy frame which encompasses the whole. As the eye wanders over this wilderness of graceful design and cunning workmanship, it will discover no cause for surprise that Forment should have devoted to this superb altar-piece no less than thirteen years, the last of his life. The cost of its construction was 110,000 *sueldos* of Arragon.[1] When this superb altar-piece was finished, he was invited by the Emperor to enter his service; this was, however, prevented by his death in 1533. The liberal patronage of the Church enabled him to leave an estate, entailed on his family, worth 60,000 Castilian ducats. His school was thronged with scholars, of whom he never had fewer than twelve, and who received at his hands both instruction and kindness. To the memory of one of them, Pedro Muñoz, his countryman and friend, he erected a monument in the cloister of the Cathedral of Huesca, where his own ashes also repose, which commemorates both master and scholar in its simple and touching inscription:

D. O. M.
LEX MI NATVRÆ, ET TE PETRE OFFENSA
TVLERVNT NVMINA: QVOD POSSVM DO
LAPIDEM ET LACHRYMAS. PETRO MONYOSIO
PATRIA VALENTINO DAMIANVS FORMENT
ARTE STATVARIA PHIDIÆ, PRAXITELISQVE
ÆMVLVS: ALVMNO SVO CARISSIMO, AC
CLIENTILI SVO B. M. FLENS, POSVIT.
VIX. AN. LXVII. MENS. X. DIES XXVIII
OB. KAL. JAN. MD. XXII.

---

[1] *Fundacion Excelencias Grandezas y Cosas Memorables de Huesca*, por Fran Diego de Aynsa y Iriarte.—Fol., Huesca, 1619, p. 510. Twenty *sueldos* made a libra, or nineteen reals.

Pedro Machuca, painter, sculptor, and architect, likewise studied in Italy. His birthplace is not known, but he resided chiefly at Granada. In painting he is said to have followed the style of Rafael, with what success time, which has spared none of his pictures, has not permitted us to judge. As a sculptor, amongst his best works was the marble fountain, richly adorned with bas-reliefs on historical subjects, which still exists, though in a very dilapidated condition, near the Alhambra gate, to attest his skill and the munificence of its founder, the Marquess of Mondejar. Seville possesses a better preserved proof of his powers, in the three fine medallion alto-relievos, representing Faith, Hope, and Charity, and full of Italian grace and feeling, which are placed over the door of the church of the Hospital de la Sangre,[1] and have escaped the brush of the whitewasher, who, in Andalusia, is no respecter of marbles. But his fame rests chiefly on his great architectural effort, that superb fragment of a palace that forms so fine a feature in distant prospects of Granada, crowning the hill, and contrasting with the red towers, of the Alhambra.

---

[1] *Handbook for Spain* [1845], p. 274 [3rd edition, 1855, p. 203]. Cean Bermudez, who has written a tract on this Hospital, does not mention the name of the sculptor who executed these marbles; but remarks that their merit is such that they might be ascribed to Torrigiano, had he not died forty years before the portal in question was built. See his *Descripcion Artistica del Hospital de la Sangre*, 12mo, Valencia, 1804, p. 22.

The fear of earthquakes, or the fickleness of royal taste, interrupted its building; and though it was never roofed in, it has been a ruin for three centuries. But its simple and majestic fronts, and the noble circular court and Doric colonnade within, will be admired so long as the crumbling fabric shall withstand the winters and rough weather of the Sierra Nevada. Its stately façades form a striking contrast to the mean rough-cast walls that enshroud the delicate bowers of the Moslem. Since the Emperor had the rashness to let loose his architects in the precincts of that enchanted palace—

> "Del Rey chiquito la encantado estancia
> De alabastro azur y oro inestimable"—[1]

he was fortunate in finding so skilful a master to undertake the dangerous changes. It is also well for Granada that the structure of its Castilian Cæsar may claim a certain meed of praise, beside the last exquisite relic of its Arabian Sultans.

Machuca was one of the first masters who introduced into Spain the Italian, or, as it was called, the Greco-Romano, style of architecture. The rich pointed architecture of the Christian, having taken the place of the light towers and arcades of the Moor, in turn gave way to a style founded on the

---

[1] Vicente Espinel, quoted by Cean Bermudez, *Arquitectos de España*, tom. i. p. 221.

models of classical antiquity. Edifices of a foreign aspect now showed themselves in street or market-place, or amongst conventual groves and gardens, rising upon the ruins of the Moorish mosque or palace, and contrasting with the grey religious structures of Castile. The first work on architecture in the Castilian language was written for the purpose of explaining the classical proportions. It was entitled, "The Measurements of the Roman," and was composed by Diego de Sagredo,[1] chaplain to Queen Juana, a man of learning and observation, who had cultivated his taste by travel in Italy. His remarks are cast in the form of a dialogue, wherein one Campeso, a servant of the Cathedral of Toledo, communicates the fruits of his researches to Picard, a painter, probably the Leo Picard who was painter to the Constable of Castile at Burgos, and who has obtained a place in history by sharing his olla with the imprisoned Count of Salvatierra, one of the unhappy leaders in the wars of the commons.[2] The work, illustrated with coarse woodcuts, is dedicated to Archbishop Alfonso de Fonseca of Toledo, where it was first printed in 1526; and it became so popular, that two

Diego de Sagredo's "Medidas del Romano."

---

[1] Medidas del Romano necesarias a las oficiales que quieren seguir las formaciones de las bases, columnas, y otros edificios antiguos (then a cut of a Corinthian capital over the words), con privilegio, 4to, Toledo; en casa de Ramon Petras. 1526.

[2] Fr. Prud. de Sandoval, *Historia de la vida y hechos del Emp. Carlos V.* 2 tom. fol., Amberes, 1681, tom. i. p. 365.

new editions appeared at Toledo and two at Lisbon, as well as a French translation at Paris, within forty years.[1] Italian architecture, thus introduced, rapidly gained ground, and soon blossomed into that florid style, known as the *plateresque*, or style of the silversmiths, which has never been surpassed in luxuriance of decoration. Engrafting the fanciful adornments of the old architecture on the simpler forms of the new, the plateresque builders covered their cornices with flowers, and wreathed their columns in garlands and arabesques, until the fronts of church and monastery rivalled in fretwork and chasing their own sacramental plate, "as if the wealth within them had run o'er." In interiors, as in the great sacristy of Seville Cathedral, this prodigality of decoration has a sumptuous effect, nor is it unpleasing in exteriors, when the buildings are complete in themselves, and not patchings added to venerable piles. In these latter lay the chief sins of the new

---

[1] The second and third editions were printed at Lisbon, by Luis Rodriguez, in January and June 1542,* and the fourth and fifth at Toledo, in 1549 and 1564, by Juan de Avala, all in black letter. I know the book only by the copy of the fifth edition, bought from the Heber library by Mr. Ford. The French translation is entitled, *Raison d'Architecture antique extraite de Vitruve, et autres anciens architecteurs, nouvellement traduit d'espaignol en françois, a l'utilité de ceulx que se delectent en edifices.* Paris, imp. par Simon Colines, 1542, 4to. *Los Arquitectos*, tom. i. p. 175. An admirable account of the plateresque architecture will be found in the *Quarterly Review*, vol. lxxvii. No. cliv. p. 521 [by Richard Ford.—ED.].

* [In a later note the author says, "This I suspect is wrong. Dn. Val. de Calderora has a copy printed at 'Lisbona, June 1541.'"—ED.]

architects, sins which were doubly offensive in the works of their degenerate successors. Thus, in the Cathedral of Valencia all styles contend, with such evenly-balanced forces, that two English travellers, bewildered in the confusion, describe it, the one as a large Gothic pile,[1] the other as a pleasing Grecian structure.[2] Nor were their fancies always in good taste. The Cathedral of Seville is encased in a mass of Greco-Romano buildings of which the heavy outlines are slightly broken, but hardly relieved, by tripods crested with flames flickering in solid stone. It would have been well, had contemporary architects imitated the graceful simplicity of Machuca.

Alonso Berruguete, who for his genius in the three arts of painting, sculpture, and architecture, may be called the Spanish Michael Angelo, was born at Paredes de Nava, in Old Castile, about 1480. His early years were passed in the atmosphere of art,[3] for he was second son of the painter Pedro Berruguete, and one of his sisters—known as "La Toledana," was married to Juan Gonzalez Becerril, a painter of Toledo. His parents, however, designed him for

---

[1] Swinburne's *Travels in Spain*, London, 1779, 4to, p. 100.
[2] Townsend's *Journey through Spain*, 3 vols. 8vo, Lond., 1791; iii. 257.
[3] *Handbook* [1845], p. 613 [3rd edition, 1855, p. 555] (quoting Morales, *Viaje*, p. 26), says: "His dormant genius was first called into action" by the study of an antique sarcophagus (on which was sculptured the history of the Horatii and Curatii in some fifty figures), existing or once existing at Husillos, a poor place, one and a half leagues from Valencia.

the legal profession, and obtained for him the post of solicitor (*Escribano del Crimen*) in the Royal Chancery of Valladolid[1]—an office of which he still retained the title in 1526,[2] although he had probably long ceased to discharge its duties. He received his first instructions in painting from his father;

and at the death of that master he passed into Italy to study in the school of Michael Angelo at Florence. There he early distinguished himself, in both painting and sculpture. In 1503 he made a copy of his master's famous cartoon of the Battle of Pisa, exe-

---

[1] Bosarte, *Viaje*, p. 156.
[2] Cean Bermudez, *Los Arquitectos*, tom. ii. p. 169.

cuted in competition with that by Leonardo da Vinci, and, with its rival, destroyed in the fire of the Great Council Chamber. He accompanied Michael Angelo, in 1504, to Rome, where he was amongst the sculptors chosen by Bramante to model the Laocoon, for the purpose of having it cast in bronze—a trial of skill which sufficiently proves the proficiency of the Spaniard, though Sansovino gained the day. On his return to Florence, he was employed to complete, for the nuns of St. Jerome, an altar-piece, left unfinished by Filippo Lippi at his death. He lived many years in Italy, in habits of friendship with all the chief artists of the time, especially Bandinelli and Andrea del Sarto. In 1520 he returned to Spain, and resided some time at Zaragoza, where he executed a tomb and an altar for the church of Santa Engracia. Thence he went to Huesca to visit Damian Forment, who profited by his knowledge and experience, in his works for the Cathedral of that place. The talents of Berruguete soon attracted the notice of Charles V., who appointed him one of his artists, and afterwards gave him a chamberlain's key. Having married Doña Juana Pareda, a lady of Rioseco, he fixed his residence in Valladolid, where he engaged in many works for churches and monasteries. Of these, one of the finest was the high altar which he erected in the Church of San Benito el Real, attached to the great Convent of Benedictines.

The original agreement between the abbot and the artist has been printed by Bosarte,[1] and bears date 8th November 1526. It is there stipulated that the height of the altar shall be fourteen yards and a half, and its breadth ten yards; that three sorts of wood shall be used in its construction, walnut (*nogal*) for the figures, and yew (*teja*) and pine for the other parts; that the colours and gilding shall be of the finest quality; and that the whole of the paintings and the heads and hands of all the carved figures shall be executed by Berruguete himself. The structure consisted of two storeys, each supported by twelve columns, the lower row being Corinthian; between the columns were bas-reliefs, or saintly figures in niches; and the cornices and every part susceptible of ornament, were covered with flowers, foliage, and animals. In the centre of the lower storey stood St. Benedict—carved and painted as large as life—in the act of blessing; on either hand were pictures representing the "Nativity of Our Lord" and the "Flight into Egypt." In the upper storey the Virgin, attended by angels, was soaring up to heaven; and the whole edifice was surmounted by a crucifix. Berruguete spent six years in making this altar, with which, when it was finished, he expressed himself highly satisfied, in a

---

[1] *Viaje*, p. 359.

letter to Andre Naxera, a brother sculptor.[1] The abbot, Alonso de Toro, however, does not seem to have shared in his satisfaction, for they had a long dispute about the price, which was at last fixed by three arbitrators (of whom Felipe de Vigarny was one) at 4,400 ducats.

He seems to have been unwearied in the exercise of his profession, in the course of which he made several journeys to Madrid, Toledo, Granada, and other cities. In 1529, he was employed by Archbishop Fonseca, of Toledo, to execute the retablo for the chapel of the College of Santiago, founded at Salamanca by that prelate; and, within two years, though occupied, as we have seen, at home, he produced a beautiful and elaborate work, adorned with eight pictures and a variety of statues. At Toledo, he was chosen, in 1539, with Felipe de Vigarny, to carve the upper stalls of the choir, of which he executed one half, and likewise the archiepiscopal throne, over which hovers an airy and graceful figure, carved in dark walnut, representing Our Lord on the Mount of Transfiguration, and remarkable for its fine and floating drapery. The Convent of San Domingo, at Palencia, possessed a noble monument of his genius in the sepulchre of Juan de Roxas and Maria Sarmi, Marquess and Marchioness of Poza, who

---

[1] Bosarte, *Viaje*, p. 376.

Monument of Cardinal Tavera at Toledo.

knelt in effigy beneath a towering canopy of marble supported by columns and adorned with sacred sculptures. This fine tomb was finished in 1557.

His faculties remained unimpaired to a good old age; for, when near his eightieth year, he went, with his son Alonso, to Toledo, to construct, for the noble Hospital of St. John Baptist, the monument of its founder, Cardinal-Archbishop Juan de Tavera, for which the stipulated price was 1,000 ducats. It is reckoned one of his finest works, and is placed in the centre of the chapel. On a richly decorated sarcophagus, the great churchman lies in his mitre and robes; his gloved hands are crossed on his breast, and his fine and venerable features—worthy of a master's chisel—wear the pure placid expression which belongs to "the dead that die in the Lord." A portrait by El Greco hangs near, and vouches for the accuracy of the likeness. Whilst engaged in this work, Berruguete resided in the hospital, and was lodged in a chamber beneath the clock—now a receptacle for dust and rubbish—where he died in 1561. His genius gained him wealth, as well as honours and fame; for, two years before his death, he purchased from the Crown the lordship of Ventosa, near Valladolid, together with the customs of the town—possessions which were enjoyed by his family for several generations.

Berruguete is universally allowed to have been

the greatest artist of his age in Spain. He brought oil-painting to a perfection unknown in the Peninsula. For the stiff angular style of the earlier masters, and their lean haggard figures—whose ages could be guessed at only from their sizes—he substituted the free outlines and rounded contours of Italy. Pompeyo Guarico's rule for drawing the human form, which gave nine times the length of the face to the whole figure, had been followed till Vigarny changed the proportion to nine times and one-third. Albert Durer made it ten. The practice of Berruguete, founded on his studies of the antique, fixed it at ten and one-third.[1] His statues, which are generally highly finished, display much of the manner of his great master, in their grand and noble forms, and well-developed, though somewhat overcharged, anatomy. His best works in painting were executed for the Cathedral of Palencia and the Church of Ventosa, and in marble and bronze, for the Cathedral and other public buildings at Toledo. As an architect, his luxuriant fancy seduced him into the flowery paths of his contemporaries; and his façades and altars are usually fretted and garlanded, after the most approved plateresque fashion. But here, as indeed in the other arts, he has sometimes been made answerable for the extravagances

---

[1] Jovellanos, *Oracion en la Junta de la Real Acad. de S. Fernando.* 14, *Julio*, 1781, 4to, Madrid, 1781, p. 15.

of others. It has been the lot of all great masters who joined unwearied industry to prolific genius, to glean a few praises for merits, and still oftener to be made scapegoats for sins not their own. Thus almost every work of architecture, sculpture, or painting produced in Castile between 1500 and 1560, which was good, or passed for such, and of which the parentage was doubtful, has, at some time or other, been ascribed to Berruguete.[1]

Diego de Navas, sculptor.

Diego de Navas was a sculptor who executed, from a design by the licentiate Velasco, the fine high-altar of the superb convent of San Jerónimo at Granada, a noble pile, still further ennobled by the grave of the Great Captain, by whose widow it was mainly built.[2] This altar consists of a basement, adorned with bas-reliefs, and three storeys of the Ionic, Corinthian, and composite orders, profusely

---

[1] Cean Bermudez, *Los Arquitectos*, tom. ii. p. 13. I find a testimony to the fame of Berruguete—where it was little to be expected—in the Chronicle of honest Bernal Diaz del Castillo—friend of Cortes, and one of the Conquistadors of Mexico. Writing of certain Mexican artists of extraordinary skill, he says, that in his judgment they could not be surpassed even by "aquel tan nombrado pintor como fué el muy antiguo Apeles, y de los nuestros tiempos, que se dicen Berruguete y Micael Angel, ni de otro moderno ahora nuevamente nombrado, natural de Burgos, que se dice, que en sus obras tan primas es otro Apeles."— *Historia Verdadera de la Conquista de la Nueva España*, 8vo, Paris, 1837, tom. iv. p. 428. Who the Apelles of Burgos could be, is not very clear. Perhaps the valiant captain—who wrote in 1572 in his old age—may have meant Vigarny, the *sculptor* of Burgos—or possibly Morales of *Badajoz*, or Campaña of *Brussels*—both of whom must have been at the height of their reputation during his visits to Castile.

[2] *Handbook* [1845], p. 392 [3rd edition, 1855, p. 324].

decorated with statues, of which the principal are, in the first storey, Our Lady of the Conception, in the second, St. Jerome doing penance in his cavern, and in the third, Our Lord on the Cross. The bas-reliefs represent passages from the life of Our Lord and the Virgin. The most graceful and pleasing of them are the Annunciation, and the Maries bending over the dead body of the Saviour. On brackets, at each side of the altar, kneel figures of the Great Captain and his wife, the Duchess of Sesa—about life-size—tolerably designed, and curious for costume, but hardly so good as the sculpture of the retablo. Each statue and bas-relief, says Cean Bermudez, is designed with grace and finished with elaborate care; and from the general character of the work it is probable that Navas, if he did not study in Italy, was one of the ablest scholars of Berruguete.

Gaspar de Tordesillas was one of the ablest sculptors formed in the school of Berruguete. One of his best works is the monument of the Comendador Pedro Gonzalez de Alderete,—wrought in alabaster, for the parish church of Tordesillas—a sarcophagus, supported by caryatides and rich with sculptured niches, on which lies the armed figure of the soldier, with his morion at his feet, and cherubs weeping around him.[1] For the Church of San Benito

---

[1] Cean Bermudez, *Los Arquitectos*, &c., tom. ii. p. 22.

CH. III.

el Real, at Valladolid, he executed, in 1547, the rich plateresque retablo of the chapel of St. Anthony the Abbot, of which the painted statue of that saint was reckoned superior to the San Benito of the high altar—the work of Berruguete himself.[1] From some documents belonging to a tedious law process respecting the tomb of Alderete, preserved by Cean Bermudez,[2] it appears that Tordesillas could not write, or even sign his name.

Xamete.

Xamete was a sculptor who may have been either the scholar or the rival of Alonso Berruguete. Of his life nothing is known; and it is a matter of dispute whether his name be Catalonian or Valencian, Italian or Moorish. He, however, proved himself one of the ablest artists of his day, by his magnificent portal of the Cathedral cloister at Cuença, carved in Arcos stone, at the expense of Bishop Sebastian Ramirez, between 1546 and 1550. It is in the florid plateresque style; it rises twenty-eight feet in height, is supported by Corinthian columns, and profusely adorned with sculpture, in which Tritons and Cupids, masks, heads of lions, harpies, and other heathen devices set off the statues of Judith and Jael, the Virgin and St. John, and bas-reliefs representing the life of Our Lord.

Fernando Gallegos.

Fernando Gallegos was born at Salamanca, between

---

[1] Bosarte, *Viaje*, p. 187.
[2] Cean Bermudez, *Los Arquitectos*, &c., tom. ii. p. 178.

the middle and the end of the fifteenth century. Some authors say that he studied painting in Germany, in the school of Albert Durer,—on account of the resemblance of their styles, in drawing and exact finish. Cean Bermudez, however, though of opinion that his paintings might pass for those of Durer, thinks it more probable that he learned his art under Pedro Berruguete, at Toledo. He mentions, with peculiar praise, his picture on panel in St. Clement's Chapel in the Cathedral of Salamanca, representing the Virgin with the infant Saviour on her knees, and attended by St. Andrew and St. Christopher. The style of Gallegos had sometimes the softness of Rafael's second manner, and some of his designs seem to have been borrowed from prints by Marc Antonio.[1] He died at Salamanca, at a great age, in 1550.

Juan de Villoldo was a distinguished painter at Toledo about the same time. He studied in the school of his uncle, Alonzo Perez de Villoldo, a scholar of Juan de Borgoña. His series of forty-five pictures on subjects of sacred history, executed in 1547-8, for the Carbajal chapel in the Church of St. Andrew at Madrid, by order of its restorer, Don Gutierre de Carbajal, Bishop of Plasencia, is commended by Cean Bermudez, as being designed with

---

[1] Cook's *Sketches in Spain*, ii. 149.

great correctness, and in a style of antique purity. He died sometime after 1551.

Francisco Comontes was son of Iñigo, and nephew of Antonio Comontes, both of whom were scholars of the elder Rincon. Iñigo was the instructor of Francisco, who first distinguished himself as an artist, in the Cathedral of Toledo, in 1533, by executing the principal retablo of the splendid Chapel "de Los Reyes Nuevos," from the designs of Felipe de Vigarny. For the winter chapter-room he painted, in 1545, the portrait of Cardinal-Archbishop Tavera, and in 1547 that of Archbishop Siliceo, for each of which he received 6,375 maravedis. In 1547 he was named Painter to the Cathedral—an office which he held till the 10th of February 1565—the day of his death. Of his many works for various altars and chapels, some have been removed by succeeding chapters, to make way for novelties; those which were considered the best were his highly-finished pictures, on panel, of the Virgin and St. Bartholomew, placed, in 1559, in a retablo, gilt by his own hands, in the Chapel of the Tower. Comontes was one of the best of the many artists of his age, whose whole lives and labours lay within the shadow of that great Toledan Church; whose genius was spent in its service, and whose names were hardly known beyond its walls.

Correa is an artist whose name has been preserved

by a series of pictures painted for the Bernardine Monastery of Valdeiglesias, representing passages from the lives of Our Lord and St. Bernard. Some of these are now in the National Museum at Madrid, and bear the signature "D. Correa, 1550." Cean Bermudez thought he detected the same hand in twelve pictures on the History of the Virgin, in the convent of San Vicente, at Plasencia. From the resemblance of Correa's style to that of the early Florentine masters, it is very probable that he studied at Florence. His figures and draperies are often Perugino-like; his skies, like the skies of St. Petersburg, are of that uncertain hue which hovers between blue and green; his colouring is rich, and his conceptions have much of grace and feeling.

Juan de Iciar, or Yciar, was a Biscayan, who was born at Durango in 1525, and who practised painting, says Cean Bermudez, as an amateur, apparently at Zaragoza. Having printed in that city, in 1549, a work on arithmetic,[1] he published there, in the following year, his book on the art of penmanship,[2]

---

[1] *Arithmetica practica*, 4to, Zaragoza, 1549, a volume which I know only from the notice in Antonio; *Bib. Nova*, tom. i. p. 712.

[2] *Arte subtilissima por la qual se enseña a escrevir perfectamente, hecho y experimentado y agora de nuevo añadido*, por Juan de Yciar Vizcayno; en Çaragoça en casa de Pedro Bernuz, año de 1550, 8vo, consisting of 11 sheets, A to L inclusive, but not paged. I have never seen any copy of this exceedingly scarce work but that in the rich Spanish library of Mr. Ford, which the fortunate possessor bought at Mr. Heber's sale.

CH. III.

His "Arte de Escribir."

the earliest work of the kind produced by a Spaniard, and one of the rarities of Spanish bibliography. It contains a great variety of alphabets and specimens of various sorts of writing, embellished with flowers, knots, and scrolled borders designed by himself, and well engraved on wood by Juan de Vingles,[1] a Frenchman, whose signature will be found on the plates, generally thus,

 or thus,

The book opens with a dedication to Philip, Prince of Spain, which is followed by an address to the "most benign reader," wherein the author craves forgiveness for his seeming presumption in inscribing his name on each of his plates, and pleads in extenuation of the offence the example of the Italian writers on the same subject, Ludovico Vicentino, Antonio Tagliente, and Gianbattista Palatino. Next comes his own boldly-executed and pleasing portrait, and then a sort of essay, more tedious than long, in which he proves out of Plato, Solomon, and Quinc-

---

[1] There was a printer at Lyon in 1497, named Jehan de Vingle, who printed "Quatre filz de Aymon." See Brunet, *Manuel de Libraire*, tom. iii. p. 883.

tilian, the importance of the nice conduct of the pen. In his alphabets he has borrowed freely from Italian writers, as for example, his beautiful series of ribbon-letters[1] from Ludovico Vicentino, who, at Venice in 1533, published rules for writing.[2] In some of his knots, scrolls, and other ornaments, he seems also to have availed himself of hints from those, now rare and precious, black-letter pattern books, printed in Germany and Flanders,[3] for the use of fair dames who amused their leisure, or cunning workmen who gained their bread, by weaving the matchless lace and sumptuous arras of the olden time. No succeeding professor of caligraphy, in Spain at least, has eclipsed his book, which seems to have furnished all that is most worth notice in the later works of Lucas,[4] Morante,[5] and Casanova.[6]

---

[1] In sheet F. They have been beautifully reproduced in Mr. J. Jobbins' elegant volume entitled *Polygraphia Curiosa*, 4to, London, 1847; Plate 25.

[2] *Regola da imparare scrivere varii caratteri de lettere con li suoi compassi et misure, et il modo di temperare le penne*, ordinato per Ludovico Vicentino; 4to, Venetia, 1523.

[3] Such as Ein new Modelbüch auff aussnehen und porten wircken in der laden und langen gestell. mit 105 andern mödeln; Gedruckt in der fürstliche Stadt Zwickau durch Hanns Schönsperger, 1524, 4to, which was reprinted in 1526; Modelbüch aller art Nehens und Stichens; sm. 4to, Franckfort, 1535. Ein new kunstlich Modelbüch; sm. 4to. Cöllen. 1545, &c.

[4] Francisco Lucas, *El arte de escribir*; 4to, Sevilla, 1570, and Madrid, 1608.

[5] Infra, chap. x.

[6] *Primera parte de la arte de escrivir todas formas de letras*, escrito y tallada por Joseph de Casanova; fol., Madrid, 1650. The second part does not appear to have been published.

CH. III.

His "Nuevo Estilo de Screvir Cartas."

It appears to have been printed three times within the author's life, the second edition, including the treatise on arithmetic, having been published in 1553,[1] and the third, apparently a reprint of the second, in 1559, both at Zaragoza.[2]

Having thus given to the world rules for the manual part of writing, he published nineteen years afterwards, in 1569, a small work entitled "The New Style of Writing Letters," and consisting of models of epistles to persons of various degrees.[3] This curious and very rare[4] little black-letter volume is dedicated

---

[1] This is the only edition mentioned by Antonio. The title, so far as he gives it, is the same as the following.

[2] Libro sutilissimo por el qual se enseña a escrivir i contar perfectamente, el qual lleva el mesmo orden que lleva un maestro con su discipulo; por Juan de Iciar, Vizcayno, en Caragoça en Casa de la Viuda de Barth. de Nagera. Impresso a costas de Miguel de Suelves, alias Zapila Infançon; Zaragoza, 1559, 4to. I find it thus entered, as *liber utilis et rarissimus*, in the *Specimen Bibliothecæ Hispano-Majansianæ*; 4to, Hannover, 1753, p. 102. Mr. Salva has a copy with the title altered as I have done it, with date 1564. On back of title is a small portrait of Philip II., a profile, in an oval on a shield, surmounting the doubleheaded eagle. The book on arithmetic has separate title. Of this Mr. Salva has an earlier edition, in folio, Libro titulado Arithmetica Practica, muy util y provechoso para todo persona que quiriere exercitarse en aprender a contar, agora nuevamente hecho por Juan de Yciar, Vizcayno —Cæsaraugustæ, 1549, folio, black letter. It has a very fine woodcut title, signed, *Anno* 1548 *DIEGO*; and the portrait of himself on a large scale, like that in the *Arte de Escrivir*.

[3] Nuebo Estilo de screbir Cartas mensageras sobre bibersas materias. Sacabas a luy por industria de Juan de Yciar Viscayno: En Çaragoça en casa de la biuda de Barth. de Nagera, ano MD.LXIX. sm. 4to of 76 leaves, including ornamental title, two leaves of index, and a woodcut at the end.

[4] It is not mentioned by Antonio, nor, so far as I know, by any other bibliographer.

to Ruy Gomez de Silva, Prince of Eboli, by whom, it seems, the idea had been suggested to Yciar, when he presented him with a copy of his former work. The headings of a few of these model epistles will be sufficient to explain their contents. There is one "from a King or Prince to a Cardinal in recommendation of a gentleman," another is a "recommendation for a man of letters and virtue to a lord-prelate professing both;" a letter "to a friend who had asked the writer to compose for him a love-letter, which he began, but would not finish," is followed by one "to a young man, hard to advise or correct;" there are several epistles of condolence on the deaths of wives, husbands, and brothers, and on the birth of a law-suit, a petition to an abbot on behalf of a penitent monk wishing to return to a convent from which he had deserted, a curious series of letters between two gentlemen on the qualification of servants, and a strange correspondence carried on between the body and the soul. In 1575, the fiftieth year of his age, he took orders, and went to spend the rest of his days at Logroño.[1] The date of his death is not known. He was the instructor of Pedro de Madriaga, likewise a Biscayan and an author of a book on

---

[1] Pedro Diaz Morante, *Segunda Parte del arte de escrivir;* fol., Madrid, 1624; Prólogo.

writing,[1] which, however, is very inferior to that of Yciar.

Tomas Pelegret was a Toledan by birth, and studied in Italy under Balthazar Peruzzi, and Polidoro Caravaggio, famous at Rome for their designs in *chiaroscúro*, representing buildings or street perspectives, bas-reliefs or groups of sculpture, cornices or other architectural ornaments, with which it was then the fashion to adorn the façades, courts, and halls of palaces. On his return to Spain—probably about 1530—he settled at Zaragoza, where he decorated the façades of many palaces and churches with paintings in the style of his masters, and enjoyed a high reputation. These works have, however, all perished by time, or in the troubles of the turbulent and ill-fated city. At Huesca he painted, about 1550, the Sacristy of the Cathedral, and the Monument for the Holy Week, works of much merit, in which he was assisted by one Cuevas, a native of the town, and his scholar, who excelled him in the grace and spirit of his figures. Cuevas died in his thirty-third year—doubtless before his master, who attained the age of eighty-four, and,

---

[1] *Honra de Escrivanos; arte para escrivir bien presto; ortographia de pluma;* 8vo, Valencia, 1565. See *Reflexiones sobre la verdadera arte de escribir,* por el Abate Don Domingo Maria de Servidori, Romano; 2 tom., folio; Madrid, 1789; tom. i., p. 66; an elaborate work which contains a complete history of the Spanish and other masters of penmanship, and specimens of their letters.

though the date of his death is not known, must have lived far into the reign of Philip II. It is not certain whether he ever painted in oils, though some pictures in the Convent of Santa Engracia, at Zaragoza were attributed to him. The decorative art which he practised did not survive him in Arragon. His facility of hand and fecundity of invention must have been remarkable; for, even in the last century, many of his drawings and designs —made for painters, sculptors, architects, goldsmiths, and other artists—were still to be found at Zaragoza.

Ezpeleta was an Arragonese painter, contemporary with Pelegret, who excelled in illuminations and miniatures. He was born at Alagon, and died at the age of sixty, about the middle of the century, at Zaragoza, where he chiefly resided, and where he illuminated with great delicacy many choir-books for the Cathedral. He likewise attempted oil-painting, but his style was so dry and hard that he soon returned to his miniature and more congenial labours on vellum.

Hernando Yañez was a painter of whom nothing is known beyond the fact that he painted, about 1531, a series of pictures on panel for the Chapel of the Albornoces—conspicuous for its portal overhung by a skeleton of stone—in the Cathedral of Cuença. He was employed for this purpose by Don Gomez

Carillo de Albornoz, prothonotary, treasurer, and canon of that church, a man of fine taste, who had visited Bologna and Rome, and who enriched the chapel of his house with many jewels and works of art. Don Gomez died in 1536; in his will these pictures by Yañez were mentioned, and that artist was called "a remarkable painter" (*pintor singular*). In the principal retablo the centre pieces represent the Nativity, Crucifixion, and Resurrection of Our Blessed Lord; and a pope, a bishop, and sundry prophets and saints fill up the side compartments. "In all these figures," says Cean Bermudez, "there is expression and lofty character; the drawing is correct, and the attitudes are highly devotional; the colouring is good, and the execution elaborate, like that of many Italian pictures of the time." In another altar are a "Pietà, or Dead Christ," and an "Adoration of the Kings," which, in their fine drawing and composition, resemble the works of Leonardo da Vinci, and favour the idea that Yañez may have studied in the school of that master.

Pedro Rubiales, a native of Estremadura, acquired great distinction at Rome in the school of Francisco Salviati, whom he assisted in many of his works in that city. He was a friend of Vasari, who relates that he painted for the Church of the Holy Ghost a "Conversion of St. Paul," which was placed beside a "Visitation of the Virgin" by Salviati, and that the work of the pupil could hardly be distinguished by its style and merits from that of the master.[1] He likewise assisted Vasari himself in his allegorical frescoes at the Palace of San Giorgio.[2] The learned Spaniard, Dr. Juan de Valverde, who was in Rome in 1553-4, superintending the engraving of the plates for his book on anatomy, cites in that work, as examples of the value of anatomical knowledge in painting, "Michael Angelo the Florentine, and Pedro Rubiales the Estremaduran, who by giving themselves to anatomy as well as painting, have come to be the most excellent and famous painters that our great times have seen." As no works of Rubiales are known to have existed in the cathedrals and galleries of Spain, it is probable that he lived and died abroad.

The love of art and the munificence of its patrons kept pace with the increasing number and excellence of its professors. The splendid Church was ever ready to encourage and reward; her new and growing temples were each day demanding fresh embellishment, and opening wider fields for artistic enterprise. In 1538, the Chapter of Seville had already paid 90,000 ducats to the brothers Arnao, of Flanders, Carlos of Bruges, and other artists, for

---

[1] Vasari, tom. iii. p. 94. The latter fact must be taken on the authority of Cean Bermudez.
[2] Ibid., p. 391.

the gorgeous painted windows of their cathedral, which were not completed till twenty years later.[1] The Cardinal Juan de Tavera was inferior in taste and magnificence to none of his predecessors on the archiepiscopal throne of Toledo. He had for his confidential secretary Bartolomé Bustamente, distinguished in the University of Alcalá for his scholarship, and one of the most classical architects of his day. By the prelate's orders, this artist designed the Hospital of St. John Baptist, without the walls of Toledo—a majestic structure of granite, remarkable for its noble cloister, supported on Doric colonnades—of which the enemies of the princely founder were wont to say that it was far too stately and sumptuous for the poor inmates, and would secure for the extravagant architect a warm place in purgatory.[2] It may have been to balk this prophecy that Bustamente assumed in his old age the habit of the Jesuits; in which garb, with his friend St. Francis Borja, he visited the retired Emperor at San Yuste. The South had its Mæcenas in Francisco de los Cobos, Commander of Leon, and Secretary to Charles V. At his town of Ubeda, this statesman built, not only his own beautiful palace, which was, as we have seen, the cradle of fresco-

---

[1] Ponz, ix. p. 4. See Cean Bermudez's remarks on his statements in the article on Arnao de Flandes, in his *Dictionary*.
[2] Cean Bermudez, *Los Arquitectos*, tom. ii. p. 31.

painting in Andalusia, but also the noble Chapel of the Saviour, both from the designs of Pedro de Valdevira, who rivalled Berruguete in rich plateresque architecture.

Men of rank no longer confined themselves to the mere patronage of the fine arts. Don Felipe de Guevara, a scion of the noble house of Oñate, and Commander of Estriana in the Order of Santiago, was no less distinguished for his taste and talent in painting than for his scholarship, and for his valour as a cavalry officer in the expedition to Tunis in 1535. He had, in 1530, accompanied the Emperor in his journey to Bologna to receive the imperial crown from Clement VII., and there first acquired the friendship of Titian. With that master, and others of Italy and Flanders, he lived in habits of familiar intercourse, and a careful study of their works made him an excellent amateur painter. He was also the author of "Commentaries on Painting," written in his old age to amuse the tedious hours of sickness: they consist chiefly of anecdotes of the painters of antiquity, gleaned from his classical reading, and interspersed with recollections of travel; and in tone and style they will remind the English student of the Essays of our own Sir William Temple. They are dedicated to Philip II., whom Guevara exhorts to make his galleries accessible to lovers of art, "for," says the old scholarly soldier, "painting and sculpture, in my opinion, are in some sort like riches, which Boethius hath said are fruitless and of no effect when heaped together and hidden, but not so when they are shared and imparted."[1] Like the philosopher of Sheen, Guevara is much a "*laudator temporis acti*," and a defender of the divine right of ancient genius. He laments the modern practice of painting on canvas instead of panel, as making the art too easy, and its productions too cheap.[2] The MS. was long forgotten, and was at last found by Dean Josef de Roa, in a bookshop at Plasencia, and published soon afterwards at Madrid, by Ponz, in 1788. Guevara possessed a fine collection of Roman coins—used and praised by the learned Ambrosio Morales, in compiling his "Antiquities of Spain"—and he wrote a treatise on the subject, now unfortunately lost, which must have preceded those of Agustin and Ursino, and was probably the earliest essay of the kind in Castilian.[3] He died at Madrid, in 1563, and was buried in the chapel of his family, in the Church of St. Jerome.

The art of illumination flourished in convents and

---

[1] *Comentarios de la Pintura de Don Felipe Guevara, con discurso y notas* de Don Antonio Ponz, 8vo, Madrid, 1788, p. 4. Ponz—ecclesiastic though he was—has a hit, in a note on this passage, at the nunneries, "where," he says, "*he has heard some works of art exist*, which few people ever see." But French marshals and principles "*ont changé tout cela.*"

[2] Id. p. 51.   [3] Id. p. 244.

cathedrals long after the printing-press had taken away the occupation of the copyist. Their great vellum missals and books of the choir employed many skilful hands in the embellishment of their ample pages. Of Antonio de Holanda, a famous Portuguese artist in this style, Charles V. said that the miniature portrait for which he had sat to him at Toledo was better than that which Titian painted at Bologna—a remark which his son Francisco, in his work on painting, avers to have been addressed to himself at Barcelona, in the presence of three Dukes. Diego de Arroya was another illuminator, whose delicate portraits in miniature gained him the place of painter-in-ordinary to the Emperor. He died at Madrid in 1551.

Francisco de Holanda was born at Lisbon in 1515, and was the son and scholar of Antonio de Holanda, the painter of illuminations. His own merits and his father's interest obtained for him, while still a lad, the post of drawing-master to the Infants of Portugal, the sons of John III., and he was employed by that sovereign to illuminate various books for the royal library. While engaged in these delicate labours at Evora, and in painting miniature pictures of the Annunciation and the Holy Ghost for the King's breviary, he discovered a new and brilliant method of laying on the colours, which had long eluded the experiments and researches of his father.

This discovery had been anticipated at Rome, as he afterwards found, by Giulio Clovio, but it seems to have gained him so much credit that the King sent him to study his art in Italy. Passing through Valladolid on his way thither, he had the honour of being presented to the Empress Isabella, who charged him not to sail from Barcelona till he had executed the portrait of her husband. On reaching the Catalonian capital, he found all the world preparing for the expedition to Tunis, and the court busied with the Infant Don Luis of Portugal, who had come from Evora, without the knowledge of his father, to join the armament, and who, with his galley, first dashed through Barbarossa's chain into the harbour of Goletta.[1] It might be supposed that the presence of the Portuguese prince, who had some taste for arts and letters, would have facilitated his access to the Emperor, but it seems that Don Luis, as well as the great officers of the household, disliked to see any ignoble foot profane the presence chamber. Holanda had recourse, therefore, to a friendly chamberlain, Don Luis de Avila, who conducted him one evening to a little room, where was a single candle burning on the table, and where he left him for a few moments. Presently entered the Duke of Aveiro, a Portuguese grandee, who was

---

[1] Diego Barbosa Machado; *Bibliotheca Lusitana histórica, crítica, e chronologica;* 4 tom., fol., Lisboa, 1731-59; tom. iii. p. 45.

greatly surprised to see the painter, and whose company the latter could well have spared. The door opening once more, the Emperor himself appeared, leaning on the arm of Don Luis de Avila, who carried another candle, and followed by the Dukes of Alba and Albuquerque, both covered. Holanda stepped forward, and having knelt to kiss his sovereign's hand, repeated the order which he had received from the Empress, and the expression of homage which he was charged to deliver on the part of his father. "The Emperor," says the artist, describing the scene, in his work on painting,[1] "smiled and gave me an excellent reception; he addressed me with compliments which he might fitly have spoken to an ambassador; he indeed knows how to honour those who have a skill in the art of design; but, for my part, I did not deserve such gracious words. Scarcely permitting me to kiss his hand, he strongly recommended me to go to see the pictures at Bologna, where he was crowned, and said that no one had succeeded better in taking his likeness than my father, not even Titian, who had also painted it. Then he seated himself on the table, where the two candles were, and made the Duke of Aveiro sit down also, leaving the other two Dukes to stand, near the door. He then began a

---

[1] Raczynski, *Les Arts en Portugal*, p. 71. See infra, p. 192.

second time to excuse himself from complying with the Empress's wish that he should sit for his portrait, saying he was too old.[1] Upon this the Duke of Aveiro, seeing that the Emperor made so much of me and would not talk on other subjects, put in some words in my favour. The Signor Orazio Farnese, nephew to the Pope, and brother to Signor Octavio and the Cardinal, now came in. After receiving permission from the Emperor to be covered, he was standing before me; but seeing that his Majesty kept looking my way, he stood aside, placing himself near the Dukes, while I drew back modestly. But, as my evil fortune ordered it, just at this instant entered the Infant Don Luis, and two or three gentlemen after him. The Emperor, who, till then, had thought of nothing but me, made him sit down. The Infant, who of right should have been favourably disposed towards me, began to look at me very hard, and to seem angry and very much astonished to find me in that place. I understood this and retired on the sudden. To Don Francisco de Pereira, who

---

[1] The Emperor must have been joking, or the painter forgetful; for his Majesty was only five-and-thirty at this time. Nor can his health have been much broken, for four years afterwards, having outstripped the rest of the chase, and having slain a stag, about two leagues from Madrid, he received the following reply from an old woodman, whose ass he wished to hire to convey it home: "Excuse me, brother, the deer weighs more than my ass and load of wood put together; you are young and strong, so take it upon your own back, and God be with you." Sandoval, *Historia del Emp. Carlos V.*, tom. ii. p. 276.

demanded how I had got in, I made no reply, but that I would answer for my conduct to the Infant, which indeed I did; for passing through the corridor, I went to the room where he was to sup, and stood there with my hand on the back of his chair, resolving within myself not to remove it until I had spoken to him. He came in due time, and ate his supper with his usual appetite, I standing there all the time holding his chair. At last I told him all that had passed with the Empress, the order my father had given me, and how I made my way into the presence. I also said that having been informed by Don Luis de Avila of the pretensions of some of our people, I had not craved leave of his Highness to kiss the hand of his Majesty, who however had done me great honour, as did likewise Signor Orazio Farnese; while his Highness, who had known me from my childhood and might have come to my aid, had crushed and mortified me before the Emperor, who was on the point of speaking to me when his Highness came in. The Infant, like a good excellent prince as he was, seemed sorry for what he had done, and immediately sat down to write letters for me to carry to the Pope, the King of France, and the Marquess del Guasto."

It does not appear whether he ever painted the Emperor's portrait. But he pursued his journey to

Rome, and there devoted himself with great ardour to the study of architecture and painting. One of the works upon which he chiefly valued himself was a copy of the celebrated picture of Our Lord, executed by the holy hands of St. Luke, and preserved as one of the most precious relics in the church of St. John Lateran. This task, undertaken by desire of the Queen of Portugal, he was obliged to achieve by stealth, for neither the Pope, nor the monks of St. John, would allow it to be copied, although leave had been asked by the King of France and many devout ladies of princely rank. He remained at Rome for more than a year, and mingled in the most intellectual society, for he enjoyed the friendship of Michael Angelo, the Marchioness Vittoria Colonna, and many of the remarkable personages who graced the court and pontificate of Paul III. But during his residence at Rome, and his two years' subsequent travel through Italy and France, the study of art was the object with which he permitted nothing else to interfere. "My palace, my tribunal, about which I lingered," he says, "was now the solemn Pantheon, now the Mausoleum of Adrian, or the Coliseum, or the Baths of Diocletian, or the Capitol. If I were sometimes found in the magnificent chambers of the Pope, I was attracted thither by my admiration for Rafael d'Urbino, whose noble hand had adorned them. I preferred the ancient men, the men of marble, standing amongst arches and columns, to the ever-changing beings that buzz around us; for from their solemn silence I learned higher lessons than were to be found in the vain babble of busy men."[1] An unwearied draughtsman, he made sketches of almost everything that he saw. For the Archbishop of Funchal he executed a careful plan of the whole city of Rome,[2] and for the Infant Don Luis, a series of drawings of the splendid military shows which took place at Nice, where Francis I., Charles V., and Pope Paul III. met on a sort of Ligurian Field of the Cloth of Gold.[3] In order to bring back portfolios stored for the amusement, or military use, of his master, he not only made copies of the subterranean paintings at Rome, Pozzuoli, and Baii, but also executed careful plans of all the principal castles and fortresses in his route, such as St. Elmo at Naples, the citadels of Florence, Ancona, and Milan, and many other fortified places both in Italy and France. At Pesaro, indeed, his zeal led him into danger, for he was imprisoned by the governor for committing his defences to paper.[4]

He returned to Portugal by way of Catalonia, where he paid his devotions at the shrine of Our

---

[1] Raczynski, *Les Arts en Portugal*, p. 7.
[2] Id. p. 86.   [3] Id. p. 66.   [4] Id. p. 67.

Lady of Monserrate, and seems to have traversed Spain as far as Seville. On settling himself at Lisbon, he was employed by the King to illuminate the choir-books for the great convent of Thomar, and in other works of a similar kind. In 1548 he composed a treatise on ancient painting, which was translated into Castilian so early as 1563 by Manuel Denis, a Portuguese painter, who had been brought up in Spain.[1] He afterwards accompanied the Infant Don Luis, grown old and devout, in a pilgrimage to Santiago; and on his return he spent eight days in the house of one Blas Perea, a painter and architect living in Spain. The conversations which he held with this artist induced him to write another essay, on the art of drawing from nature, which, being added to his former work, was likewise translated by Denis.[2] At some period of his life he visited the monastery of Guadalupe in Spain; and he may perhaps have been employed by Philip II. to work for the Escorial, for its library possessed a volume of highly finished drawings, by him, of views and antique monuments in Italy and France, and commencing with portraits of the Pope and Michael Angelo. In 1569 he wrote some poetical pieces which he called Eternal Praises,[3] and

---

[1] *De la Pintura Antigua.*
[2] *El sacar por el natural.*
[3] *Louvores eternos.*

dedicated to his guardian angel, and two other little works in verse, entitled Love of Aurora[1] and Ages of Man,[2] and adorned with pious reflections and precious illuminations. His last work was a Memorial, respecting the state of art in Portugal,[3] addressed to King Sebastian, and dated in 1571. It is written in a strain of querulous disappointment, and laments, no doubt with great justice, the apathy of his countrymen, who, in matters of art, he avers, are behind every other people in Europe. While he expresses thankfulness for the favour of King John III., the Infant Don Luis, and the Infant Don John, father of the reigning prince, he by no means lavishes compliments on the taste and munificence of the house of Avis. From his rural retreat, between Lisbon and Cintra, where he lives unknown and neglected, he calls upon the King to bestow some protection on art for the sake of the glory of his crown. For himself he wants nothing, being arrived at an age when the smiles of the world would be a misfortune, and awaiting the final stroke which is to put an end at once to his life, and to the existence of painting in Portugal. It is probable that the expected blow fell shortly afterwards, for we hear of him no more.

---

[1] *Amor de Aurora.*   [2] *Idades do Homen.*
[3] *Fábrica que fallece á cidade de Lisboa.*

CH. III.
Writings on art.

His dialogues.

Holanda's writings on art have never yet been printed in the original Portuguese. They exist in manuscript in the library of Jesus at Lisbon, where a French translation of a portion of them was made by M. Roquemont, and published in 1846 by the Count Raczynski, Prussian minister in Portugal.[1] A copy of the Castilian translation by Denis, which belonged to Felipe de Castro, the sculptor, was, in the days of Cean Bermudez, and probably still is, in the library of the Academy of St. Ferdinand at Madrid.[2] The most curious part of his manuscripts, as given to the world by M. Raczynski, is the second book of his treatise on ancient painting, which consists of four dialogues on art, supposed to be held by the author and his friends at Rome. The first three of these dialogues are held in the church of

---

[1] Infra, chap. xii.
[2] Having thus touched on the arts in Portugal, it may be as well to notice the few works on the subject in Portuguese. The printed books treating of art are the *Arte Poetica e de Pintura e symetria con alguns principios da Perspectica*; 4to, Lisbon, 1615, by Filippe Nunes, a painter who became a Dominican monk by the name of Fr. Felippe dos Chagas, wrote various religious works, and died after 1633 ; *Carta Apologetica e analytica pela ingenuidade da Pintura em quanto sciencia*; 4to, Lisboa, 1752, by Jozé Gomes da Cruz, a knight of Christ and a learned jurist, born at Lisbon, 1683 ; Vieira's *Autobiography* (noticed infra, chap. xv.); *As Memorias*; Lisboa, 1815, by José da Cunho Taborda, painter to the King of Portugal, born 1766 ; and the *Collecaõ de Memorias* (noticed, chap. v.), by Cyrillo Volkmar Machado, likewise painter to the King, who died shortly before its publication in 1823. The names of some MSS. by Felix da Costa, Pedro de Carvalho, Francisco Xavier Lobo, Arcangelo Fosquini, and Taborda, will be found in *Les Arts en Portugal*, p. 445.

San Silvestre after sermon, and the speakers are the Marchioness Vittoria Colonna, Michael Angelo, Lactantio Tolomei, Diego de Zapata a Castilian gentleman, and Fra Ambrosia de Sienna a celebrated preacher; the fourth takes place in the house of Giulio Clovio, the painter of illuminations, who is entertaining there, besides the author, Valerio de Vicenza the engraver, and some other gentlemen of Rome. Into the mouth of Michael Angelo is put a long discourse on the relative merits of Flemish and Italian painting, in which he rebukes the Flemings for their slavish attention to detail, and claims the arts of design as the exclusive birthright of Italy.[1] He also is made to accord the palm of supremacy to painting as the "universal queen and absolute mistress" of the arts,[2] although in the very year in which Holanda finished his manuscript the great artist in his letter to Varchi expressed a contrary opinion.[3] He allows that of all foreign painters only one or two Spaniards, amongst whom he doubtless includes Berruguete, have ever succeeded in catching the true tone and feeling of the Italian pencil.[4] But this compliment to the national genius is balanced by a sneer at the national parsimony. The great Castilian lords, he complains, "love to parade their noble sentiments, fall into ecstasies

[1] *Les Arts en Portugal*, p. 14. [2] Id. p. 25.
[3] Infra, chap. xv.   [4] *Les Arts en Portugal*, p. 15.

of admiration before pictures, and praise them to the skies; yet they decline to order or purchase the most trifling work of art, and marvel at the munificent prices given for pictures by Italian nobles."[1]

Artists in gold and silver.

The goldsmiths of Spain had been famous for the beauty and splendour of their works,[2] even before the Genoese mariner had dreamed of a western world. The discovery of America supplied fresh vigour and double resources to their sumptuous craft. In those days of wealth and piety, when the hero of Mexico, fresh from the pillage of Montezuma, sent his proud offering of a golden culverin[3] to the Castilian Cæsar, not a few of the ablest Spanish artists left their labours in bronze and marble to work for the Church in the precious metals of the Indies. The reign of Charles saw revived the glories of Solomon. Almost in the words of the sacred chronicler,[4] it might be said that "the kings of the west and the governors of the country brought gold and silver to the emperor, besides that which the merchants and chapmen brought; and he made silver as stones in the streets of Valladolid and Leon; it was nothing accounted in the days of

---

[1] *Les Arts en Portugal*, p. 33.
[2] Supra, p. 97.
[3] Bernal Diaz del Castillo. *Verdadera Historia*, tom. iv., p. 84.
[4] 1 Kings, ch. x., and 1 Chronicles, ch. ix.

Charles." To the Church, her own adventurous missionaries, as well as the soldiers of fortune, lustful of barbarian treasure, and hoping for the pardon of their crimes, "brought every man his present, vessels of silver and vessels of gold, raiment, harness, and spices." The vast masses of bullion which came into the hands of the silversmiths of Spain would have excited the wonder and envy of Cellini, even amidst the wealth of his royal workshop in the Tour de Nesle; and their shrines, chalices, and croziers might have vied in delicacy of workmanship with the fairest salt-cellars and vases of that vainglorious Florentine. Of these artificers, one of the most skilful was Henrique d'Arphe, a native of Germany, who had early in the century settled at Leon, where he founded a family of goldsmiths, or rather sculptors and architects in plate. For the Cathedral of that city he wrought in silver the celebrated Custodia,[1] of Gothic design, and ten

---

[1] I have already explained the meaning of this term, but may here add the quaint stanza of Juan d'Arphe (grandson of Henrique), descriptive of the use and origin of the Custodia. (*Varia Commensuracion*. Folio. Madrid, 1795, p. 287.)

" Custodia es Templo rico, fabricado
  Para triunfo de Christo verdadero,
  Donde se muestra en pan transustanciado
  En quo esta Dios y Hombre todo entero,
  Del gran Sancta Sanctorum fabricado
  Que Beseleel, Artifice tan vero,
  Escogido por Dios para este efecto,
  Fabricó, dándole él el intelecto."

" Custodia" is a temple of rich plate,
  Wrought for the glory of our Saviour true,
  Where, into wafer transubstantiate,
  He shows his Godhead and his Manhood too,
  That holiest ark of old to imitate,
  Fashion'd by Bezaleel, the cunning Jew,
  Chosen of God to work his sov'ran will,
  And greatly gifted with celestial skill.

feet in height,[1] consisting of five storeys, profusely adorned with small saintly figures, and culminating in a tapering spire. This noble temple of silver, so worthy of the not less delicate temple of stone which it adorned, was melted down by the French in the War of Independence. In 1517 the artist was called to Toledo, to execute another Custodia, which happily still exists, having been saved to the Cathedral by the friendly arms of England. It is a Gothic edifice, nine feet high, and somewhat resembling the Scott Monument at Edinburgh, which, however, it far exceeds in richness of design and luxuriance of decoration. From an octagon base rise eight piers and pointed arches, supporting as many light pinnacles clustered round a beautiful filigree spire. Within the chamber beneath is placed a smaller shrine, for the Host, formed of the purest gold and blazing with gems. The whole is a dazzling mass of fretwork and pinnacles, flying buttresses, pierced parapets, and enriched niches, among which are distributed two hundred and sixty exquisite statuettes. Each ornament and chasing seems different from all the rest; the eye is not cheated or wearied by the recurrence of the same moulds or models, but is regaled with ever-new variety, the brilliant offspring of genius and toil. The

---

[1] Ponz, tom. xi., p. 224. The Castilian foot is less than the English, by one inch.

price of this superb work is stated by Cean Bermudez to have been only 1,033,357 maravedis—or about £415—a sum which, even taking into account the higher value of money in those days, seems astonishingly small. In 1599 a plinth was added to the base, and the whole was parcel gilt, as it still remains,—the most beautiful piece of plate in the world. A smaller Custodia of the same kind, and the work of the same hand, is preserved in the Cathedral of Cordoba. Antonio d'Arphe, son of Henrique, discarded the Gothic, and adopted the Greco-Romano style, on which he engrafted many of the rich decorations of the former. His works were, therefore, exquisite models for the lovers of plateresque architecture. The best of them were the Custodia of the Cathedral of Santiago, that of the church of Medina de Rioseco, and the great processional reliquary (*las andas*) of the Cathedral of Leon—all of which have fallen victims to French rapacity or Spanish indigence. He executed the woodcut coat-of-arms for Gudiel's History of the House of Giron, which bears his signature.[1] Juan Ruiz, another excellent goldsmith, is supposed to have been a native of Cordoba, where he learned his art under the elder d'Arphe, when employed on the Custodia of that Cathedral. In 1533, he began his

---

[1] Gudiel (Yerónymo), *Compendio de algunos historias, donde se tratan de la antigua familia de los Girones*, fol. Alcalá, 1577.

A., F., and C. Becerril.

Greco-Romano Custodia, for the Cathedral of Jaen, which he took four years to complete, and which gave the name of "*Calle de la Custodia*" to the street where he had his workshop. Cuença produced three famous silversmiths, the brothers Alonso and Francisco Becerril, and Cristobal, son of the latter, who made for the Cathedral its great Custodia, which was one of the most costly and celebrated pieces of church plate in Spain. They began it in 1528, and though ready for use in 1546, it was not finished till 1573. It was a three-storeyed edifice, of a florid classical design, crowned with a dome, and enriched with numberless groups and statues, and an inner shrine of jewelled gold; it contained 616 marks of silver, and cost $17,725\frac{1}{2}$ ducats, a sum which can barely have paid the ingenious artist for the labour of forty-five years. In the War of Independence this splendid prize fell into the hands of the French General Caulaincourt, by whom it was forthwith turned into five-franc pieces bearing the image and superscription of Napoleon.

Goldsmiths permitted to wear silk.

Charles V. showed his favour to the goldsmiths of Spain by permitting them and their wives to wear silk attire, a luxury forbidden by the sumptuary laws to tailors, shoemakers, and artizans of the honest callings, which, in those wise old times, were considered ignoble and degrading. This boon was granted by an imperial rescript, dated 30th September 1552, and issued in reply to the petition of Cristobal Alvarez and the goldsmiths of Palencia.[1]

---

[1] Gutierrez de los Rios, *Noticia de los artes*, p. 205-210, where it is printed at full length.

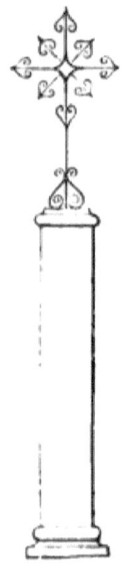

CHAPTER IV.

REIGN OF PHILIP II.—1556-1598.

THE Emperor's love of art descended in full measure on his son Philip II. It is the redeeming feature in the forbidding character of that prince; and in reviewing the bloody annals of his reign, it is refreshing to turn from the dismal exploits of viceroys and commanders to the nobler and more enduring achievements of painters and architects.

Despising the arts of courtesy practised by his father, as well as the golden opinions which they won, Philip valued the immortality conferred by the hand of Titian. Gloomy and morose in court and council, with his family, and even in his amours, he maintained towards his artists a gracious and familiar demeanour which might have gained him the imperial diadem had it been extended to the Electoral Princes. Soon after his accession to the throne, having received a memorial from Titian, praying for the payment of his pension, which had fallen into arrears, he replied with promptitude and kindness, and addressed a peremptory order for payment, under his own hand, to the Viceroy of Milan. A similar wrong suffered by the imperial recluse of San Yuste remained unredressed, and his complaints unheeded. To Anthony More he is said to have shown still greater favour, in overlooking a gross breach of etiquette, and conniving at the bold Fleming's escape from the scandalised familiars of the Inquisition. He delighted in the conversation of artists as well as friars; to both he was always accessible; and he would frequently enter the chapel or the studio, unexpected and unattended, to join in the matins or the evensong, or to note the progress of the picture on the easel.

But while he devoted far more of his time and treasure than Charles to the promotion of the fine arts, his taste was less catholic and expansive. The Emperor could appreciate the wit of Aretin as well as the pictures of Titian, the poetry of Garcilasso as well as the architectural designs of Machuca. Philip, on the contrary, though he wrote well, and was a purist in matters of style and grammar, had little knowledge or love of literature. His favourite reading was books of devotion and the writings of the martyr-mystic, Raymond Lully.[1] Mariana dedicated to him his history, yet narrowly escaped the sharp criticism of the Inquisition.[2] Luis Ponce de Leon, in spite of his genius and high birth, languished in its dungeons during five years of this reign, for no other crime than that of translating the Canticles into classical Castilian verse[3] for the use of a friend who lacked Latin. Though the epic poet, Ercilla, entered life as page to Prince Philip, he was neglected by the King;[4] and if Jorge de Montemayor attended his early travels, it was in the capacity of a musician.[5]

In that remarkable composition,[6] which records the dalliance of Philip of Austria and Anne of Eboli,[7]

---

[1] Balthasar Porreño—*Dichos y Hechos de el Señor Rey Don Phelipe II.*, sm. 4to, Madrid, 1748, p. 165—a work dedicated to the "Most holy Empress of Heaven and Earth, Mary Mother of God."

[2] Bouterwek's *History of Spanish Literature*, translated by Thomasina Ross, vol. i. p. 157.

[3] Id. p. 240.   [4] Id. p. 407.   [5] Id. p. 218.

[6] Now in the Fitzwilliam Museum, at Cambridge. There are two pictures very similar in subject, by Titian, in the Queen of Spain's gallery at Madrid, in one of which Venus plays with a little spaniel, and in the other with a Cupid; in neither are the features of the musician like those of Philip II. They are not to be found in the Catalogue, but are kept in what is called the council-room, where royal visitors are served with refreshments, and where hang many tiresome repetitions of the foolish face of the Spanish Bourbons.

[7] Mr. Ranke (*Fursten und Volker von Sud-Europa im sechszehnten und siebzehnten Jahrhundert*, 4 bänder, 8vo. Berlin, 1837; band. i., p. 190, note 3) has treated the amours of Philip and the young wife of Ruy Gomez de Silva as a mere fable; they have, however, been placed beyond a doubt by Don Salvador Bermudez de Castro, in his agreeable volume,

Titian has sufficiently indicated the favourite recreations of the royal lover. Reclining near the couch, whereon reposes the voluptuous and unveiled form of his high-born Venus, he touches the strings of a theorbo; and a vista of trees in the background is closed by a stately architectural fountain, like those of the gardens of Aranjuez. Music, painting, and architecture were the chief amusements of his leisure. Nurtured among the works of Titian, he could hardly have failed to acquire a fine perception of the beauties of painting. He is even said to have used the pencil with considerable skill. In the choice of his painters, and in the allotment of their several tasks, he displayed much discernment and discrimination. A severe, though candid, critic, the faults of a picture no more eluded his eye than the errors of orthography or punctuation in a state-paper;[1] nor was painter or secretary ever excused the task of correction.

Architecture, however, was Philip's most cherished pursuit, and the art of which he possessed most

---

Antonio Perez; estudios historicos, 8vo, Madrid, 1841, and are confirmed by the more recent French work, *Antonio Perez et Philippe II.*, 8vo, Paris, 1845, by M. Mignet, who tells us (p. 33) that that fine and fascinating woman was not blind of an eye, according to the old slander of history, but merely squinted; and (p. 37) that her connection with Philip was so notorious, that at court her son, the Duke of Pastrana, was universally held to stand in the same relation to his reputed father, the Prince of Eboli, as that in which Philip Faulconbridge stood to old Sir Robert.

[1] Porreño, p. 149; and Bermudez de Castro, *Ant. Perez*, p. 43.

practical knowledge. In his progress to Portugal, in 1580, he spent fifteen days at Merida, with his favourite architect, Juan de Herrera, examining the bridge, aqueduct, temple, and other Roman remains.[1] At Madrid, in a tower of the Alcazar, he fitted up a cabinet with carved presses of walnut, wherein he kept the plans of his palaces, and other architectural drawings.[2] Here at a stated hour each day he gave audience to his architects, whom he liked to have about his person, and two of whom, Herrera and Francisco de Mora, held the dignified post of Quartermaster-general of the royal household (*Aposentador mayor del palacio*). He loved to make designs of palaces, castles, and gardens, and we are told that when the plans of others were laid before him, he would add, take away, or alter with the judgment of a Vitruvius or Sebastian Serlio.[3] It is said that he made with his own hand the plan for the convent of the Trinity at Madrid, and that the original drawing was long preserved in the archives of the house.[4] This convent, now the National Museum, is a large building of brick, with a good inner court, designed in so plain and severe a style as to manifest that the royal architect, if the design be indeed his, defied the plateresque builders and all their fancies, and was equally austere in temper and in taste.

---

[1] *Los Arquitectos*, tom. ii. p. 139.   [2] Carducho, *Dialogo* viii.
[3] Porreño, p. 161.   [4] Id. p. 209.

The royal residences and establishments of Spain underwent constant alterations and additions during the reign of Philip. He enlarged and embellished the Alcazar of Madrid, and added a stately tower to the palace at Lisbon; he built the royal mint of Segovia, and the chapel and great part of the palace of Aranjuez; and to the hunting-seat of the Pardo he added four towers, some galleries, the fosse, and the gardens, in imitation, it is said, of a country-palace which had pleased him during his short residence in the realms of his English Queen.[1] "He was equally zealous," says his panegyrist, Porreño, "in building churches, colleges, and convents, as castles and batteries."[2] On the site of the confiscated mansion of Secretary Perez he founded, at Madrid, the College of St. Isabel. At the same time that he displayed his munificence to Flanders in the rising walls of the University of Douay, and to the Castiles, by erecting the Cathedral of Valladolid, and the Royal Monastery of the Escorial, the Algerine rover might note from the Mediterranean the magnificent piety of the Catholic King in the aspiring and majestic tower of the still unfinished Cathedral of Malaga.

Such works as these afforded ample scope for distinction to artists of all kinds. The great monument, however, of Philip's reign is the Escorial, a

---

[1] Porreño. p. 199.   [2] Id. cap. xiii. passim.

monastery which casts into the shade every other architectural work of the age, and peculiarly deserves the attention of the student of Spanish art, not only for its own sake, but also as opening in its vast walls the finest field ever offered to the painters of Spain. This huge gridiron of granite—as it is commonly considered, of which the frame and bars are a palace-convent, and the handle a monastic-palace—was thirty-one years in building, and cost upwards of six millions of ducats. To watch and hasten its progress was, for many years, Philip's ever-present care and his chosen recreation. It were hard to decide which object lay nearer his heart, the aggrandisement of his house or the completion of the Escorial. His armies might pine for supplies, or mutiny for pay, but the sinews of war were never wanting to his architects. When he could steal a few hours from statecraft, he would climb the overhanging Guadarrama, and, seated on a rock, still known as the "King's Chair," would contemplate the maze of granite walls growing into order and grandeur at his feet. At all times and distances, at Burgos, Valladolid, or Lisbon, he was intent on the work. As old age and infirmities crept upon him, his anxiety became ever more feverish. Wars and intrigues, and the fortunes of the House of Austria, he could leave to his successors; not so his favourite monastery. Treasure was, therefore, lavished, that time might be economised; but his artists would be stinted of neither. Thus, although Leoni, the Italian sculptor, employed chiefly in the decorations of the church, had engaged to complete the high altar in four years, at the cost of 20,000 ducats, ten years passed away, the money was spent, and the work remained unfinished in his studio at Milan. The poor King, oppressed with gout and melancholy, wrote piteously from Madrid, entreating that some part of it might be sent, were it only a single statue. In thirteen years, instead of four, the altar was at last finished; much, however, remained to be done to the chapel. The adornments of the gospel-side[1] were not completed for four years more, till April 1597, when the increasing maladies of the King made time doubly precious. Leoni was, therefore, compelled to bind himself to fit up the epistle-side in eighteen months, and spurred on by a promised largesse of 200 ducats for every month by which the wearisome time of expectation should be shortened. Thus urged, creative art kept pace with decaying nature, and the proud chapel, with its rich garniture, stood ready for the funeral rites of the founder in 1598.

With the Escorial is blended much of the history of Philip II. He redeemed his vow to St. Lawrence,

---

[1] The gospel-side of a chapel is to the left hand of the spectator who faces the altar, the epistle-side to his right.

offered up amid the roar of battle at St. Quentin, by rearing this superb edifice in all the pomp and beauty of holiness on the site of a miserable convent, the chapel of which had once been a bedchamber, and could boast no better altar-piece than a crucifix sketched in charcoal on the wall.[1] Whilst performing his devotions in the unfinished temple, he received tidings of the great naval victory at Lepanto, and returned thanks for the overthrow of the Turk.[2] Here he joined in the Te-Deum for the conquest of Portugal, and offered up solemn prayers for the discomfiture of the heretics of Holland, and for the success of his "Invincible Armada."[3] Hence, too, he derived one of those lessons which Providence sometimes reads to conquerors; for this his house of pride, planned in the hour of victory, was not complete until the decline of his power, and the very year of its consecration (1595) was memorable for the overthrow of the Spanish arms at Fontaine-Françoise. Here he performed those acts of humility and devotion which gained him, amongst friars and inquisitors, the character of a crowned saint, and enjoyed the converse of his artists and monks with so little of royal show and state, that, being met in the cloister one day by a countryman, he was taken for

---

[1] Porreño, p. 64.   [2] Id. p. 29.   [3] Id. p. 73.

a dependant of the establishment—an idea which the King humoured by showing the stranger the wonders of the place. From the Escorial, too, he issued the decrees which were law on the banks of the Po and the shores of the Pacific; and here, in a little alcove adjoining the church—on the wall of which hung a grim allegory of the Seven deadly Sins, by Jerome Bos[1]—amidst the solemn sounds of the organ and the choir, and clasping to his breast the veil of Our Lady of Monserrat[2]— he died.

The Escorial is, without doubt, one of the most interesting edifices in Europe. Castilian writers are never weary of extolling it, as an eighth wonder of the world, "or rather," says Villegas, the Hagiologist, "all the seven comprehended in one."[3] In point of size it will bear comparison with the mightiest works of the Pharaohs or the Cæsars, with Karnak and the Coliseum; and it is probably the greatest architectural undertaking ever conceived and executed by one man. No Egyptian or Roman builder is recorded to have completed a pile of which the doors, like those of the Escorial, if we may credit Fray Francisco de los Santos, required

---

[1] Guevara (*Comentarios*, p. 43) describes this picture; and Ponz, in a note, mentions that it hung in the chamber in which Philip died.
[2] Porreño, p. 192.
[3] "—o, por mejor decir, todas siete encerradas en una."—*Flos Sanctorum*, p. 381.

1,250 pounds weight of iron to make their keys.[1] The church and palace on the Vatican Mount have been three centuries and a half in growing

---

[1] A few of the leading measurements of the Escorial will give a better idea, than any description can, of its magnitude. The monastery, or the gridiron itself, is a parallelogram of 740 feet by 580; the palace, or handle, affixed to one of the longer sides, projects about 200 feet, and has a front of about 160; the four spires, or feet of the instrument, at the corners, are each 200 feet high; the two spires rising above the entrance of the church which occupies the centre of the building 270, and its crowning dome 330, with an interior diameter of 66; the height of the pediment over the grand portal in the principal or western front is 145 feet; and the general height of the monastery to the cornice, whence springs the high pitched roof, 60 feet. The windows in the grand front exceed 200 in number, those in the palace-front are 376, and the whole number of external windows in the building about 1100.

The best works on the Escorial, to most of which my pages are indebted, are the *Descripcion del Real Monasterio de San Lorenzo del Escorial, unica maravilla del mundo,* por el padre Fr. Francisco de los Santos, Profesor de la misma real Casa, &c., y Historiador General de la Orden de San Jeronimo, folio, Madrid, 1657 and 1681, of which a small abridgment and translation, "by a servant of the Earl of Sandwich, in his extraordinary embassy to Spain," was published in London, in 4to, 1671, and of which the *Descripcion*, by Fr. Andres Ximenes, another Jeronymite friar, fol., Madrid, 1764, is little more than a reprint, with a few additional plans and drawings. I have a copy of the *Descripcion* of Padre Santos, which bears the date 1667. A second and more complete English translation is the *Description of the Royal Palace and Monastery of the Escorial,* from the Spanish of F. de los Santos, by George Thompson, of York, Esq.; 4to, London, 1760, with plates, which, says the translator in his preface (p. xi.), are better and more numerous than those in the original, and may perhaps compensate for the want of "that lofty and elegant pomp of diction which characterises the writings of the Spanish author." Ponz devotes the greater part of his *Viaje,* tom. ii., to the Escorial, and there is also a *Descripcion Artistica* por Damien Bermejo, 12mo, Madrid, 1820. Townsend and other English travellers describe its splendours down to the French Invasion; and the late Mr. Beckford's account of his promenade through the building, with the proud Lord Prior, is one of the most graphic passages in his admirable travels (*Letters from Spain,* X. and XI.). The cream of all these writers, and an exact picture of the present condition of the monkless, kingless, palace-

Works on the Escorial.

to their present magnitude, under the rule of fifty Popes, with a treasury recruited by oblations from all parts of Christendom. Excepting its Pantheon, or Royal Cemetery—which was built in its present form by Philip IV.—the Escorial owes nothing of importance to the successors of Philip II. There is a peculiar grandeur in its five-fold purpose as a convent, a college, a church, a palace, and a royal mausoleum. No great structure was ever more strongly stamped with the character of its founder and the spirit of his age. Seated amidst the rocks and deserts of the Guadarramas, it was the fitting abode of the austere brotherhood of St. Jerome; and its dim halls and cloisters are the scenes which imagination most loves to people with the ecstatic monk, and the iron-visaged inquisitor, and the dark and terrible figures of the ancient fanaticism. The cheerless prison-like palace seems adapted solely to shelter the old age of that relentless prince, who, in the prime of his manhood, welcomed to Spain his young and beautiful bride, Isabella of Valois, with fire and faggot, and the human sacrifices of an Auto-de-fe.[1] Where is the mind in which

---

convent, may be found in the brilliant and accurate *Handbook* [1845], pp. 809-820 [3rd ed., 1855, pp. 750-763.—ED.]. An excellent collection of views of the Escorial, twelve in number, were drawn and engraved by Josef Gomez de Navia, and published, in 1800, at the Estamperia Real at Madrid.

[1] Held at Toledo, 25th February 1560. See Llorente, *Historia Critica de la Inquisicion de España*, 12mo, Barcelona, 1836, tom. iv. p. 202.

the very name of the Escorial does not awaken thought and evoke high associations? For the student of history it stands like a landmark on the hills of Castile; a relic of the days that are gone, when it was the pride of the Spaniard and the envy of the foreigner, an outward and visible type of the glory and pre-eminence of Spain.[1] To the pious Catholic it is an object of affectionate reverence as the noblest monastic foundation ever consecrated by his Church "to daily and nightly prayer and praise, to contemplation and holiness, to alms-deeds and study,"[2] and to the honour of his faith. The scholar may still regard it with interest as once the stately home of learning and research, and as a mine, not yet exhausted, of Arabian and Castilian lore; and the artist as one

---

[1] Thus Malherbe, in his ode on occasion of Etienne de Lisle's attempt on the life of Henry IV., makes the Escorial the symbol of the pride and glory of Spain. Invoking the Divine favour and protection on the head of the boy-Dauphin, afterwards Louis XIII., he thus winds up his aspirations for him and his royal parents:—

"Et pour achever leurs journées,   Fais leur ouïr cette nouvelle,
Que les oracles ont bornées,   Qu'il a rasé l'Escurial."
Dedans le trône impérial,   —POESIES. Paris, 1842, 12mo, p. 83.
Avant que le ciel les appelle,

So also the English proverb—

"My house, my house! tho' thou be small,
Thou art to me the Escariall!"

Jacula Prudentum; or, Outlandish Proverbs, Sentences, &c., selected by Mr. George Herbert, late Orator of the University of Cambridge, 12mo. London, 1651, p. 26.

[2] Porreño, p. 153.

of the greatest shrines of painting, for which Titian and Velazquez laboured, where Rubens and Murillo studied, and where a line of kings for two centuries hived the treasures of European art.

Strange as it may seem, it has been disputed who planned this famous pile. The slender claims of certain Italians have been put forward by Italian writers; but the most impudent assertion of all was that of one Louis Fox or Foix, a French maker of water-pipes and pumps, employed at Toledo, who, on his return to Paris, gave himself out as the architect of the Escorial. His audacious story, told perhaps in jest, was repeated by the President de Thou, and gained easy credence with Voltaire.[1] To the question, which is indeed sufficiently set at rest by inscriptions on the building, Ponz devotes a tedious letter in his volume on the Escorial, and decides it on clear documentary evidence in favour of two of his countrymen. The first of these, Juan Bautista de Toledo, was born at Madrid, and after studying his

---

[1] And with Lord John Russell, who, in the preface to his tragedy of *Don Carlos* (8vo, London, 1822, p. i.), quotes De Thou's tale of the Infant's love for his stepmother (*Thuanus*, Lib. xliii. c. 8), "on the authority of Louis de Foix, *a Parisian architect, employed by Philip to build the Escurial.*" The play, however, eclipses the error of the preface, for the noble dramatist there (Act I., sc. 2, p. 18) makes Philip boast, in 1568, of his magnanimous reply, when told of the loss of the Armada, exactly twenty years before that armament sailed from the Tagus—a most intolerable poetical license, worthy of the imaginative pump-maker himself, to whose invention almost every European language owes a play or romance on the story of Don Carlos.

profession at Rome, where he gained the name of the "able Spaniard" (*el valiente Español*), he spent the best part of his life at Naples, in the service of the Viceroy, Don Pedro de Toledo. Besides the viceregal palace and the church of Santiago, he there designed that noble street, the main artery of the city, which still preserves in its name the memory of both the founder and the architect. On a summons from the King in 1559, he repaired to Madrid, leaving behind his wife, Ursula Jabarria, and his two daughters, who were afterwards lost at sea as they followed him to Spain. His yearly salary, as chief architect to the Crown, was at first no more than 220 ducats; Philip's policy, with his Spanish artists at least, being to assign them moderate allowances until he had tested their abilities. Toledo soon began his plans of the Escorial, of which he saw the first stone laid on the 23rd April 1563, and superintended the works till his death in 1567. The building was carried on, and the masonry finished in 1584, by his scholar, Juan de Herrera, an Asturian, to whom Ponz, on the authority of a medal, attributes the plan of the church. This architect was a scholar and a good mathematician; he contrived a crane, on an improved principle, to facilitate the work; and with the same end in view he caused the stones to be dressed in the quarry—not without much opposition from the change-hating masons—so that, under his rule in the

Escorial, as in the temple of Solomon, "there was no tool of iron heard in the house when it was in building."[1] Of the other architectural works of Herrera, the Cathedral of Valladolid, a stately temple in the Greco-Romano style—and the imposing but somewhat heavy Exchange (*Lonja*) at Seville, are amongst the most important. He executed a series of eleven plans, perspective views, and sectional drawings, of the Escorial—engraved in 1587 by Pedro Perret—of which he published, in 1589, a descriptive Catalogue or "Summary."[2] This excellent architect died in 1597, having been rewarded by the King for his long services with a pension of 1,000 ducats, the place of Aposentador-Mayor, and the Cross of Santiago. His original drawings, and those of Toledo, for the Escorial, long remained in the King's Cabinet in the Alcazar of Madrid. Many of them were rescued from the conflagration in 1734, and dispersed, and

---

[1] 1 Kings, ch. vi., v. 7.
[2] *Sumario y Breve Declaracion de los diseños y estampas de la Fabrica de San Lorencio el Real del Escurial.* Sacado a luz por Juan de Herrera, Architecto General de su Majestad y Aposentador de su Real Palacio. Con privilegio, en Madrid por la viuda de Alonso Gomez, Impresor del Rey nuestro Señor, año de 1589, sm. 8vo, containing 32 leaves, including the title, and beginning "Lo que esta planta contiene en si," and ending "considera bien la medida de esta fabrica." This is one of the rarest volumes in Spanish bibliography—of which see a notice in the *Cartas Españolas*,—a Madrid periodical—for July 12, 1832, from the pen of Don Bartolomé José Gallardo, by whom I was informed that he had seen only three copies of it—one of which is in the library of the British Museum.

were sometimes offered for sale till late in the century.[1]

Like all other great works, the Escorial has been the theme of every variety of criticism; the object of praise warm as the sun that glares upon it at midsummer, and of blame bitter as the wintry whirlwinds that sweep down from its snowy Sierra. Fray Francisco de los Santos,[2] its inmate and historian, conceived that its grand proportions and harmonious design must affect the eye as a service of solemn music affects the ear, and dissolve the soul in ecstacy. Cumberland,[3] on the other hand, quotes the good father with infinite contempt, and does not hesitate to describe his beloved pile as a "graceless mass." But the lover of art, as he first beholds—from the road that winds downward through the pine-forest of Guadarrama, or from the ramparts of Madrid—the grey convent-palace enthroned on its terraces of rock, majestic amidst the majesty of nature, with the clear sunlight of Castile on its dome and clustering towers; or, as he pauses before the awful portal that opens only to admit the royalty of Spain to the font or the tomb, will feel more sympathy with the enthusiasm of the Spanish friar than with the flippancy of the

---

[1] Cean Bermudez, *Los Arquitectos*, tom. ii. p. 80.
[2] Of the grand Court, he says that it "toca en la vista, como la música en el oydo, y causa una gustosa suspension en la alma, que la recrea ensancha y engrandece," p. 10.
[3] *Anecdotes*, vol. i. p. 47.

English envoy. It is not till the first amazement and delight produced by the solid vastness of the building has abated that the faults of the Escorial become visible. The eye then discovers that the windows are too small, and the projections wanting in boldness, and wishes for more relief and variety in the long grey façades. Displeased with what he considered the vicious style of contemporary Spanish architects, Toledo has fallen into the opposite errors. They delighted in sudden curves and unexpected angles, intricate mouldings and wreaths of flowers, twisted columns and broken pediments, perplexing the eye with perpetual variety. He, on the other hand, had acquired a better taste amongst the purer models of Italy, and loved breadth and simplicity, and the grandeur of continuous lines and recurring forms. To majesty—certainly the first merit of a great building—he was content sometimes to sacrifice beauty; and hence the monotonous sternness of the fronts of the Escorial. The grand southern front, facing the mountain, is somewhat varied by the imposing height of its central portion, and by the state entrance; that which looks over the plain to Madrid is the most faulty of them all, being broken, yet not relieved, by the palace—a mere excrescence, inferior to the rest of the pile in elevation. Without, as within, the mean proportions of the royal residence contrast strangely with the regal magnificence of the monastery. The gridiron of St. Lawrence could hardly have been furnished with a more inconvenient or unsightly handle.

It is not until the threshold of the Escorial is crossed that the genius of the architect is fully comprehended. Then as the courts and cloisters successively unfold themselves, it is discerned that Toledo, to a feeling for form fine as Palladio's, united much of the bold spirit of Michael Angelo. Perhaps no collegiate or conventual building in Europe can show a quadrangle equalling in chaste and solemn grandeur the Court of the Evangelists, with its Doric cloisters and stately fountain, embosomed in the massive walls, and shadowed by the great dome, of the Escorial. The church is one of the happiest examples of classical architecture adapted to Christian ends. So admirable are its proportions, that St. Peter's itself—in spite of its unapproached magnitude—does not at first sight impress the mind with a stronger sense of its vastness, or awaken a deeper feeling of awe. The sternness of the Doric design, and the sombre ashy hue of the granite pervading the pavement, the walls, and the overhanging depths of the dome, invest this church with a grave religious air, somewhat like that of a Gothic Cathedral, and never to be found amongst brilliant mosaics and many-

CH. IV.

Capilla del Altar Mayor.

coloured marbles, seen by the unsoftened light of day. All the pomp of decoration—the slabs of porphyry and agate, and the capitals and cornices of burnished gold—has been wisely reserved for the high altar and its chapel, placed apart and raised on many broad steps of dark jasper,

"Ascending by degrees magnificent."[1]

There rises the lofty retablo of the four orders, gleaming with statues of gilded bronze and columns of precious marble. And there in marble oratories, on either hand, Charles and Philip, with their consorts and royal children, sculptured in bronze, kneel uncrowned before the holy place, forming a group of historical monuments unsurpassed in interest and in execution, and worthy of a chapel which is perhaps the most splendid and beautiful in the world.

Materials and decorations of the Escorial brought from all parts of the world.

Minutely to describe the Escorial in its palmy days would be to review the elegant arts and manufactures of the age of Philip II., and to enumerate half the products of his superb monarchy—the first that could vaunt that the sun never set on its shores. Italy was ransacked for pictures and statues, models and designs; the mountains of Sicily and Sardinia for jaspers and agate; and every sierra of Spain furnished its contribution of marble. Madrid,

---

[1] *Paradise Lost*, B. iii. l. 502.

Florence, and Milan supplied the sculptures of the altars; Guadalajara and Cuença, gratings and balconies; Zaragoza, the gates of brass; Toledo and the Low Countries, lamps, candelabra, and bells; the New World, the finer woods; and the Indies, both East and West, the gold and gems of the Custodia and the five hundred reliquaries. The tapestries were wrought in Flemish looms; and for the sacerdotal vestments there was scarce a nunnery in the empire, from the rich and noble orders of Brabant and Lombardy to the poor sisterhoods of the Apulian highlands, but sent an offering of needlework to the honoured fathers of the Escorial.

Of the artists employed in the subordinate parts of the building, Pompeyo Leoni most deserves notice, as the sculptor of the high altar and the royal monuments. Born in Italy, he came to Spain with his father, Leo Leoni, who had been sculptor to Charles V.; he there amassed a fortune, became a patron of art, and died at Madrid in 1610. Giacomo Trezzo,[1] a Milanese, executed, from the designs of Herrera, the glorious Custodia, a domed temple, sixteen feet high, of gilt bronze and agate (for which Arias Montano wrote the Latin inscription) —a work which cost him seven years' labour, and

---

[1] His name is still preserved, though in a corrupt form, in that of a street at Madrid, the "Calle de *Jacometrenzo.*" See Ponz, tom. ii. p. 53.

which was demolished, in 1808, in half that number of minutes, its metal being mistaken for gold by the French troopers of La Houssaye. The matchless marble crucifix behind the prior's seat, in the choir, was sculptured at Florence, in 1562, by Benvenuto Cellini, and was the offering with which the gallant artist surprised the grand Duke Cosmo I. and his Duchess when they honoured him with a visit.[1] The Duke afterwards presented it to Philip II., who caused it to be conveyed from Barcelona on men's shoulders.[2] The figure is of life size, finely modelled, and well relieved by the black marble of the cross; the head droops on the shoulder; "It is finished" has just parted from the lips, the eyes are closed, and the body, with all its muscles and anatomy developed, and still quivering with the last convulsion of the Divine agony, hangs heavily on the arms, and settles into the stillness of death. Never was marble shaped into a sublimer image of the great sacrifice for man's atonement. The chaste woodwork of the choir and library was carved by Josef Frecha; and the indiffe-

---

[1] B. Cellini; *Vita*, tom. ii. p. 423. [Symonds' translation, 1889, p. 484. In a note to the passage, Symonds says, "The Duchess would not take the crucifix as a gift. The Duke bought it for fifteen hundred golden crowns, and transferred it to the Pitti in 1565. It was given by the Grand Duke Francesco, in 1576, to Philip II., who placed it in the Escorial."—ED.]

[2] *Handbook* [1845], p. 817 [3rd edition, 1855, p. 759]. For an anecdote of Philip's reception of this noble marble, see supra, chap. i. p. 37.

rent colossal statues of St. Lawrence (over the great portal) and the Hebrew kings and Evangelists (in various external parts of the building) were hewn, each from a single block of granite, by Juan Bautista Monegro, both of them Spaniards and sculptors of repute.

Clemente Virago was an Italian sculptor and engraver, likewise in the service of Philip II., for whom he executed on a diamond an intaglio portrait of the unfortunate prince Don Carlos, which was considered a prodigious feat. At his death, in 1591, his place and annual salary of 200 ducats were transferred to one Cristobal Cambiaso, his nephew.

It is now time that we should turn our attention to the painters employed by Philip. In their case only, he seems to have forgotten his usual Spanish predilections. His over-anxiety, perhaps, to secure perfection in all the furniture and decorations of his favourite edifice, induced him to bring to the Escorial, at vast cost, Flemish and Italian painters, of whom some doubtless infused new and valuable spirit into the school of Castile, while others might have learned far more at Toledo, Seville, or Valencia, than they were able to teach at Madrid. On the whole, Philip would have better attained the object which lay so near his heart had he more fully entrusted to native genius the embellishment of his beloved monastery.

In age, as in fame, the venerable name of Titian stands first on the list of Philip's painters. Although he never set foot in Spain, he may fairly enough be ranked amongst the artists of the Escorial. For his noble "Last Supper," one of the grandest of his religious works, on which his pencil lingered lovingly for seven years, was painted for the convent, and beheld many generations of monks sit at the long table of the Refectory, whence it has passed into the Queen of Spain's gallery at Madrid.[1] The greater part of the many pictures which he had executed for his imperial and royal friends were collected in the Escorial, filling long suites of conventual rooms with life and beauty. In the palace of the Pardo hung his famous picture, known as the "Venus del Pardo,"[2] but in reality representing Jupiter disguised as Satyr, feasting his eyes on the beauties of the sleeping Antiope. The hall of portraits contained no less than eleven from his easel—likenesses of the Emperor and Empress, Philip II., the great captains, Duke Emmanuel Philibert of Savoy and Fernando Duke of Alba, and several princely personages of Germany—all of which perished by fire in the next reign. The person of Philip—that "little man with vast gigantic thoughts in

---

[1] [The picture is still in the Refectory of the Escorial. *Handbook*, 1855, p. 758. *Titian*, by Richard Ford Heath, 12mo, London, 1879, p. 95.—ED.]
[2] [Now in the Louvre, No. 449, Catalogue 1889.—ED.]

him"[1]—and those marble features that brightened not at the news of Lepanto, nor grew darker on the announcement of the fate of the Armada, have been made familiar to the world by the pencil of this great master. In the days when he sat to Titian, his face, always haughty in expression, was not unhandsome; his complexion was fresh and clear; and his hands, which in the portraits usually dally with his sword-hilt or twirl the silken tassels of his girdle, are remarkable for beauty and delicacy of form. Still the curling lip and cold grey eye betray the false and callous heart within; and beneath the velvet and miniver of the princely gallant we can detect the sceptred friar of the Escorial.

Sofonisba Anguisciola,[2] a noble lady of Cremona, was one of six sisters so amiable, and so distinguished in arts and letters, that Vasari calls the house of their father Amilcar, "l'albergo della pittura anzi de tutte le virtù."[3] The year of her birth has not been noted by any of her numerous biographers, but we gather from her history that it must have been between 1530 and 1540. She displayed her

---

[1] Howell's *Letters*, 8vo, London, 1726, p. 166 [5th edition, 12mo, London, 1678, Sec. II. letter xxxv. p. 149].

[2] The facts of this lady's life, which have not been recorded by Cean Bermudez, I have taken for the most part from "*Le Vite de' Pittori, Scoltori et Architetti Genovesi, e de' Forastieri che in Genova operarono; con alcuni ritratti de gli stessi;* opera postuma dell' Illustrissimo Signor Rafaelle Soprani, nobile Genovese." 4to, Genova, 1684.

[3] Vasari, tom. iii. p. 17.

CH. IV.

Picture by Sofonisba Anguisciola.

taste for drawing at a very tender age, and soon became the best pupil in the school of Antonio Campi —a good painter of Cremona. One of her early sketches, of a boy with his hand caught in the claw of a lobster, and a little girl laughing at his plight, was in the possession of Vasari, and by him esteemed worthy of a place in a volume which he had filled with drawings by the most famous masters of that great age. Portraiture was her chief study; and Vasari commends a picture, which he saw at her father's house, of three of the sisters and an ancient housekeeper of the family playing at chess, as a work "painted with so much skill and care, that the figures wanted only voice to be alive."[1] He also praises a portrait which she painted of herself, and presented to Pope Julius III.,[2] who died in 1555, which shows that she must have attracted the notice of princes while yet in her girlhood. At Milan, whither she accompanied her father, she painted the portrait of the Duke of Sessa, the Viceroy, who rewarded her with four pieces of brocade and various rich gifts.

Her name having become famous in Italy, the

---

[1] Vasari, tom. iii. p. 15. This picture came into the possession of Lucien Bonaparte, and will be found in the collection of outline engravings entitled *Choix de gravures à l'eau forte d'après les peintures originales et les marbres, de la galerie de Lucien Bonaparte;* 4to, Londres, 1812. No. 116.

[2] Id. p. 133.

King of Spain, in 1559, ordered the Duke of Alba, who was then at Rome, to invite her to the Court of Madrid, where she arrived the same year, with a train of two waiting gentlewomen, two ushers, and two lackeys, and was received with the highest distinction, and lodged in the palace. The first work undertaken by Sofonisba, after reposing from the fatigues of her journey, was the portrait of the King, who was so pleased with the performance, that he rewarded her with a diamond worth 1,500 ducats and a pension of 200 ducats. Her next sitters were the young Queen Elizabeth of Valois, known in Spain as Isabel of the Peace, then in the bloom of bridal beauty, and the unhappy boy, Don Carlos. By the desire of the Pope, Pius IV., she made a second portrait of the Queen, sent to his Holiness with a dutiful letter, which Vasari has preserved, as well as the gracious reply of the Pontiff, who assures "his dear daughter in Christ" that her painting shall be placed amongst his most precious treasures. While in Spain she received from Cremona a portrait of her mother, Bianca, painted by her sister Europa, which was no less approved by the critics of the Castilian court than grateful to her filial feeling, as a

"Faithful remembrancer of one so dear,"[1]

---

[1] Cowper's lines on receiving his mother's portrait.

from whom she probably was parted for ever. It is possible that her sister Lucia may have sent, at the same time, her admirable portrait of Piéro Maria—a famous Cremonese physician—a grave elderly personage in a furred robe—praised by Vasari, and worthy of the best Florentine master, which now adorns the Queen of Spain's gallery, where, strange to say, it is the sole specimen of the powers of the highly-gifted Anguisciolas.[1] Sofonisba held the post of lady in waiting to the Queen, and was for some time governess to her daughter, the Infanta Isabella Clara Eugenia, an appointment which proves that she must have resided in Spain for some years after 1566, the year of that princess's birth.

Her royal patrons at last married their fair artist, now arrived at a mature age, to Don Fabrizio de Monçada, a noble Sicilian, giving her a dowry of 12,000 and a pension of 1,000 ducats, besides many rich presents in tapestries and jewels. The newly-wedded pair retired to Palermo, where the husband died some years after; Sofonisba was then invited back to the Court of Madrid, but excused herself, on account of her desire to see Cremona and her kindred once more. Embarking, for this purpose, on board of a Genoese galley, she was entertained with so gallant a courtesy by the captain,

---

[1] *Catalogo de los Cuadros del Real Museo* [1843], No. 720 [edition of 1889, No. 15].

Orazio Lomellini, one of the merchant princes of the "proud city," that she fell in love with him out of sheer gratitude, and, if her biographer belie her not,[1] offered him her hand in marriage, which he accepted. It is not recorded whether she ever revisited her native Cremona. At Genoa she continued to pursue her art, and her house became the resort of all the polished and intellectual society of the republic. Nor was she forgotten by her royal friends of the House of Austria. On hearing of her second nuptials, their Catholic Majesties added 400 crowns to her pension. The Empress of Germany paid her a visit, on her way to Spain, and accepted a little picture, one of the most finished and beautiful of her works. She was also visited by her former charge, the Infanta—now the wife of the Arch-Duke Albert, and with him co-sovereign of Flanders. That princess spent many hours in talking with her of old times and her family affairs, and honoured her by sitting for her portrait, for which, when it was finished, she presented her with a gold chain enriched with jewels, as a memorial of her friendship. Thus courted in the society of Genoa, and caressed by royalty, she lived to an extreme old age.

---

[1] "Dal quale," says Soprani (p. 309), meaning the seducing Orazio, "durante il viaggio receve tali gratie e tanti favori che obligata si stimò, no solo a darle segni di aggradimento, mà molto più a dedicarle se stessa con offerirsele sposa. Al che havendo acconsentito quel generoso Signor si celebrarono con reciproca sodisfattione le nozze."

A medal was struck in her honour at Bologna; artists listened reverentially to the opinions, and poets sang the praises of

> "— la bella e saggia dipintrice
> La nobil Sofonisba da Cremona."[1]

Though deprived of sight in her latter years, she retained to the last her other faculties, her love of art and her relish for the society of its professors. Vandyck was frequently her guest during his residence at Genoa in 1620 or 1621, and used to say of her that he had been more enlightened in painting by a blind woman than by his own master—no mean praise from the favourite scholar of Rubens.

The works of Sofonisba are now rarely to be met with. In 1824 one only was known to exist at Cremona—a small picture of the "Virgin giving suck to her Divine Infant"—in the collection of the Signors Bresciani-Carena, which was engraved by Cerasa for a work entitled "La Pittura Cremonese," published in that year.[2] In portraiture her skill was little inferior to that of Titian. Of this evidence is afforded by that beautiful portrait of herself —probably one of those seen by Vasari, in the wardrobe of Cardinal di Monte, at Rome, and at

---

[1] Graziani, quoted by Grasselli. *Abecedario Biografico dei Pittori Scultori ed Architette Cremonese*, 8vo, Milano, 1827, p. 22.
[2] Grasselli, p. 22.

Piacenza, in the house of the Archdeacon, or that noticed by Soprani[1] in the palace of Giovanni Geronimo Lomellini at Genoa,—which is now no mean gem amongst the treasures of the galleries and libraries at Althorp. She has here drawn herself in what the Germans conveniently name a "knee-piece," and perhaps rather under life-size. Her head is small and finely formed, and well set on a graceful neck, and its dark hair dressed smoothly and simply; her features are quite Italian and regular, her complexion a clear olive, and her black eyes large and liquid. The dark close-fitting dress is relieved only by small white frills at the throat and wrists, and two white tassels hanging on her breast; and her delicate and most exquisitely painted hands are seen over the keys of a spinnet. To her right, in deep shadow, stands an old woman—perhaps she who played at chess with her sisters—wearing a kerchief twisted turban-wise round her head, and resembling a St. Elizabeth or a St. Anne in a religious composition of the Caracci. The whole picture is painted in the clear firm manner of the best pencils of Florence.

Another Sofonisba is mentioned by Palomino, but by no other authority, amongst the foreign painters of this reign. Sofonisba Gentilesca, says that writer,[2]

---

[1] Soprani, p. 310.   [2] Palomino, tom. iii. p. 386.

was a lady illustrious in art, who came from France in the train of Queen Isabel of the Peace, to whose household she belonged. She painted miniature-portraits with remarkable skill, and had for sitters their Majesties, the Infant Don Carlos, and many ladies of the Court of Madrid, where she died in 1587.

Giovanni Battista Castello was born at Bergamo, early in the sixteenth century, and became the scholar of Aurelio Buso, a Cremonese painter, by whom he was brought to Genoa. There he obtained the patronage of the family of Pallavicina, who sent him to Rome, whence he returned, a painter and architect of great skill. At Genoa he painted many works in conjunction with Luca Cambiaso—the most famous artist of the proud city. Of these, one of the most noted was the "Last Judgment," in the Church of the Nunziata di Portoria, of which Cambiaso painted the multitudes expecting their doom, and the Bergamese the Judge and His attendant angels, which was reckoned the finest part of the composition.[1] Castello drew and composed in the style of the Roman school, and his colouring had something of the splendour of the Venetian masters. He painted many works in fresco—representing architectural perspectives, then fashionable decorations of the stately halls of Genoa. The Grillo palace pos-

---

[1] Lanzi. *Storia Pittorica della Italia*, 8vo, Bassano, 1818, tom. v. p. 302.

sessed many good specimens of his powers in this style, and of his fine taste in architecture, especially in the chamber in which he painted the "Banquet of Dido and Æneas." Invited to Spain in 1567, he fixed his residence at Madrid, and received from the King an annual salary of 300 crowns, besides payment for his works. In the palace of Madrid he painted several ceilings; and he also designed the great staircase of the Escorial—by which he proved himself a worthy compeer of Toledo and Herrera. Dying at Madrid in 1569, he left behind him a young son, Fabrizio, and a stepson, Nicolao Granelo, who had also been his scholar. Granelo was named painter to the King in 1571—with the slender allowance of fifteen ducats a month, and the younger Castello, having acquired his art from his brother, received the same appointment in 1584, with the yet smaller monthly salary of 6,000 maravedis. At the Escorial they painted in concert several ceilings, and in the gallery known as the hall of battles the "Moorish Rout at Higueruelas"—borrowing from an old painting of that subject found at Segovia [1]—and the "Battle of St. Quentin," frescoes which deserve little praise, and for stiffness are worthy of the venerable days of Dello. They were afterwards employed to paint in fresco three other battles in the armoury

---

[1] See supra, chap. ii. p. 92.

_{Nicolao Granelo.}

of the ducal palace at Alba de Tormes. Granelo died at Madrid in 1593; and Fabrizio Castello in 1617, having been continued in his post of painter by Philip III.

Francisco de Viana accompanied Castello from Genoa to Madrid, assisted him in his works at the Alcazar, and finished some of them after his decease. He was made painter to the King in 1571, with a monthly salary of twenty ducats, which he enjoyed till his death at Madrid in 1605.

Florence furnished to Madrid an excellent painter in the person of Romulo Cincinato—who had studied under Francisco de Salviati at Rome. He was sent to Spain, in 1567, by Don Pedro de Requesens, Spanish ambassador at Rome, and was engaged for the King's service for three years—at the monthly salary of twenty ducats. He was first employed in painting some frescoes in the Alcazar of Madrid, and afterwards at the Escorial in various works, of which some of the best were the pictures of two oratories in the principal cloister. One of these represented the "Transfiguration of Our Lord;" and here he introduced a youth under the influence of a demon, in which he imitated the similar figure in Rafael's great Transfiguration. For the spaces over the seats of the choir he painted, in imitation of fresco, four large canvases, of which one had for its subject the tutelar of the monastery, St. Lawrence, Archdeacon of Rome, following his Bishop, St. Sixtus, to prison; and another, the same saint in the presence of the Roman Prefect, who demands of him the treasures of his church, and is shown, in reply, a company of the Christian poor. The remaining two pictures represented passages in the life of St. Jerome. In 1571 Cincinato was allowed six months' leave to go to Cuença, where he painted, for the Jesuits' church, three altar-pictures,[1] representing St. Peter, St. Paul, and the "Circumcision of Christ," now in the Academy of St. Ferdinand at Madrid. The "Circumcision" is well composed, the draperies are broad and graceful; the male heads have the noble air which belongs to the school of Rome, but the heads of the Virgin and the other women are not so pleasing. The High Priest, in a robe of curious pale blue, is the most conspicuous figure; he is seated with his back to the spectator, and performs the operation with a long, sharp-pointed knife, like the murderous weapons still made at Albacete for the girdles of the peasantry. The background is filled up with a high arch, supported on pillars, and crossed by an airy gallery, in which three figures are standing. This "Circumcision" is reckoned Cincinato's masterpiece, and was so considered by himself; for, when his

---

[1] Ponz, tom. iii. pp. 97-98.

friends praised his works at the Escorial, he would say—"There is a shin at Cuença that is worth them all." This celebrated shin belongs to the High Priest's left leg, which is thrust out behind him, as he sits with his back turned, so as to display the heel and ankle. It is an accurate representation of a rather clumsy model. Cincinato was afterwards employed by the Duke of Infantado to paint a variety of frescoes in his palace at Guadalajara. About 1591 he became a cripple, and disabled from pursuing his profession; but the King permitted him to enjoy his pension till 1600, when he died at Madrid, "universally deplored by the artists," says Palomino,[1] "for his amiable manners and eminent ability," and leaving behind him two sons, whose names will appear in a later reign.

With Romulo Cincinato, the Spanish ambassador sent from Rome, in 1567, Patricio Caxesi, or Caxes, a native of Arezzo, whom he had engaged for the King's service, on the same terms as his companion. They at first painted together in the Alcazar of Madrid; Caxes was not, however, employed at the Escorial, nor does he seem greatly to have distinguished himself as a painter. The Queen of Spain's gallery possesses only one of his works—a large picture of the Madonna, with the infant Saviour asleep on her

---

[1] Pal., tom. iii. p. 403.

lap, and surrounded by adoring angels;[1] the sleeping babe is pretty, but the rest unpleasing and poorly executed. Having some taste for architecture, he was, in 1570, employed to design a high altar for the Church of San Felipe el Real, at Madrid. He long laboured on a translation into Castilian of Vignola's book on the Five Orders, which was at last published in 1593, in folio, with an architectural title-page designed and engraved by himself, and an epistle dedicatory to Prince Philip, who afterwards mounted the throne as the third monarch of the name.[2] By order of that prince he painted certain works at the Pardo in 1608; and he died at an advanced age, in 1612, leaving a son by whom he was eclipsed.

Antonio and Vincenzo Campi were the second and third sons of Galeazzo Campi, a painter of reputation at Cremona, whose profession they followed, under his instruction and that of their

---

[[1] *Católogo*, 1843, No. 162. In the *Católogo Descriptivo é Histórico*, 1872, No. 698, it is attributed, following Cean Bermudez, to *Eugenio Caxes*. It does not appear in the Catalogue of 1889.—ED.]

[2] "*Regla de las cinco Ordenes de Architectura de Jacome de Vignola, agora de nuevo traduzido de Toscano en Romance* por Patritio Caxesi, Florentino, Pintor y Criado de su Magestad. Dirigido al Principe Nuestro Señor. En Madrid. Patricius Caxiesi fe. et tulsit A.D. 1593. Se vende en casa de Antonio Mancelli." This title I have copied from a copy of the first edition, the only one which I have seen, in the Cathedral Library of Seville. It wants the Epistle Dedicatory, and is a good deal mutilated. The impressions are much better than in the later editions, and the engraving neatly executed. The architectural first order is the worst of the plates. It is curious to find the author's name spelt in two ways on the title of his book, "*Caxesi*" and "*Caxiesi*."

elder brother, Giulio. They visited Spain in 1583, and were for some time in the service of the King. The best works of Antonio, in his native city, were a "Holy Family,"—in which the Divine child was represented as playing with a dove—painted in 1567 for the church of St. Peter; and the "Decollation of St. John Baptist," and other pictures, executed, with the stucco bas-relief ornaments of a chapel, in 1577–1581, for the church of St. Sigismund.[1] At the Escorial he painted, for the Vicar's chamber, a large picture, on panel, of the "great Doctor," St. Jerome, wearing, in defiance of all civil chronology, the purple robe of a cardinal, and seated, with a pen in his right hand and his eyes fixed on a crucifix, his left arm resting on an open volume, and its hand twined in his bushy beard; near him were his inkhorn, red hat, and the usual skull and domesticated lion.[2] Antonio was likewise a writer of some reputation, and

---

[1] Grasselli, p. 80.
[2] Fray Francisco de los Santos (*Descripcion del Escorial*, p. 68), describes the saint's beard as "*muy poblada*"—"well peopled," an expression which, though it is merely equivalent to "thick," sounds alarming to English ears. He states the height of the panel at four yards, and its width at two. In the Museo Real, at Madrid, there is a picture exactly answering the above description, except in its measurement, which is given (*Catálogo*, No. 459), as 7 feet 8 inches high by 5 feet 1 inch wide, and ascribed to *Bernardino* Campi. The friar and the catalogue-maker doubtless mean the same picture—the former probably being wrong in his figures, and the latter in the name of the artist. [Now No. 72. In the *Catálogo descriptivo é histórico* of 1872, the name *Bernardino* was retained, but in the editions of 1873 and 1889, *Antonio* has been adopted.—ED.]

printed, in 1585, a "Chronicle of Cremona," enriched with some fine engravings by Agostino Caracci, his friend and admirer, and dedicated to Philip II.[1] Pope Gregory XIII. also employed him as an architect, and decorated him with the order of Christ. As a painter, grace was his distinguishing merit, and Correggio the model of his imitation.[2] The works of Vincenzo Campi at the Escorial, or at least their names, have not been preserved. For his brother's book he engraved the topographical plan of Cremona; and his best picture in that city was a "Dead Christ, in the arms of the Virgin," executed for the church of San Facio. Though his colouring was good, he was inferior to his brothers in invention and power of drawing; his best historical works were generally of a small size, and he excelled in portraiture and in painting fruit and flowers.[3] He died in 1591.[4]

Luca Cambiaso,[5] one of the most famous and most diffuse of the painters of the Escorial, is

---

[1] *Cremona fedelissima citta et nobilissima colonia de' Romani rappresentata in disegno col suo contado et illustrata d'una breve historia delle cose più notabili appartenenti ad essa, et dei ritratti de duchi et duchesse di Milano, e compendio delle lor vite* da Antonio Campo pittore e cavalier Cremonese, al potentissimo e felicissimo Re di Spagna; fol., Cremona, 1585. Engraved title, with a portrait of Philip II., and the arms of his various kingdoms, on the back of it; and an excellent portrait of the author on the leaf before p. 1.

[2] Lanzi, tom. iv. p. 137.   [3] Grasselli, p. 81.

[4] Lanzi, tom. v. p. 138.

[5] For the life of this artist I am in many particulars indebted to Soprani, pp. 35 to 51, where his portrait is engraved.

also esteemed the head of the school of Genoa. His parents having retired from that city on the approach of the Constable Bourbon's army in 1527, he was born on 18th of October of the same year at Moneglia—a white town that sparkles on its hill-top on the eastern shore of the Ligurian gulf, —and was called after the Evangelist painter, to whom the day is dedicated. He began to paint at the age of ten years, under the eye of his father, Giovanni Cambiaso, who evinced good taste in setting him to copy certain works of the correct and noble Mantegna. His progress was so rapid that, at the age of seventeen, he was entrusted to decorate some façades and chambers of the Doria palace at Genoa, where he displayed his rash facility of hand by painting the story of Niobe on a space of wall fifty palms long, and high in proportion, without cartoons or any drawing larger than his first hasty sketch on a single sheet of paper. While he was engaged on this work, there came one morning to look at it some Florentine artists, who, seeing a lad enter soon after and commence painting with prodigious fury, called out to him to desist. His mode, however, of handling the brushes and the colours, which they had imagined it was his business merely to clean or pound, soon convinced them that this daring youngster was no other than Luca himself; whereupon they crossed themselves and declared that he it was who should one day eclipse Michael Angelo. Cambiaso early acquired great skill in fore-shortening, which he seized every occasion, however difficult, of displaying, quite regardless, if aware, of Rafael's precept, that it should be used sparingly, in order to cause the greater wonder and delight.[1] His knowledge of perspective, composition, and colours, was much improved by the instructions of Castello, in conjunction with whom, as has been already mentioned, he painted for twelve years, "in which space of time," says Soprani, "was produced the flower of his works." Amongst his best pictures of this epoch were the "Martyrdom of St. George," in the church of that saint at Genoa, remarkable for its composition, light and shade, and force of expression; and the "Rape of the Sabines," in the palace of the Imperiali at Terralba, a large work full of life and motion, passionate ravishers and reluctant damsels, fine horses and glimpses of noble architecture, and with several episodes heightening the effect of the main story. Of this latter picture the fastidious Mengs said that he had never been more vividly reminded, by any other work, of the chambers of the Vatican.[2]

---

[1] Lodovico Dolce, *Dialogo della Pittura*, 12mo, Vinegia, 1557, fol. 36, a work said to have been composed from notes left by Rafael. [*Aretin: or a Dialogue on Painting*, from the Italian of Lodovico Dolce, 12mo, Glasgow, 1770, p. 130.—ED.]

[2] Lanzi, tom. v. p. 30.

CH. IV.
Death of his wife, and its effects.

While in the zenith of his fame and prosperity Cambiaso had the misfortune to lose his wife; a loss which he endeavoured to remedy in some degree by committing the management of his household and children to her sister. This lady, by whose assistance he hoped to lighten his sorrows and his cares, proved, however, a fertile source of distress; for, as she plied the needle, or whipped the boys, she displayed so close a resemblance to the dear departed, that the widower conceived for her a violent passion, which the canons of the Church did not permit him to gratify by marriage. In 1575, the year of jubilee, he therefore set out for Rome, to crave a dispensation from the Pope. Passing through Florence, he was entertained by Signor Giovanni Battista Paggi, a young Genoese noble, and amateur painter, who carried him, by the desire of the Grand Duke, Francesco I., to meet his Highness in the Gardens of the Prato. The interview was arranged without the knowledge of Cambiaso, who was a man of shy and retiring disposition; and, being unexpectedly ushered into the presence of royalty, he was utterly confounded by the surprise, and by the fine speeches and compliments of the Duke. The circumstance shows, however, the renown which he had acquired. Arriving at Rome, he had an audience, and kissed the holy feet, of Gregory XIII., to whom he presented two fine pictures as a peace-offering, and then, not without blushing, unfolded his case. But the Pontiff, although he graciously accepted the pictures, was not to be moved by the prayers of the painter, who was therefore obliged to return home, having taken nothing by his journey but the papal benediction, and advice that he should dismiss the beloved sister-in-law from his house; which, like a good son of the Church, he did, with many tears.

Thus disappointed, he sought to forget his sorrows in his art, which he pursued with an invention so inexhaustible, and hands so dexterous, that he sometimes painted with two pencils at the same time. His fame obtained for him an order from the King of Spain to paint for the high altar of the Escorial church the "Martyrdom of Saint Lawrence"—a subject which he treated so much to the royal satisfaction that he received an invitation to the Spanish court. Being averse to leaving home, he was induced to comply with Philip's request only by the entreaties of his friends, and by the hope that Castilian interest at Rome might perhaps enable him to accomplish the marriage after which he was still yearning. He arrived, therefore, at Madrid in 1583, attended by his son, Orazio, and another scholar, Lazaro Tavarone, both of them good fresco painters, and was sent to the Escorial with an annual salary of 500 ducats,[1] besides the price of his works, which were to be paid for on a valuation. The vault of the choir was assigned to him as the field of his first labour, for which he made a sketch of the required subject, "the Glory of the Blessed in Heaven." This was submitted to Philip, who rejected it, "not understanding," says Soprani, "Cambiaso's extravagant foreshortenings and figures hovering in the air; and listening to the counsels of his monks, who recommended that the heavenly host should be drawn up according to their hierarchies and degrees in due theological order." A design, "more pious than picturesque," being at last agreed on, the artist fell to work with his wonted fury, and so speedily covered vast spaces with a multitude of figures, that the King, according to the expressive Italian phrase, "remained stupid," not being able to believe that the master, with only one assistant, could have accomplished so much. Philip and his fourth Queen, Anna of Austria (who was also his niece), often visited Cambiaso when at work; and the artist, immersed in his task, sometimes felt a hand laid on his shoulder, which proved to be that of the King of the Spains and the Indies, a discovery that at first must have caused no small discomposure

---

[1] Soprani (page 49) says he received "la somma de scuti cinquecente il mese per il proprio manteniento"—which seems *more* than is probable, while that in the text seems rather *less* when compared with the allowances given to artists of similar reputation at the Escorial.

to the man who had so quailed before the advances of a mere Grand Duke. His Majesty one day remarking that the head of St. Anne, amongst the blessed, was too youthful, the painter, with four strokes of his pencil, so entirely altered its air, and so seamed the face with wrinkles, that the royal critic once more "remained stupid," not knowing whether he had judged amiss, or the change had been effected by magic. By means of thus painting at full speed, frequently without sketches, and sometimes with both hands at once, Cambiaso clothed the vault with its immense fresco in about fifteen months. Though sprinkled over with noble heads and fine figures, the composition, of which the colours are still fresh, cannot be called pleasing. The failure must be attributed mainly to the unlucky meddling of the friars, who have marshalled

> "The helmèd cherubim
> And sworded seraphim"[1]

with exact military precision, ranged the celestial choir in rows like the fiddlers of a sublunary orchestra, and accommodated the congregation of the righteous with long benches, like the congregation of a Methodist meeting. The artist pourtrayed himself standing with Fray Antonio de Villacastin, master of the works, who had probably no small hand in the

---

[1] Milton, Hymn on Christ's Nativity, stanza xi.

design, on the threshold of the heavenly mansions. The King was so well pleased with the fresco, that he paid Cambiaso 12.000 ducats, being 3,000 more than the award of the valuers.

The condescensions of Philip now emboldened the love-sick artist to think of craving the royal interposition with the Pope in behalf of his long-wished-for marriage. He was cautioned, however, by his acquaintances at Court, against preferring so impious a petition, which they said would infallibly cost him the favour of the pious monarch. This fresh disappointment, added to the fatigue and ill effects of painting for many hours together in constrained attitudes, brought on a severe illness, in which he was carefully attended by the royal physicians. But, in spite of their skill, an abscess gathered in his chest, for which they hit upon the singular remedy of causing some of his friends to burst suddenly into his room, and revile him as he lay, in the hope that a hearty fit of rage might break the obstruction. The poor man's spirit, however, had sunk under chagrin and disease; he heard, but heeded not; the rough messengers of mercy confessed the deception with tears; and the patient expired soon after, of a broken heart and an unbroken imposthume, to the great regret of the King.

Besides his great fresco, Cambiaso found time to paint, at the Escorial, two others for the grand staircase, representing "The Risen Saviour appearing to the Apostles," and several altar-pieces in oil-colours, of which "The Martyrdom of St. Ursula and the Eleven Thousand Virgins," and the "Triumph of the Archangel Michael," were so indifferent that the King would not permit them to be placed in the proposed sites. So careless and hasty was their execution that Father Siguenza said of them, that they seemed to have been done, like the coarse daubs sold in the streets, for a dinner. "The Martyrdom of St. Lawrence," painted at Genoa, for some time occupied the chief place in the high altar, but was removed after the artist's death to make room for another, by Zuccaro. Cambiaso was a man of amiable character, and liberal to poor artists, and on one occasion gave a dowry to the portionless daughter of a brother painter. His works suffered much from the careless haste of their execution; his drawings were easily recognised by collectors by their free bold style, and were so infinite in number and so negligently preserved, that, in his own house, they were often used by his maid-servant for kindling fires. Of some of them which fell in the way of Tintoretto, who rivalled the Genoese in rapidity, that artist remarked that they might be of service to an experienced painter, but were enough to ruin the style of a beginner.[1]

Character.

Merits as an artist.

---

[1] Ridolfi, part ii., p. 59.

The younger Cambiaso was employed for a short time at the Escorial, in painting with the sons of Castello the Bergamese, but returned to Italy in 1586, receiving 50 ducats to defray the cost of the journey. His companion, Lazaro Tavarone, was named painter to the King in 1585, with a monthly salary of 20 ducats, and had a hand in the ungainly frescoes in the hall of battles.[1] He afterwards assisted Tibaldi, and finally received, in 1590, 200 ducats for his travelling expenses to Genoa, where he arrived, says Lanzi, "rich in drawings by his master, ready money, and honour."[2] Cambiaso had been accompanied or followed by a third disciple, Giovanni Battisto Castello,[3] a skilful painter of illuminations, who was employed upon the choir-books of the Escorial. He was called in Castile the "Genoese," to distinguish him from Castello of Bergamo;[4] and he returned to Genoa about the end of the century.

On the death of Cambiaso, Philip invited Paul Veronese to the Escorial, but that fine master could

---

[1] Supra, p. 233.
[2] Lanzi, tom. v. p. 304.
[3] Cean Bermudez mentions a fourth pupil of Cambiaso—one "Juan Bautista Scorza"—as his companion in Spain, whom I take, however, to be identical with this Genoese Castello, from the curious concidence of the facts of their lives. Both were painters of illuminations, and died at Genoa, in 1637, aged ninety; and each of them is said to have had a son, "who, from a mere merchant, became a prince in Sicily." "Scorza" may have been a nickname of Castello, and by some mistake converted into a rival artist.
[4] Supra, p. 232.

DON GASPAR DE GUZMAN, COUNT OF OLIVARES.

not be induced to quit Venice. The Count of Olivares, Spanish ambassador at the Vatican, then sent over Federigo Zuccaro, a painter whose reputation, acquired not only in Italy, but also in England, France and Flanders, exceeded his merits as much as it fell short of his inordinate vanity. He was the son of Ottaviano Zuccaro, a second-rate painter of San Angiolo in Vado, in the duchy of Urbino, and was born there in 1543. Having learned somewhat from his father, he was sent, at an early age, to study at Rome, under his elder brother Taddeo, who had earned considerable distinction as a painter of frescoes. There he made rapid progress, and soon despised the fraternal counsels; for Taddeo having presumed to correct some parts of a fresco with which his scholar was adorning the front of a house, the retouchings were immediately cut out of the plaster by the exasperated tyro. A consequent quarrel led to a separation between the brothers, who, however, were afterwards reconciled; for Taddeo dying in 1566, was buried near Rafael, in the Pantheon; and Federigo inscribed a boastful and fulsome epitaph on his tomb. The frescoes of the cupola of Santa Maria in Fiori, at Florence, being left unfinished by the elder brother at his death, they were completed by the younger, much to the satisfaction of the Grand Duke, and probably were the cause of his being appointed by Gregory XIII.

to execute some paintings in the Pauline Chapel at the Vatican. Sustaining, however, some real or imaginary injury from certain of his acquaintance, Zuccaro took his revenge by painting an allegory on the subject of calumny, wherein he pourtrayed the offenders with the auricular head-gear of Midas. This he irreverently hung over the portal of St. Luke's Church, on a day of festival; an outrage for which he lost the papal favour, and was forced to leave Rome. His patron, the Cardinal of Lorraine, befriended him in his difficulty, and sent him to Paris, where he obtained employment for some time, and whence he went to Antwerp, to make cartoons for the tapestry-workers. He afterwards visited Holland, and also passed into England, where, says Horace Walpole,[1] he arrived in 1574, but did not long remain. It appears, however, that he was in this country in 1580, that being the date on his portrait—now at Hampton Court—of Queen Elizabeth's huge porter—" the jolter-headed giant" of the pleasures of Kenilworth in Scott's romance. He likewise painted the Queen herself, and her prisoner, the unhappy Mary of Scotland. Two of his portraits of the English princess are now at Hampton Court, and one of them—that wherein she is drawn at full length, fantastically attired, and musing in a forest

---

[1] *Works*, 4to, London, 1798, vol. iii. p. 121.

—is inscribed with some mysterious Latin mottoes, and some bad English verses of her own composition.[1] Many old English houses still possess portraits by Zuccaro of their members who figured at the Court of Elizabeth. From London the roving artist seems to have moved southward to Venice, where he painted with Paul Veronese and Tintoretto in the Great Council Chamber of the Doge's palace. Thence he ventured to return to Rome, where he found the Pope's anger mollified by time and distance, and was permitted to finish his labours in the Pauline Chapel.

It was now that he attracted the notice of Olivares, who sent him, in 1585, to Spain, as the best artist that Rome could furnish. He was engaged at the large annual salary of 2,000 crowns, and, arriving at the Escorial early in 1586, was received by the prior with almost regal honours.[2] His first works were six paintings on canvas for the high altar—"The Martyrdom of St. Lawrence," "Christ at the Column," and "Christ bearing His Cross," for the compartments of the second storey; and the "Assumption of the Virgin," "Our Lord's Resurrection," and the "Descent of the Holy

---

[1] Horace Walpole, *Works*, vol. i. p. 271, and also Mrs. Jameson's agreeable *Handbook to the Public Galleries*, London, 1845, p. 406.

[2] A letter dated 29 May, 1586, written by himself from the Escorial, will be found in Dennistoun's *Memoirs of the Dukes of Urbino*, 3 vols. 8vo, London, 1851, vol. iii. p. 343.

Ghost," for those of the third, which were all fixed in their places before the King saw them. But observing that neither the courtiers nor the monks said anything in praise of these pictures, but preserved a doubtful silence, Zuccaro bestowed far greater pains on the "Nativity of the Saviour," and the "Adoration of the Kings," intended for the lowest division of the altar, which lay more fully than the others within the ken of criticism. When finished he submitted them to the inspection of the King, confident of applause, and modestly remarking that the force of painting could no farther go. Philip, however, was neither to be blinded by his fame, nor awed by the assurance of this spoiled favourite of courts. Looking at the pictures for some time in contemptuous silence—in which Titian has left evidence that his aspect must have been sufficiently chilling—he at length inquired whether those were eggs in the basket of a little shepherdess, in the "Nativity," who seemed hastening to lay her offering at the feet of the Virgin-mother. The artist answering yes, the King quietly hinted that the said eggs, besides being ill-painted, were somewhat out of place in the basket of a damsel running at full speed, and purporting to be a shepherdess coming at midnight from the fold, unless, indeed, her flock consisted of fowls; and, turning on his heel, left the Italian not a little disconcerted by the unusual event of meeting with criticism which was not flattery.

In fresco-painting, to which he next applied himself, Zuccaro was not more fortunate. Six pieces, which he executed in the cloisters, were condemned by the King, and afterwards effaced, excepting one representing the "Incarnation of Our Lord." Having laid the blame of this failure on his disciples who had assisted in the work, he was ordered to execute, entirely with his own hand, the "Mystery of the Conception," which proved, however, as unsatisfactory as the rest. It must be admitted that Philip behaved on the occasion with great kindness and generosity: dissembling his displeasure, and having borne with the artist for three years, he finally sent him away rejoicing, with payment, says Palomino, at the rate of 6,000 ducats a year,[1] or, according to Cean Bermudez, with a present of 900 over and above his pension, a gold chain, a string of pearls, and undiminished self-esteem. His "St. Lawrence" was dismissed from the high altar to a small chapel of the palace, and the "Nativity" and "Epiphany" to the hall of the convent; while his other pictures, which their lofty position rendered less obnoxious, were suffered to retain their places. On the painter's departure, his friend, Fray Antonio de Villacastin,

Condemned frescoes.

---

[1] Palomino, tom. iii. p. 402.

kissed the King's hand, and thanked him for the munificence he had shown. "It is not Zuccaro who is to blame," replied Philip, "but those who brought him hither." Zuccaro's failure in Spain does not appear to have damaged his reputation in Italy. There he was caressed by the great, and employed by the Church as before, founded, and was chosen first president of, the Academy of St. Luke, at Rome, under the patronage of Sixtus V., built himself a fine house there on the Pincian hill, became a member of the literary Academy, "dell' Insensate," under the whimsical title of "Il Sonnachioso;" published several works on the arts,[1] and, dying at Ancona in 1609, was buried there with great pomp. His portrait, engraved in Walpole's "Anecdotes of Painting in England," represents him in the prime of life as a handsome man, with regular features and a fair complexion.

Zuccaro brought with him from Italy his Florentine disciple, Bartolomeo Carducci,—or Carducho, as he was called in Spain,—who was born in 1560, and who practised in Castile, during two reigns, the three arts of painting, sculpture, and architecture, of which he had studied the two last under Bartolomeo Ammanati at Florence. He was re-

---

[1] Of these the best is entitled, *L'Idea de' Pittori, Scultori et Architetti del Cavalier Federigo Zuccaro*, folio, Torino, 1607, in which (p. 5) he informs us of his adoption of the style of "The Drowsy."

tained by Philip II. at the yearly salary of 50,000 maravedis (somewhat under £20) besides the price of his works—slender emoluments, which, however, he declined to resign, although invited to the court of France by Henry IV. At the Escorial he painted several altar-pieces in oils, and the frescoes which fill the spaces between the book-cases and the cornice of the library, and which illustrate, and are not unworthy of, Tibaldi's allegorical ceiling that overhangs them. Each compartment relates to the science allegorised immediately above it, and some of them display a curious choice of subject. Thus the force of eloquence is symbolised by a Hercules, out of whose mouth proceed chains of silver and gold to bind the nations; and Arithmetic is represented by the wise King of Israel, seated at a table and resolving the problems proposed by the Queen of Sheba. He likewise painted for the church of San Felipe el Real a "Descent from the Cross," which reminded Cumberland of the style of Rafael.[1] On the death of his royal master, Carducho was confirmed in his post of painter by Philip III., whose esteem he enjoyed, and at whose court he lived and laboured at Valladolid till 1606. He was then sent to the palace of the Pardo to paint the ceiling and model the plaster ornaments of

---

[1] *Anecdotes*, vol. i. p. 122.

the southern gallery, and died there in 1608. His works were distinguished by their accurate drawing, harmonious colouring, and imitation of the antique. A fastidious taste led him to touch and retouch his pictures repeatedly, in order to attain his own high ideal of excellence, of which he was wont to say that he wished those profoundly versed in art, and not the vulgar herd, to judge. "Prudence and disinterestedness," a rare and happy combination, "were," says Cean Bermudez, "his peculiar virtues." Expressing, one day, his admiration of a picture, newly finished by a brother artist, a scholar of his own drew his attention to a badly drawn and misplaced foot. "I did not observe it," replied he, "it is so concealed by the difficult excellence of this bosom and those hands,"—a piece of kindly criticism that deserves to be recorded. Carducho left two daughters, but no sons. The honours of his name, however, were worthily worn and extended by his younger brother and disciple, Vincenzio, who became one of the most eminent painters in Castile. The picture of the "Last Supper," in the Queen of Spain's gallery at Madrid,[1] is one of the best works of Bartolomé Carducho. The head of Our Lord is noble in character, and there is considerable variety in the heads of the apostles.

---

[1] *Catálogo*, No. 925 [edition of 1889, No. 81].

Judas is distinguished from the other eleven by his customary red hair, obnoxious to Castilian taste,[1] and here of an unusually fiery shade. The tablecloth, with its folds accurately marked as in the pictures of Paul Veronese, is laid on a rich Turkish rug, the brilliant border of which peeps out, and is painted with Flemish minuteness.

Antonio Rizi, born at Bologna, was another of the scholars of Zuccaro, who accompanied that master to Spain. He is said to have assisted his chief in executing some of the unfortunate frescoes at the Escorial, removed by order of Philip II. Soon after his arrival at Madrid, he married, on the 18th of September 1588, at the church of San Gines, Doña Gabriela de Chaves, by whom he had two sons who became painters of reputation in the reign of Philip IV., although he himself appears to have died before they were of sufficient age to handle the pencil. The only work of Antonio Rizi, discovered by Cean Bermudez at Madrid, was a picture of St. Augustine, in the nunnery of Santo Domingo el Real.

Pellegrino Tibaldi was born in 1522, or, according to another account, in 1527, at Valdelsa, a village in the Milanese, where his father followed the trade of a mason. Being early removed to Bologna, he there studied painting, sculpture, and architec-

---

[1] Infra, chap. vi. p. 425, note 3.

ture, the first, it is said, under the elder Ramenghi, a pupil of Rafael. In 1547 he went to seek improvement in the galleries and churches of Rome, where he addicted himself to the study of Michael Angelo, and to the imitation of his style. Having painted some works in the castle of St. Angelo, he returned to Bologna, and there executed in the Institute a series of frescoes, on subjects taken from the Odyssey, which fixed his reputation. He afterwards went to Loretto to paint the chapel of the Cardinal of Augsburg, and he also painted some esteemed works in the Merchants' House at Ancona. Twenty years of his life were devoted to the study and practice of architecture and sculpture; he was chosen by St. Charles Borromeo to build his college, or "Palace of Wisdom," at Pavia; and at Milan he became intendant of works in the renowned Cathedral, which, begun in the days of the old Visconti, owes its splendid crest of marble spires to the magnificence of Napoleon. Here he designed the choir; and he has also left other proofs of his architectural powers in the churches of Milan. In sculpture his name stood so high that some of his plaster designs were used as models by Annibal Caracci, in painting the gallery of the Farnese palace.

Invitation to Spain.

Invited to Spain by Philip II., this distinguished master arrived, in 1586, at the Escorial, where his first works were some frescoes, in the Camarin, or little chamber behind the high altar, representing "Abraham paying tithe to Melchizedek," and "Elias fed by an Angel in the Desert." The King was much pleased with these specimens of Tibaldi's powers, and directed him to supply the place of Zuccaro's condemned frescoes in the great cloister with others on subjects belonging to the legend of the Blessed Virgin. For the same cloister he painted several other works, amongst which three oil pictures, adorning an oratory, and representing "The Raising of the Cross," "The Crucifixion," and "Our Lord taken down from the Cross," were remarkable for the skill of their difficult fore-shortenings. He also painted in oils, for the high altar, the "Martyrdom of St. Lawrence," the "Nativity," and "Epiphany," which still exist there, having superseded those by Zuccaro. This gorgeous altar must have been built under an evil star, for these pictures were little better than their predecessors. St. Lawrence, extended on his gridiron, is ill painted, and far too large; for had he really been of that gigantic stature, the pigmy Roman cooks, who stand around, and whom he facetiously requested to turn him that both sides might be equally broiled and fit for eating,[1]

---

[1] "Mira miserable," said the valorous martyr to his executioner, "que ya tienes assada una parte de mi cuerpo: buelvele, paraque la otra se asse, paraque sazonadas mis carnes puedas comer de ellas," &c. Villegas, *Flos Sanctorum*, p. 380.

Frescoes in the library.

would have found their functions dangerous as well as difficult. The King approved of his work when he saw it on the easel, but was disappointed with its effect in the altar. Tibaldi's greatest achievement at the Escorial was the fresco of the ceiling (194 feet long by 32 wide) of the noble library, where the books still glitter in their cases, with their gilt edges turned outwards, as they were left by the first librarian, Arias Montano. This ceiling is divided into seven compartments, each of which contains an allegorical representation of a science. It displays a profusion of various and beautiful figures, brilliantly coloured, and of colossal size; the design is adapted with admirable skill to the archings of the roof; and the whole affords a proof of the artist's acquaintance with the frescoes of the great Florentine. The Caracci were wont to call Tibaldi, on account of the combined grandeur and softness of his style, "the reformed Michael Angelo,"[1] a proud but hardly merited title, for he had not proved the giant's armour which he had assumed, and when he copied the exaggerated forms of his illustrious model, the mighty soul that inspired them was too often wanting. For his labours at the Escorial Philip rewarded Tibaldi with 100,000

---

[1] Lanzi, tom. v. p. 46.

crowns,[1] and the dignity of Marquess in the Milanese states, by the title of Valdelsa, the hamlet where his father had carried the hod. He did not long enjoy these gifts, for he died soon after, at Milan, in 1592.

Bernardino del Agua was a Venetian painter, who executed, in the cloister of the Court of Evangelists at the Escorial, and under the direction of Tibaldi, some frescoes from the sketches of that master. The defects, from which these works were by no means free, were attributed by the designer not to the carelessness of Agua, but to the haste with which Philip II. insisted that they should be finished.

Flanders, as well as Italy, furnished to the King of Spain its contingent of painters. Sir Anthony More, one of the best portrait-painters of his day, and no less famous in London than at his native Utrecht (where he was born in 1512), was the scholar of John Schoorel, and afterwards travelled in Italy. Cardinal Granvelle introduced him to the service of Charles V., by whom he was sent to Portugal to paint some of the royal family. He had previously painted Prince Philip, and his pencil was the means of making that marrying monarch and the first two of his four queens, the Maries

---

[1] Pacheco (p. 94) states the sum at 50,000 crowns, in which he is followed by Palomino (tom. iii. p. 408); Cean Bermudez, however, whom I have taken as my authority, is borne out in his statement by Malvasia; *Vite dei Pittori Bolognesi*, 4to, Bologna, 1678, tom. i. p. 170.

of Portugal and England, acquainted with each other's persons. In England, More was munificently entertained, and probably received his knighthood; he frequently painted Queen Mary, who presented him with a hundred pounds and a gold chain, and allowed him a hundred pounds a quarter whilst he remained in her service; and he was largely employed by the Howards and the Russells and other grandees of the court.[1] His portraits of the Queen accord with the earlier ones by Holbein, and represent her as not handsome, yet not unpleasing, of a fair complexion and dignified presence, and bearing in her somewhat pensive eyes nothing akin to the horrible epithet which history — justly, perhaps, but most invidiously — has wedded to her name. One of these, a half-length, is in the Queen of Spain's gallery; another, a fine full-length picture, adorns the collection of the Duke of Wellington at Apsley House. More was much about the person of Philip, then King of England and Naples, and probably painted that portrait of him—in armour, and bareheaded, out of deference to the Queen—which poor Mary, who privately suspected her husband of cowardice, begged for, in her joy and surprise at hearing of his

---

[1] For this life I have consulted Horace Walpole's *Anecdotes of Painting in England, Works*, vol. iii. p. 106; and Descamps, *La Vie des Peintres Flamandes*, &c., tom. i. p. 98.

presence at the field of St. Quentin.[1] When Philip went to Spain to take possession of the throne, More followed him to Madrid, and for some time basked in the full sunshine of royal favour. All of a sudden he withdrew to Brussels with a haste that betokened disgrace and alarm, and for some cause which has never been satisfactorily explained. One account is that the King, visiting More according to custom, laid his hand upon his shoulder as he stood at the easel, a familiarity which the artist returned by rudely rapping the royal knuckles with his maulstick, or, according to another version of the story, daubing them with carmine. The attendants stood aghast, and the story getting wind, the officers of the Inquisition prepared to apprehend the playful Fleming. Philip, however, treated the matter as a jest, good-naturedly gave the painter warning of his danger, and enabled him to escape; and some time after even invited him back to court, an invitation with which More did not think it safe to comply. Neither Palomino nor Cean Bermudez, however, mention this coarse and dangerous pleasantry, and they allege the jealousy and dislike of the courtiers as the cause of the painter's sudden evasion. The former[2] asserts that More was so much an object of royal favour and courtly envy, that he

---

[1] Gregorio Leti, *Vie d'Elizabeth, Reine d'Angleterre*, 8vo, Amsterdam, 1703, tom. i. p. 397.   [2] Palomino, tom. iii. p. 361.

had like to have been cast into the prison of the Inquisition on a charge of bewitching the King. The latter writer describes him as being "very much the courtier, and living like a gentleman of grave and majestic manners,"—a sort of person not likely to play tricks on a King of Spain. Whatever were his reasons for leaving Madrid, he was kindly received at Brussels by the Duke of Alba, governor of the Low Countries, and painted the portraits of that iron commander and some of his mistresses. To the artist's sons lucrative posts were given by the Duke, who is said to have even suppressed the letters which invited him back to Madrid, that he might not be deprived of his society and services.[1] His declining years were spent in ease and opulence — the fruits of successful toil at the Courts of England, Portugal, and Spain; and he died, aged seventy-six, at Antwerp, in 1588. The hall of portraits in the palace of the Pardo contained sixteen of his pictures of royal and noble personages, which perished with those of Titian. Though he addicted himself chiefly to portraiture, he executed some pictures on religious subjects, and was engaged, when he died, in painting the "Circumcision of Our Lord," for the Cathedral of Antwerp. His works are usually finished with great care, and

---

[1] Descamps, tom. i. p. 100.

sometimes are coloured in the rich style of Titian. In the long gallery at Althorp there is a fine specimen of his powers, in the portrait of himself; from which we learn that he was a tall stately man, with a good, though somewhat rugged, countenance, and red hair and beard; that he wore a dark doublet with sleeves of shining black satin, and a heavy gold chain passed twice round his neck; and that he went attended by a huge brindled wolf-hound.

Michael Coxein or Coxie[1] was born at Mechlin in 1497, and first studied there under Van Orlay, and afterwards went to Rome. Thence he returned with an Italian wife, and a portfolio filled with sketches from the works of Rafael, which, as occasion served, he reproduced as his own, a piece of audacious larceny at last exposed by his countryman Jerome Cock, who published an engraving from the school of Athens, and thus whispered to the Flemish churchmen the source whence Coxie had stolen saintly figures for their shrines. Philip II. employed him to make a copy of Van Eyck's picture, at Ghent, of the "Triumph of the Lamb," a work which the dexterous plagiary carried with him to Madrid, where it was placed over the altar of the chapel at the Alcazar. At the Escorial he painted several pictures for various altars and oratories, such

---

[1] Descamps, tom. i. p. 57.

as "Christ and the Virgin interceding with the Father Eternal," "St. Joachim and St. Anne," and "David cutting off Goliath's head." He likewise painted the "Resurrection of Our Lord" for the barefooted Carmelites of Medina del Campo. Returning to Mechlin with considerable wealth, he built himself three houses, and adorned them with his own pictures. He retained his faculties and industry to the age of ninety-five, and died in 1597, of a fall from a scaffold while painting in the Hôtel de Ville at Antwerp. Notwithstanding his pilferings, he was an artist of considerable skill, and left in the Church of Our Lady, at Antwerp, a "Holy Family," which was praised by Rubens. The royal gallery of Madrid possesses two of his works, of which one is "the Death of the Virgin,"[1] a large panel, bought for a great sum by Philip II., from the Cathedral of St. Gudule, at Brussels. The other is "St. Cecilia playing on the organ,"[2] a composition in which imitation of Rafael is very evident, especially in his occasional poverty of colour; the saint's hands are clumsy, the heads commonplace, and none of the figures is pleasing, except a pretty little amber-haired angel in the act of singing.

Antonio Pupiler was a Fleming whom Philip took into his service in 1556, at the salary of 350 crowns

---

[1] *Catálogo* [1843], No. 1598 [edition of 1889, No. 1300].
[2] Id. No. 499 [edition of 1889, 1299].

REIGN OF PHILIP II.

annually, and employed at the Pardo, and afterwards, in 1567, to copy a retablo at Louvaine. It is not known whether he returned to Spain, nor have any of his works survived the ravages of time, and the fire at the Pardo.

In Ulric Staenheyl, a soldier of his German bodyguard, Philip II. found an artist conversant with painting on glass; and he accordingly, in 1566, employed him for that purpose, with an annual salary of 260 ducats, and exemption from military duty.

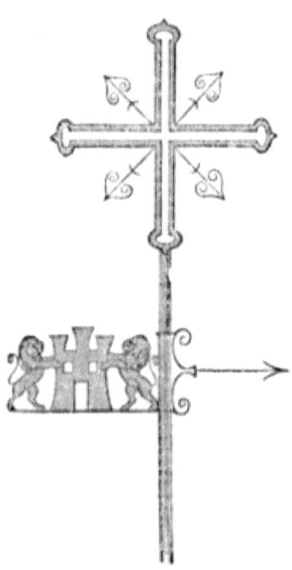

CHAPTER V.

REIGN OF PHILIP II. 1556-1598—(*continued*).

CASTILE in this long reign produced many painters, who neither were excelled in skill, nor have been eclipsed in fame, by the ablest of their Italian or Flemish rivals.

First in age, and perhaps also in reputation, comes Luis Morales, upon whom the admiration of his country, or the devotional character of his works, has conferred the title of "the Divine." He is the first Spaniard whose genius and good fortune have obtained for him a place amongst the great painters of Europe. Like many of those who have most strongly influenced the mind or taste of their age, he lived and laboured in obscurity, and the records of his life are meagre and contradictory.

Born at Badajoz about 1509, he is absurdly said by Palomino[1] to have been, at Seville, a pupil of Campaña, a master who did not arrive in Spain till 1548. Cean Bermudez, with more probability, supposes him to have studied his art at Toledo or Valladolid; and he seems to have practised it for the greater part of his life in Estremadura, painting chiefly for churches and for the oratories of private mansions. By a baptismal entry in the register of the Cathedral of Frexenal, a small town on the Andalusian border, it appears that he was residing there in November 1554, when his son Cristobal was baptized in that church, and that the name of his wife was Leonora de Chaves. In, or shortly before, 1564, he was commanded by Philip II. to repair to court, to paint some pictures for the newly-founded monastery of the Escorial. Presenting himself in magnificent attire, little suited to his condition, his ostentation is said to have displeased the King, who at first ordered his dismissal with a sum of money, but was mollified by the gallant painter's declaration that he had spent all he had in order to appear in a manner befitting the dignity of his Majesty.[2] He seems, however, to have painted, during his residence at court, only a single picture, "Christ going to Calvary," given by Philip

Visits the Escorial.

---

[1] Pal., tom. iii. p. 384. [2] Id., tom. i. p. 178.

to the Church of the Jeronymites, at Madrid; nor did any work of his form part of the original decorations of the Escorial. After his return to Estremadura his fortunes began to decline. As old age drew on he lost the steadiness of hand so necessary in his profession, his eyesight failed him, and he fell into extreme poverty. By a writing, discovered by Cean Bermudez in the archives of the Cathedral of Frexenal, we find him, in February 1575, selling for 100 ducats some vines which he possessed in the Vega of Merida. His wretchedness was somewhat relieved, in 1581, by the timely visit of the King to Badajoz, as he returned from taking possession of his newly-acquired kingdom beyond the Guadiana. The poor, disabled painter, appearing in the royal presence in a garb very different from that in which he had flourished at the Escorial, attracted the notice of Philip. "You are very old, Morales," said he. "Yes, sire, and very poor," replied the artist. Turning to his treasurer, the King immediately ordered the old man a pension of 200 ducats, out of the crown rents of the city, "for his dinner;" when Morales interposed with the question, "And for supper, sire?"—a stroke of dexterous begging which Philip, being in a humour to be pleased, rewarded with another hundred ducats. "Here may be seen," says Palomino, "the liberality of that great monarch, and the discreet wit of the vassal in profiting by the occasion, and speaking at the right time, which is a great felicity."[1] Morales did not long enjoy the royal bounty; for he died five years afterwards, in 1586. Badajoz has done honour to the memory of its great painter by naming after him the street in which he lived.[2] It is a street of considerable length, which takes a downward course from the centre of the city, widening as it approaches its termination on the terraced bank of the Guadiana, a little way above the great hospital. The houses are mean, especially near the river, and the population gipsy and disreputable.

Morales was the first artist born and bred in Spain who invested the religious thought and feeling of his native land with the beauties of Italian expression. Pure and graceful in design, and rich in the harmonies of colour, his works might have been painted in the schools of Rome, amongst the models of ancient art and in the inspiring companionship of Rafael and Fra Bastiano. But, as pictures by the great foreign masters were rarely to be met with out of the royal collections, it is probable that his acquaintance with the creations of Italian art began and ended with his short residence at court, when his style was doubtless

---

[1] Pal., tom. iii. p. 385.   [2] Ponz, tom. viii. p. 162.

as mature as his age. He may, indeed, have benefitted in his youth by the instructions of travelled artists, and may have been numbered amongst the scholars of Berruguete. Nothing, however, is certain, except that he far excelled any painter who could possibly have been his instructor. He stands, therefore, in art, amongst the few of whom it can be said that each was

> "author of himself,
> And knew no other kin."[1]

He discovered for himself many of the secrets of his craft, and triumphed over its difficulties by the mere force of genius. At the distance of three centuries we may still regret that his noble pencil, not excelled at the Escorial, and not unworthy of the Vatican, should have been doomed to ill-requited and inglorious toil in the wilds of Estremadura.

The subjects of Morales are always devotional, and those few by which he is known out of Spain are generally of a doleful cast. It is not, however, with the ghastly sufferings of the body that, like Spagnoletto, he chiefly deals, but with the nobler sorrows of the soul. The Virgin whom he offers to the contemplation of the pious is never the fair young mother, smiling on the beauty of her Babe Divine, but the drooping Mater Dolorosa, wan and weary with unutterable

---
[1] *Coriolanus*, act v. sc. 3.

anguish. His Christ is in every feature "the Man of Sorrows and acquainted with grief," wrung with the agonies of the garden, or bearing on His brow the damps and paleness of death. Here the prostration of physical force and the wasting frame are drawn with terrible truth, as if Morales had groped his way into the vaults of the Inquisition, and there chosen for a model some lean heretic Carthusian (if such there were) writhing in the grasp of the tormentor.[1] Our Lord fainting under His cross was a theme which often engaged his pencil and finely displayed his powers. His conception of this sublime subject recalled to the recollection of Cumberland[2] Rafael's famous "Spasimo," and his execution the manner of Da Vinci. The Louvre possesses a very fine picture of this kind, by his hand, in which the head of the Saviour much resembles that striking head of "Christ with the crown of thorns" in the Queen of Spain's gallery,[3] perhaps the finest of all his works for richness of colour and intensity of feeling. So few of his larger works have found their way out of his native province, that it has been said that he never painted a full-length figure. This, however, is disproved by his "Crucifixion," overlooked by

---

[1] [*Notice des Tableaux*, édition 1889, No. 537. A steel engraving of it is given in *Murillo and the Spanish School of Painting*, by Wm. B. Scott, 4to, London, 1873.]

[2] *Anecdotes*, vol. i. p. 76.

[3] *Catalogo*, No. 120 [edition of 1889, No. 851].

the French in stripping the Cathedral of Badajoz; and still more by the altars of the once proud temple of the military monks at Alcantara, and of the village church of Arroyo del Puerco, a desolate hamlet on the road from Alcantara to Truxillo. The first of these contains a St. Michael and St. John, and other pictures by Morales; the second, sixteen of his grandest works, which, though noticed in the Dictionary of Cean Bermudez—Soult's handbook for Spain—escaped the keen glance and iron gripe of that picture-pilfering commander, whose troops long occupied the place. The best of them are the grand "Christ and Joseph of Arimathea," "St. John," and "Christ bound"—three-quarter length —"Christ at the Column," and the "Descent from the Cross." "Though chilled and dirty, they are at least pure,"[1] and uninjured by either care or neglect. "The Saviour's Circumcision," in the Queen of Spain's gallery,[2] though defective in composition, and injured by the stiffness of some of the figures, is remarkable for the serene beauty of the female

---

[1] *Handbook* [1845], p. 546 [3rd edition, 1855, p. 490], which contains the single account of these fine pictures that I have met with in any foreign work on Spain. Cean Bermudez, who probably never saw them, merely notices them in his list of the works of Morales as "sixteen historical subjects;" and, in Ponz, I find no mention at all of their existence.

[2] *Catálogo* [1843], No. 110 [edition of 1889, No. 849, where it is now called "The Presentation of the Child Jesus in the Temple" (St. Luke, chap. ii.). Engraved in wood, in *Murillo and the Spanish School of Painting*, p. 28. —ED.].

_{CH. V.}

_{Careful finish.}

heads, especially those of the taper-bearing maidens who attend upon the Blessed Virgin.[1]

The works of Morales were always painted on panel. The labour bestowed on their execution fully accounts for their scarcity. His pencil lingered on a head, or on a fold of drapery, with the fond and fastidious care of the early Florentine masters. He finished his faces with a smoothness sometimes excessive, and in the curious elaboration of the hair he was rivalled neither by Durer, delighting in hyacinthine ringlets, nor by Denner, matchless in depicting the stubbly chins of grey-beards and old women. Like Parmegiano, he worked on the amber locks of his cherubs till "they curled like the little rings of the vine;"[2] each particular hair was expressed, and the whole seemed ready to wave at a breath.[3] His colouring, rich though sober, is sometimes cold and greyish; and in his full-length figures the drawing is too often incorrect. But the fine feeling of his countenances, and the roundness of his forms, give his works a charm which seldom belongs to those of his Spanish contemporaries.

_{Scholars.}

_{Morales the younger.}

He had few disciples, and those few—amongst whom was his son, possibly the Cristobal whose birth

---

[1] [A beautiful example is now in the National Gallery, "The Virgin and Child," *Catalogue*, 1889, No. 1229; acquired in 1887.—ED.]

[2] Jeremy Taylor, *Sermon on Marriage*. *Works*, 15 vols. 8vo, London, 1828, vol. v. p. 259.

[3] Palomino, tom. iii. p. 384.

has been recorded—were mere feeble imitators of his style, who exaggerated his faults and were devoid of his inspiration. Their dismal Madonnas, and chalky Ecce-homos have, however, frequently been laid at his door, to the damage of his reputation. The best of the band was Juan Labrador, who chose a humbler walk of art, and painted fruit and flower pieces, which were admired for their truth and brilliancy of colour, and their fresh-gathered leaves empearled with transparent dew-drops. He died at Madrid in 1600.

Alonso Sanchez Coello,[1] the first of the great Spanish portrait-painters, and the Velazquez of the court of Philip II., has been erroneously called by several writers a Portuguese. Cean Bermudez, however, reclaims him for Spain, and, on the authority of the heralds of Santiago, asserts that he was born at Benifayrò, in Valencia, early in the sixteenth century.[2] Nothing of his early history has been preserved, nor is it known where he acquired the rudiments of his art. His style, however, appears to have been formed on Italian models, and he left several careful and excellent copies of the works of Titian. In 1541, he was residing at Madrid, where

---

[1] Pacheco, p. 589, and Palomino, tom. i. p. 178—ii., p. 388.
[2] To the fact of his being a Spaniard a doubting and reluctant assent is given by Dom Cyrillo Volkmar Machado,—the Portuguese Pilkington,—in his *Collecção de Memorias relativas c's vidas dos Pintores, e Escultores, Architectos, e Gravadores Portuguezes, e dos Estrangeiros, que estiverão em Portugal*—4to, Lisboa, 1823, p. 66.

he married Doña Luisa Reynalte. In 1552 he accompanied Anthony More to Lisbon, and there entered the service of the Infant Don Juan of Portugal. A miniature portrait, the handsome head of the ill-fated King Sebastian, probably painted at this time, is now in the collection of the Duke of Palmella in his palace of Calhariz at Lisbon. On the death of that prince he was recommended by his widow, the Spanish Infanta Juana, daughter of Charles V., to her brother Philip; and, returning to Spain, he became painter-in-ordinary to that monarch, on More's hasty retreat from Madrid. There his genius and address obtained for him a distinguished position at court; he enjoyed the full confidence of the King, and was usually in attendance on his person. Philip was wont to call him "his Portuguese Titian," in allusion to his residence at Lisbon; and from any royal progress, in which the favourite painter did not accompany him, he would write to him as his "beloved son Alonso Sanchez Coello." At Madrid the artist was lodged in the treasury buildings contiguous to the palace, and connected with it by a private door, of which Philip kept a key, and by which he sometimes surprised him at table in the midst of his family. At other times the King, loosely arrayed in a morning gown,[1] would steal

---

[1] This morning gown affords Cumberland an opportunity of making a singular blunder, which I have noticed in the Preface.

softly into the studio, and laying his hand on the painter's shoulder, compel him to remain seated and pursue his labours whilst he looked on or lounged over other pictures. These familiarities, more flattering perhaps than agreeable, Sanchez Coello appears to have received with all due modesty, never forgetting, as was alleged of More, the awful distance which separated even the most playful King of Spain and the Indies from his painter-in-ordinary. More fortunate than the Fleming, he was the favourite, not only of the monarch, but also of the court and of the whole royal house and its allies. The Popes Gregory XIII. and Sixtus V., Cardinal Alexander Farnese, and the Dukes of Florence and Savoy, bestowed on him tokens of their admiration. "Seventeen royal personages," says Pacheco, "honoured him with their esteem, and would sometimes recreate and refresh themselves under his roof, with his wife and children." His table was never without some nobleman or worshipful gentleman for a guest; and the Infant Don Carlos, the Archbishops of Toledo and Seville, Cardinal Granvelle, and Don Juan of Austria, the hero of Lepanto, were amongst his familiar friends. The two large courtyards of his house were often thronged with the horses, litters, coaches, and chairs of the nobility and the ambassadors. To maintain this expensive hospitality, his pencil must have commanded a

Royal and noble friend.

noble revenue. At his death in 1590, according to Palomino, the seventy-fifth year of his age, he left a fortune of 55,000 ducats, part of which went to endow an hospital for orphans at Valladolid.

An anecdote related by Porreño,[1] the biographer of Philip II., shows how high the artist stood in the estimation of the court. Don Diego de Cordoba, chancing to see exposed for sale some wretched portraits of the King, in a fit of loyal indignation rushed into the royal presence and besought his Majesty to follow the example of Alexander the Great, and "grant to Alonso Sanchez, or some other famous painter," the exclusive right of depicting his gracious countenance. "Let the poor daubsters live," said the King, "so long as they misrepresent our faces, and not our behaviour." Lope de Vega, who, amongst the myriad subjects of his fluent pen, frequently sang the praises of painting and its professors, has given an honourable place in the ninth silva of his "Laurel de Apolo" to

"el Español Prothogenes famoso
El noble Alonso Sanchez, que envidioso
Dejará al mas antiguo y celebrado
De quien hoy ha quedado
Honrando su memoria
Eternos quadros de divina historia."[2]

---

[1] *Dichos y Hechos*, p. 329.
[2] *Obras Sueltas* de Fray Lope Felix de Vega Carpio, xix. tomes, 4to, Madrid, 1776, tom. i. p. 171.

> The noble, fam'd Prothogenes of Spain,
> Alonso Sanchez, from whose hand remain
> Pictures, the masters most renown'd of old
> With looks of envious wonder might behold,
> Eternal scenes of history divine,
> Wherein for aye his memory shall shine.

A dark handsome head, painted by Alonso Sanchez Coello, and said to be his own portrait, exists amongst the pictures of the academy of San Carlos at Valencia.

Portrait of Alonso Sanchez Coello.

Amongst the disciples of this Spanish Prothogenes was his daughter, Doña Isabel, born in 1564, in her childhood the playmate of the Infants and Infantas of Spain, and, in after life, equally distinguished as a painter and musician. She married Don Francisco de Herrera y Saavedra, Regidor of Madrid and knight of Santiago, by whom she had a son, Don Antonio, likewise a member of that noble order. She died, like her father, at Madrid, in 1612, and was buried in her husband's family chapel in the church of San Juan.

Isabella Sanchez Coello.

Sanchez Coello almost rivals Titian himself in the number of royal and noble personages whose favour he enjoyed and whose countenances he delineated. In 1582 he executed, for the hall of portraits at the Pardo, no less than ten pieces, amongst which were an Emperor, a Queen, and five Archdukes, Infantas, and royal Princes. He painted the King many times, both on foot and on horse-

Alonso Sanchez Coello's portraits.

CH. V.

Infant Don Carlos.

back, and in every variety of costume. But time, which so frequently avenges the victims and persecutes the favourites of fortune, has dealt very hardly with his works, most of which perished in the flames of the Pardo and of the Alcazar of Madrid. Of his many portraits of the Queen of Spain's famous ancestor, Philip II.,[1] her gallery does not possess one. Sufficient specimens, however, of his powers exist there to vindicate his fame. His portraits of the Infant Don Carlos[2] and his half-sister Isabel Clara Eugenia[3] are fine works of art, and no less valuable, from the impress of fidelity which they bear, as illustrations of history. In Carlos we find little to heighten the pathos of his story; and, indeed, the pencil of Coello, like the prose of the historian, furnishes a strong contrast to the touching poetry of Schiller. The unhappy prince appears in his seventeenth or eighteenth year; and with the pallid features of his father, he has also his cold grey eye and suspicious dissatisfied expression. Both the head and the dress—a cloth of gold doublet, short-furred mantle, barrette, and trunk hose—recall Titian's early portraits of Philip. The hands, of which one rests on the sword-hilt, the other on

---

[1] [One of Sanchez Coello's portraits of Philip II. is now at Keir. A wood-engraving is given in *Don John of Austria*, vol. i. p. 33.—ED.]
[2] *Catalogo* [1843], No. 152 [edition of 1889, No. 1032].
[3] Id. No. 154 [edition of 1889, No. 1033.]

his hip, are delicately shaped and finely painted.
The Infanta Isabel—afterwards that resolute Archduchess, whose linen, unchanged during the three
years' siege of Ostend, gave the name to the tawny
tint still known to French dyers and grooms as the
"couleur Isabelle"—seems about the same age as
her brother. As she was only two years old at the
time of his death, her portrait must have been
painted many years after its companion. Her countenance, both in features and expression, strongly
resembles her father's, who loved her above all his
other children, and spoke of her on his death-bed
as "the light and mirror of his eyes;" and her
swarthy complexion somewhat justifies the sarcasms
of Pierre Leroy, and the Huguenot wits, in the
"Satyre Ménippée." These hereditary peculiarities
are far too strong for beauty, even "in the April of
her prime;" her face, indeed, appears to better advantage when invested with the dignity of matronly
years on the canvas of her friend and counsellor,
Rubens,[1] or still later, when she had exchanged the
weeds of a widow for those of a Chanoinesse, and
sat for her portrait to Vandyck.[2] But though in
neither of these royal portraits was Sanchez Coello
fortunate in his subject, they, on that account perhaps, the more display his masterly skill. He has

CH. V.

Infanta Isabel Clara Eugenia.

---

[1] In the Musée, at Brussels.
[2] Louvre, No. 436 [*Notice des Tableaux*, édition 1889, No. 145].

supplied the place of beauty, as far as possible, by something little less winning and far more difficult to be caught and described—that air of refinement and repose which belongs to gentle blood and delicate nurture. To the graceful design and fine colouring of these pictures Titian himself could hardly have added anything, beyond a softer outline and somewhat more roundness of form. Amongst the master's other portraits in this royal collection, a picture [1] of the heroine of Ostend and her sister, deserves notice, and likewise that of Queen Isabel of the Peace,[2] to whose sweet face he has hardly done justice, but whose black dress is magnificent, and her jewellery, especially the knots of pearl at the opening of the robe, worthy the imitation of the most tasteful and sumptuous of queens. The student of history will also look with interest on the well-painted head [3] of a dark, handsome, bright-eyed man, wearing a small black cap and white plume, and the cross of Santiago on his breast; for it is the gay, ambitious, intriguing, banquet-giving,

---

[1] *Catalogo* [1843], No. 193 [edition of 1889, No. 1034].

[2] *Catalogo* [1843], No. 530. [In the new catalogue of 1889 this picture (No. 925) is no longer ascribed to Sanchez Coello, but is doubtfully attributed to his pupil and friend, Pantoja de la Cruz; and Don Pedro de Madrazo adds in a note, in his *Catalogo Descriptivo é Histórico*, 1872, "En tal caso, fué ejecutado por otro retrato anterior, quizá de Sanchez Coello, pues segun queda dicho en la noticia biográfica, de Pantoja, los retratos que éste hizo de personas Reales de la familia de Felipe II, fueron por lo general copias de cuadros anteriores" (p. 506).—ED.]

[3] Id. No. 206 [edition of 1889, No. 1039].

irresistible, but unfortunate, Antonio Perez, the Bolingbroke of Castile. In the Louvre there is a portrait,[1] attributed to Sanchez Coello, of Don Juan, the bold bastard of Austria, and the terror of the Turk.

In 1570 the Court portrait-painter was employed with Diego de Urbina to execute the paintings for the decoration of the triumphal arches under which Doña Anna of Austria passed into the capital of her hoary uncle and bridegroom. Notwithstanding his avocations in the palace, he found time to paint, between 1574 and 1577, for the parish church of Espinar, a village in the territory of Segovia, nine pictures for the high altar, with the gilding and adornment of which he was also entrusted. For these works, and for a curtain or architectural drop-scene, with which the altar was veiled during the last two weeks of Lent, he was paid 3,350 ducats. In 1580, he executed a large composition of the "Martyrdom of St. Sebastian" for the church of St. Jerome, at Madrid, where it was seen by Cumberland, who praises its "great majesty of design, bold relief, and strong masterly expression."[2] For the Escorial he painted, by the King's desire, in 1582,

---

[1] Louvre, Gal. Espagn. No. 69. [Sold in the Louis-Philippe Collection in 1853, and now at Keir. A wood-engraving of it is given in *Don John of Austria*, 2 vols. 8vo, London, 1883, vol. i. p. 3.—ED.]

[2] *Anecdotes*, vol. i. p. 89.

CH. V.

Portrait of St. Ignatius Loyola.

five altar-pictures, each containing a pair of saints, and likewise an excellent portrait of his friend, Father Sigüenza, the historian of the order of St. Jerome, which has been well engraved by Fernando Selma. In 1585 he painted a portrait of Ignatius Loyola, from waxen casts taken from the dead body twenty-nine years before, and from the recollections of Father Ribadeneyra, the hagiologist, which was reckoned the best representation ever made of the stern and melancholy countenance of the great first Jesuit. The fate of this interesting picture is not known; but it may have been the original of that striking portrait which hangs in the church of San Miguel at Seville. In the royal gallery of Madrid there is one fair specimen of Sanchez Coello's powers of treating sacred subjects in his "Marriage of St. Catherine."[1] The composition and colouring are good; and although the Divine Babe is more like a small man than a child, and his mystical bride unhappily resembles an Austrian Infanta, these defects are atoned for by the exceeding grace and beauty of Mary and her attendant angels. The picture is painted on cork, and is signed "ALONSVS SANTIVS F."

Scholars.

Sanchez Coello had a number of scholars, of whom Juan Pantoja de la Cruz[2] (1551-1609) was the

---

[1] *Catalogo*, No. 501 [edition of 1889, No. 1041.]   [2] Infra, p. 316.

most famous. Cristobal Lopez became painter to King John III., of Portugal, from whom he received the order of Aviz; and, after having executed many portraits of that prince and his family, and some good pictures for the chapel-royal at Belem, died at Lisbon in 1594.[1] Juan de Urbina is said to have painted with reputation at the Escorial; none of his works, however, has been preserved to our times, and his name lives only in books and in the verse of Lope de Vega, who calls him "Generoso Urbina," and laments his death as a heavy loss to his royal patron—

CH. V.
Cristobal Lopez.

Juan de Urbina.

"Al sol del mundo, al inmortal Felipe."[2]

Another artist of the same school was Giovanni Narduck, or perhaps Narducci, an Italian, whose history is somewhat curious. Born about 1526, in the Neapolitan county of Molica, he acquired some knowledge of painting at Naples; whence, being of a devout temper, he made a pilgrimage to the various shrines of Italy, and afterwards to Santiago of Compostella. In the course of his Spanish travels he passed some time with a society of hermits who dwelt amongst the mountains of

Giovanni Narduck, or Fray Juan de la Miseria.

---

[1] Palomino (tom. iii. p. 363) gives 1570 as the date of his death, but I follow the Portuguese writer, Machado, who says of Lopez (*Vidas, dos Pintores*, p. 67), "pintou quadros de historia com maneira boa, e larga."

[2] *Laurel de Apolo*, Silva ix.

Cordoba, and with one of whom, a noble Italian named Ambrosio Mariano, he formed a close friendship. Mariano, a retired doctor of laws, being sent to Madrid on some affairs of the fraternity, was accompanied thither by Narduck, who, while the business was pending, betook himself once more to the pencil, and entered the school of Sanchez Coello. Here his piety recommended him to the esteem of the devout Infanta Juana, sister of Philip II., and other religious ladies; and Doña Leonor de Mascareñas, governess to Don Carlos, and a Dorcas amongst courtly dames, employed him to paint certain devotional pictures, which he executed to her entire satisfaction. At her house he became known to Santa Teresa de Jesus, who persuaded him and his friend Mariano to assume, in 1560, the Carmelite robe in one of her reformed convents at Pastrana, where Narduck exchanged his secular name for the humble title of Fray Juan de la Miseria, and left as a specimen of his artistic powers an "Ecce-homo." Removing some time after to a cloister at Madrid, he there closed a long life of devotion in October 1616. His body was embalmed, and was kept in the sacristy of the chapel of San Bruno, beneath a copious and eulogistic epitaph. It is doubtful whether any of his works still exist. Of Santa Teresa he made two portraits, one for Doña Leonor; the other, says Pacheco, belonged to the Carmelite nuns of Seville; he likewise pourtrayed S. Luis Beltran, and the holy Friar Nicolas Factor, whose name we shall meet with again amongst the artists of Valencia.

Gaspar Becerra, painter, sculptor, and architect, was son of Antonio Becerra and Leonor Padilla, and was born in 1520, at Baeza, in the kingdom of Jaen, revered by Spanish martyrologists as the birthplace of St. Ursula and her eleven thousand virgins. He seems to have gone early to Italy, and to have passed many of his best years in study at Rome, where he may have been a scholar of Michael Angelo. Cean Bermudez had seen a pencil-sketch by him of part of the "Last Judgment." Amongst the artists who assisted Daniel de Volterra in the embellishment of the Rovere chapel in the church of the Trinità de' Monti, Vasari records that "Bizzera the Spaniard"[1] executed a painting of the "Nativity of the Virgin," and that Pellegrino Tibaldi, afterwards famous at the Escorial, was one of his fellow-labourers. He likewise worked under the eye of Vasari himself, who enumerates him and his countryman Rubiales amongst "his young men" who aided him in the historical and

---

[1] Vasari, tom. iii. p. 102. Cean Bermudez has fallen into a slight error in relating that Becerra's work was placed beside one of Daniel de Volterra. Its companion, says Vasari, was "Christ presented to Simeon," painted by Gio. Paolo Rosetti of Volterra.

VOL. I.   T

CH. V.

Dr. Juan de Valverde, and his book, illustrated by Gaspar Becerra.

allegorical frescoes with which he adorned the hall of the Cancelleria in the palace of Cardinal Farnese. Perhaps the young Spaniards may have accompanied their chief to the reunions of artists and men of letters which were held at the supper-table of the Cardinal, where a casual remark of "Monsignor Giovio" first suggested to Vasari's mind the idea of writing his delightful "Lives of the Painters."[1] For Dr. Juan de Valverde's work on anatomy, published in 1554, Becerra designed the plates,[2] and he likewise executed about the same time two statues as anatomical studies, of which casts were used as models in the studios. In 1556 he married

---

[1] Vasari, tom. iii. p. 391.

[2] Llaguno (*Arquitecto*, tom. iii. p. 107) doubts this fact, which, he says, is not confirmed by any notice of Becerra in Valverde's book; Cean Bermudez, however, remarks, in his note on the passage, that it may be true for all that. Llaguno gives 1556 as the date of the publication of the *Anatomy*, which Brunet—always deficient in Spanish bibliography —does not mention in the last edition of his bulky *Manuel de Libraire*. The title of the book is *Historia de la composicion del cuerpo humano, escrita por Juan de Valverde de Hamusco*; Impressa por Antonio Salamanca y Antonio Lafrerii; fol., Roma, 1556. A handsome engraved title and 11 preliminary leaves, and 106 leaves paged on one side, besides the anatomical plates and their explanations. I do not find any signature of any kind in any of the plates; but Barbosa Machado, *Bibliotheca Lusitana* (tom. ii. p. 780-1), like Llaguno, attributes them to Becerra. Valverde was physician to Card. Juan de Toledo, Archbishop of Santiago, to whom his work is dedicated, and enjoyed great practice at Rome. An Italian translation of his book, executed by himself, was published at Venice, in fol., 1586, and a Latin one, by Michele Colombo, at the same place, fol., 1589, a previous Latin version, with additions, having issued from the Plantine press, fol., Antwerp, 1579. Both the Venetian editions have the author's portrait, supported by skeletons and adorned with visceral festoons, engraved by Nicolas Beatrizet; Bartsch, tom. xv. p. 242.

Doña Paula Velazquez, daughter of a Spaniard of Tordesillas, and soon afterwards returned to Spain.

He remained for some time at Zaragoza, where he lived with the younger Morlanes, the sculptor, to whom he presented some of his drawings, and a small bas-relief in alabaster of "The Resurrection of Our Lord," which may still be seen over a tomb in the old Cathedral of the "Seu." It was not long before his abilities became known to Philip II., who took him into his service, in 1562, as sculptor, with a yearly salary of 200 ducats, and in August 1563, named him one of his painters-in-ordinary, when his salary was raised to 600 ducats. In the Alcazar of Madrid he painted several corridors and chambers; and, in conjunction with Castello the Bergamese, the King's cabinet in the southern tower, and two adjoining passages—of which the lower parts, within the reach of hands, had greatly suffered, when Palomino[1] saw them, "from careless sweepers and pranksome pages," and which finally perished in the flames of the palace. Of the chambers which he painted at the Pardo, one survived the fire there, and its frescoes, representing the story of Perseus and Andromeda, were praised by Cean Bermudez for their good drawing, spirited attitudes, and noble expression.

---

[1] Palomino, tom. iii. p. 365.

When the artist was making his designs for the Pardo, the King, coming to observe his progress, and finding only a single figure—a Mercury—finished, exclaimed disappointedly, "And is this all you have done!"—"a remark," says Palomino, "which much disconcerted the draughtsman, and proves that kings do not love delay, even when conducing to greater perfection."[1]

Religious works.

Becerra was employed by the Infanta Juana, Princess-Dowager of Brazil, to design and execute the high altar for the church of the convent of barefooted nuns which she founded at Madrid in 1559. It is a chaste structure of the Doric, Ionic, and Corinthian orders of architecture, adorned with painted sculptures of the Virgin and angels, and of the Crucifixion and Resurrection of Our Lord, of which the Crucifixion is the best. He also painted on slabs of marble, for this and other altars, several pictures which are still to be seen in the church. "His most heroical work of sculpture and the crown of his studies," says Palomino,[2] was the image of Our Lady, carved for the Queen Isabella of the Peace. This princess bore, it seems, a peculiar affection for the religious order of St. Francis de Paula, to which belonged her confessor, Fray Diego de Valbuena, whom she sent soon after her nuptials

---

[1] Palomino, tom. iii. p. 365.   [2] Id.

with a donative to the friars of the Holy Sepulchre at Jerusalem;[1] and upon that monk's representation that his convent was in need of a statue of the Virgin, she ordered her master of the horse, Don Fadrique de Portugal, to cause one to be executed by the best sculptor in Spain. Becerra being chosen, was instructed to take for his model a picture in the Queen's oratory; and the brotherhood of Fray Diego offered up solemn prayers for a happy conclusion of his labours. Being himself very devoutly inclined towards St. Francis, of whose holy austerities he had heard in the misogynist's native Calabria, he addressed himself to the work with great alacrity and earnestness; but succeeded so ill, that, at the end of a year, he produced an image which did not satisfy himself, and which was at once rejected by the Queen. His next attempt was better, for it pleased not only Don Fadrique and the friars, but also his artist-friends, who pronounced it worthy of the disciple of Michael Angelo. The Queen, however, decided otherwise, and threatened to employ another hand if he should fail a third time. The Franciscans thereupon betook themselves to redoubled masses and fasting, and the poor sculptor returned to his studio and racked his memory and imagination for ideas of angelic grace and divine

Carves for the Queen the figure of Nra. Señora de la Soledad.

---

[1] Gonçalez Davila, *Theatro de las Grandezas de la Villa de Madrid*, folio, Madrid, 1623, p. 250.

beauty. Sitting one winter's night over his drawings, and fatigued with anxious thought, he fell into a slumber, from which he was aroused by an unknown voice saying to him, "Awake and rise, and out of that log of wood blazing on the hearth shape the thought within thee, and thou shalt obtain the desired image." He immediately bestirred himself, plucked the indicated brand from the burning, and having quenched it, fell to work at dawn; and the auspicious block proving an excellent piece of timber, soon grew beneath his chisel into "a miracle of art, and became," says Palomino, "the portentous image of Our Lady of Solitude, to this day had in reverence, in which are expressed beauty, grief, love, tenderness, constancy, and resignation, and which, above all, is the refuge of our sorrows, the succour in our ills, the solace of our toil, and the dispenser of heavenly mercies." When the carving was brought to the Queen in 1565, she at last acknowledged that she had been well served, and Becerra was accordingly well paid. The Virgin was dressed by her Majesty in a suit of those doleful weeds introduced by poor Queen Juana to express her mighty woe at the death of her handsome and worthless lord, and worn by all Castilian widows of rank until Queen Anna Mariana of Neuburg, loath to disfigure herself for the sake of the defunct Charles II., had the boldness to set a more becoming fashion. Thus dismally draped, Our Lady of Solitude presided in her peculiar chapel in the convent of the Minim Fathers at Madrid,[1] and became renowned for her miraculous powers, "which brought her masters much gain." Her history and achievements were printed by Fray Antonio de Ares in 1640,[2] and she remained, albeit darkened in complexion by time,[3] a star of Castilian devotion till the War of Independence. In that stormy time it is possible that Becerra's celebrated billet—so exactly realising the Hebrew prophet's description[4] of the tree-stock which "shall be for a man to burn: for he will take thereof, and warm himself; . . . and the residue thereof he maketh a god, even his graven image; he falleth down unto it, . . ."—after two cen-

---

[1] Cumberland (vol. ii. p. 29) erroneously sets up this famous image at Valladolid.

[2] *Historia de la Imagen de Nuestra Señora de la Soledad*, 4to, Madrid, 1640. Besides this there is a book by Tomas de Oña, *El Fénix de los Ingenios en la Translacion de la Virgen de la Soledad á su Capilla*, 4to, Madrid, 1664, which contains her history; and there is also the *Relacion Historial del origen de Nuestra Señora de la Soledad, de la Victoria*, 4to, Madrid, 1719. A notice of Becerra's family chapel in the convent of Victoria at Madrid will be found in Fr. Lucas de Montoya, *Coronica General de la Orden de los Minimos de San Francisco de Paula*, fol., Madrid, 1619, lib. iii. p. 98. There is a print of "Nuestra Señora de la Soledad de la Victoria de Madrid," by Pedro de Villafranca, Matriti, 1657, of which a poor impression is in Dn. B. J. Gallardo's copy of Oña's work, which was published seven years later. A very full account of the Capilla de N. S. de la Soledad, her relics, processions, and Cofradia, will be found in Lucas de Montoya, *Coronica General*, lib. iii. p. 98. See also G. Quintana, *Hist. de Madrid*, fol., Madrid, 1629, p. 158.

[3] Ponz, tom. v. p. 292.

[4] Isaiah, chap. xliv. v. 15-17.

turies and a half of worship, may have fulfilled its original destiny beneath the flesh-pot of some godless dragoon of Murat.

Works in various cities. Granada.

The time of Becerra was not wholly engrossed in the service of royalty. For the Cathedral of Granada he carved a good crucifix of life size, and for the church of St. Jerome in the same city a celebrated "Entombment of Our Lord" and a pretty little "Infant Saviour." Valladolid, Salamanca, Bribiesca, and Rioseco possessed specimens of both his painting and statuary in their churches and convents; in the church of St. Jerome, at Zamora, there was a celebrated skeleton carved by him, wrapped in a winding sheet, and grasping a scythe; and at Burgos the cathedral still retains his exquisite little figure of St. Sebastian, which was reckoned so good that it was twice stolen from its chapel, and on one of these occasions had reached Cadiz before it could be recovered.[1] The convent of Santa Cruz, at Segovia, possessed a picture by him on panel, representing a young maiden reclining on the ground with a pot of ointment by her side, that bespoke her a Magdalene. Although one of those fair creatures whose allurements tended rather to sin than to penitence, she was highly admired by Bosarte, who speaks with rapture of the grace of her head, the

Valladolid, &c.

Burgos.

Segovia.

---

[1] Cook's *Sketches*, vol. ii. p. 143.

beauty of her arms and feet, and the fine cast of her drapery.[1] In 1569 he completed the mighty high altar of the Cathedral of Astorga, which, though out of keeping with that Gothic pile, is a grand and imposing work, and is reckoned his masterpiece of architectural design and sculptural decoration. It consists of three lofty storeys of the Doric, Corinthian, and Composite orders, covered with elaborate ornament, and with bas-reliefs illustrating the lives of the Holy Virgin and Our Blessed Lord, and statues of saints and saintly virtues, of which some are not unworthy of Michael Angelo. This noble retablo has been cruelly repainted, and had suffered much from the washings and scrapings of a quack-restorer even in the days of Ponz, who nevertheless remarks that, as Velazquez can be fully appreciated only at Madrid, and Murillo at Seville, so Becerra can be judged of fairly only in the Cathedral of Astorga.[2] The Chapter paid for this work in all 30,000 ducats, of which about 11,000 fell to the share of Becerra. Returning to Madrid, he died in 1570, at the premature age of fifty, in the full vigour of his genius and in the sunshine of his fortune. From his will[3] it appears that his wife, Paula Velazquez, bore him

---

[1] Bosarte, *Viaje*, p. 77.
[2] Ponz, tom. xi. p. 263-4. See also *Handbook* [1845], p. 592 [3rd edition, 1855, p. 536].
[3] Printed by Cean Bermudez, *Arquitectos*, tom. ii. p. 261-3.

no children, or that none survived him; to that lady he bequeathed 1,100 ducats, all his clothes and jewels, and half of his funds accumulated since their marriage; to his brother, Juan Becerra, apparently a sculptor and his assistant, he gave 200 ducats and directions to complete certain of his works; and his mother, Leonor Padilla, was left residuary legatee. He further ordered that "his body, habited in the robes of St. Francis de Paula, should be interred in the chapel which he had purchased in the church of the convent of Victory," where it was accordingly laid in the keeping of his own "Lady of Solitude."[1]

Merits as a painter.

Of Becerra's paintings few good specimens seem to have been preserved. He executed no pictures for the Escorial, nor does his name appear in the Catalogue of the Queen of Spain's gallery; and his works in the church of the Royal Barefooted Nuns at Madrid were commonplace. The bust of a "Sibyl holding tablets in her left hand," said to be painted by him, and once in the collection of Mr. Coesvelt, is now in the palace of the Hermitage at St. Petersburg;[2] and amongst the Standish drawings in the Louvre there are four, executed with the pen, which are attributed to him.[3] Cean Bermudez says that he

---

[1] *Arquitectos,* tom. ii. p. 111.
[2] *Livret de la Galerie Impériale de l'Ermitage de St. Petersbourg.* Ibid. 1838, 8vo, Salle XLI. No. 107, p. 428. [*Catalogue* 1887, No. 403.]
[3] *Catalogue de la Collection Standish,* 1842, *Dessins,* Nos. 299–301. [This collection was sold in 1853 in the Louis-Philippe sale.]

followed the excellent Italian method of painting no work without cartoons of the full size required; and that his sketches, usually made with black or red chalk, and highly finished, were of great rarity and value. Pacheco considered that, as a sculptor, Becerra eclipsed the fame of Berruguete,[1] to whom Cean Bermudez also esteems him superior in spirit and grandeur of style.

Of his scholars, Miguel Barroso, born at Consuegra in 1538, became most distinguished in painting. His earliest independent work of which any notice has been preserved, was a picture executed for the Hospital of St. John Baptist at Toledo in 1585. In 1589 he was named one of the King's painters, with an annual salary of 100 ducats, and painted some frescoes in the chief cloister of the Escorial, of which that representing the "Coming of the Holy Ghost" was considered the best. His drawing was correct, but his invention feeble; he was a man of learning and general accomplishments, understood something of music and architecture, and was a friend of Father Sigüenza. He did not long survive his promotion to the King's service, but died the year after, 1590, at the Escorial. Bartolomé del Rio Bernuis was a promising young disciple in the same school at the time of Becerra's death. He

---

[1] Pacheco, p. 242.

practised his art chiefly at Toledo, where he held during the last twenty years of his life, from 1607 to 1627, the post of painter to the Chapter. Francisco Lopez and Gerónimo Vazquez were also scholars of Becerra, and painted with some credit during this reign, the first at Madrid, the second at Valladolid. Miguel Ribas, Miguel Martinez, and Juan Ruiz de Castañeda were sculptors formed under Becerra's eye, who aided him in his works, and attained some distinction after his death.

Juan Fernandez Navarrete was an artist whose genius was no less remarkable than his infirmities, and whose name—El Mudo, the dumb painter—is as familiar to Europe as his works are unknown. Born in 1526, at Logroño, of respectable—Palomino says noble[1]—parents, he was attacked in his third year by an acute disorder, which deprived him of the sense of hearing, and consequently of the faculty of speech. Cut off from the usual channels of converse, and living a century before his countryman, Bonet,[2] had invented the art of speaking on the fingers, he was compelled to express his wants

---

[1] Palomino, tom. iii. p. 370.

[2] Juan Pablo Bonet, Secretary to the Constable of Castile, one of the earliest, if not the first writer on the subject. His *Reduction de las letras y Arte para enseñar a ablar los Mudos*, 4to, Madrid, 1620, pp. 308, with 12 leaves of licenses, encomiastic verses, &c., and 2 leaves of index, an elegantly engraved title by Diego de Astor, 8 plates of the Abecedario Demonstrativo, and a folding sheet of Greek contractions, is a rare and very curious volume.

and his thoughts by rough sketches in chalk or charcoal—a practice in which he early displayed great readiness of hand,—and learned to draw as other children learn to speak. Taking advantage of this bent of his inclination, his father placed him in a neighbouring monastery of Jeronymites at Estrella, under the care of Fray Vicente de Santo Domingo, one of the fraternity, who had acquired some knowledge of painting at Toledo, and who left behind him a few pictures at Estrella, and in the convent of Santa Catalina, at Talavera de la Reyna, where he died. This worthy monk, after teaching him all that he himself knew, advised his parents to send him for further improvement to Italy, whither El Mudo, as he was called, accordingly went while still a stripling. It is probable that he remained there several years; he visited Florence, Rome, Naples, and Milan, and is said to have studied for a considerable time in the school of Titian at Venice. It was perhaps at Rome or Milan that he was known to Pellegrino Tibaldi, who used to remark, when admiring, many years afterwards, El Mudo's works at the Escorial, that in Italy he painted nothing worthy of much notice. He had acquired, however, sufficient reputation to attract the notice of Don Luis Manrique, Grand Almoner to the King of Spain, through whose recommendation he was called to Madrid, and on the 6th of March, 1568, appointed painter to his Majesty, with a yearly allowance of 200 ducats, besides the price of his works. As a specimen of his abilities, he brought with him a small picture on the subject of "Our Lord's Baptism,"—"admirably painted," says Cean Bermudez, "though in a style different from that which he afterwards followed,"—which greatly pleased the King, and became in due time an ornament of the Prior's cell in the Escorial.

He was first employed there to paint on the folding doors of an altar some figures of prophets, in black and white, and to make a copy of a large and excellent picture of the "Crucifixion," which was highly approved by the King, who ordered it to be placed in the royal chapel, in the wood of Segovia. During the first three years of his engagement, his health being feeble, he was permitted to reside at Logroño. There he found time to paint for his early friends, the monks of Estrella, four noble pictures, of one of which, representing St. Michael, Cean Bermudez remarks that it was the finest figure of that Archangel in Castile. He returned in 1571 to the Escorial, bringing with him four pictures—"The Assumption of the Virgin," "The Martyrdom of St. James the Great," "St. Philip," and a "Repenting St. Jerome." Being dissatisfied with the "Assumption," in which he thought the Blessed Mary was lost amongst the crowd of angels, he wished to cancel it, but this the King would not permit. The heads of the Virgin, and one of the apostles standing below in the foreground, were portraits of the painter's parents, his mother being remarkable for her beauty. In the "Martyrdom" it is said that he revenged himself for some affront received from Santoyo, the royal secretary, by bestowing the face of that minister on one of the tormentors of the apostle; and that, notwithstanding Santoyo's complaints, Philip would not suffer the picture to be altered, excusing himself on the ground of its great excellence.[1] According to another account, however, the original of the executioner was merely a young official of Logroño. For these pictures El Mudo was paid 500 ducats, and they were placed in the sacristy of the Escorial. He passed the next five years at Madrid, the buildings of the Escorial not being in sufficient order to receive artists. His pencil seems to have been less rapid than those of some of his contemporaries, or his labours must have been interrupted by ill health; for in 1575 he had completed only four new works,—the "Nativity of Our Lord," "Christ scourged at the Column," the "Holy Family," and "St. John writing the

---

[1] Palomino, tom. iii. p. 371.

Apocalypse," for which he received 800 ducats. Of these works, the last perished by fire, with the "St. Philip" and "Assumption" above mentioned. The "Nativity" was remarkable for the skill with which El Mudo had introduced three different lights, proceeding from the body of the Divine Infant—after the fashion first set by Correggio in his famous "Notte," now at Dresden—the glory above, and a candle held by St. Joseph. The adoring shepherds also were so finely treated that Tibaldi never looked at the picture without exclaiming "O! gli belli pastori!" In the "Holy Family" the heads were noble and expressive, and a cat and dog in the foreground stood spitting and snarling over a bone with laughable truth and spirit. "The Scourging of Christ" was admirable for the skilful foreshortening of Our Lord's figure, of which a front view was given.

Picture of "Abraham" in the "Recibimiento."

In 1576 El Mudo painted one of his most celebrated works, "Abraham receiving the three Angels," which was hung over an altar in the entrance-hall of the convent, where strangers were received by the fathers. The figures were of life size; beneath a leafy tree the Patriarch bowed himself to the ground, entreating the travellers to repose themselves from the noontide heat, and taste of his cheer; the three angels, symbolising the persons of the most Holy Trinity, and all clad in the same fashion, smiled benignly, with countenances of heavenly beauty, and accepted his proffered hospitality; and in the background, half concealed by the tent-door, was seen the laughing countenance of ancient Sarah. "This picture, so appropriate to the place it fills," says Fray Andres Ximenes, though the first of the master's works that usually meets the eye, might for its excellence be viewed the last, and is well worth coming many a league to see."[1] El Mudo was paid 500 ducats for it. In August of the same year he undertook to paint thirty-two large pictures for the side altars of the church. The contract between him and the Prior, Julian de Tricio, curious for its minuteness, is printed at full length by Cean Bermudez. The price agreed on was 200 ducats for each painting, each to be executed on a single piece of canvas, and the whole were to be finished in four years. It was stipulated that if any saint were introduced more than once in the series, he should in all cases appear with the same features and drapery; and that whenever an authentic portrait was to be had, it was to be scrupulously copied. All accessories that had no reference to devotion were excluded, and dogs and cats were expressly forbidden, probably in allusion to the excellent, but

---

[1] Ximenes, *Descripcion del Escorial*, p. 44.

indecorous, episode in the "Holy Family." Of these pictures the artist unhappily lived to finish only eight.

Sickness and death.

Towards the close of 1578 his health began to decline, and he vainly sought for relief in excursions to Segovia and some of the neighbouring villages. In February 1579 he removed to Toledo, where he died on the 28th of March, in the fifty-third year of his age. Shortly before his death, he confessed himself three times to the curate of the parish of San Vicente, by means of signs which that churchman declared were as intelligible as speech. Calling for pen and paper, he then disposed of his modest gains in a testament, which is curious, and short enough to be given entire:—

Testament.

"Jesus, Nuestra Señora.
Albacea, Nicolas de Vergara.
Anima, Pobres, 200 ducados.
Hermano frayle, 200 ducados : Pobres.
Hija monja, 600 ducados.
Estrella, Hermanos, 500 ducados : Misa.
María Fernandez, 100 ducados.
Padre, Misa, 200 ducados.
Mozo, 40 ducados.   JUAN FERNANDEZ."

Then follows an explanation of this concise will, supplied by the witnesses. The first and second clauses imply that he died in the Catholic faith, leaving Vergara for his executor; the third provides for the expenses of his burial, and for alms on the occasion; the fourth gives the sum named to his brother Fray Bautista, for his life, and afterwards to the poor of an hospital at Logroño; the fifth allots a dowry to his natural daughter, a child of four years old, at Segovia, and directs that she is to take the veil, "and that as early as possible," as the testator contrived to say to the curate, Luis Hurtado, "there being no hope of a girl of her condition getting married with so slender a portion;" the sixth remembers his old friends the Jeronymites at Estrella, on condition of their remembering him in their masses, and giving a resting-place to his bones within their walls; the seventh alludes to a married cousin living at Logroño; the eighth establishes masses for the souls of his parents in the family chapel at Logroño; and the ninth is a bequest to one Adam Mimoso, who had been his serving-man for a year and a half. He was buried at Toledo, in the church of San Juan de los Reyes; and although Cean Bermudez cites an agreement entered into between Doña Catalina Ximenes and Diego Fernandez, mother and brother of El Mudo, and the prior and monks of Estrella — that his remains should be brought thither at the cost of the former, received at the door of the court, with the cross, by the latter, and interred in the church, at the foot of the steps leading to the high altar, and that on the payment to the convent of 300 ducats, the office of the dead should be sung for his soul every St. John Baptist's day—it does not appear that the removal of his bones ever took place.

"El Mudo," says Cean Bermudez, "was a man of uncommon talent, and in no ordinary degree versed in sacred and profane history and in mythology. He read and wrote, played at cards, and expressed his meaning by signs with singular clearness, to the admiration of all who conversed with him." When Titian's celebrated picture of the "Last Supper" arrived at the Escorial, it was found to be too large for its destined place in the refectory. The King having ordered it to be cut, El Mudo manifested a lively indignation, and by means of signs offered, at the risk of his head, in six months to finish an exact copy of it of the required size; at the same time making the sign of a cross on his breast, to signify that he expected an order of knighthood as the reward of doing in six months what had cost Titian the labour of seven years. Philip was, however, too impatient to wait for a copy, and the canvas of Titian, to the great grief of his scholar, was forthwith submitted to most sacrilegious shears. Indeed, it was not until Navarrete had gone to the tomb that the King fully understood his worth. When, however, his foreign Zuccaros, engaged at immense salaries, began to cover the walls of the Escorial with some very bad paintings, he became sensible that a far finer hand lay cold at Toledo, and frequently declared that amongst all his Italian artists there was none that could equal his dumb Spaniard.

El Mudo imitated with success many of the chief beauties of his Venetian master, and for his splendid colouring alone well deserved his title of "the Spanish Titian." His works have a freedom and boldness of design that belonged to none of his contemporaries of Castile. It has been well remarked that he "spoke by his pencil with the bravura of Rubens, without his coarseness."[1] Amongst the unfinished pictures found in his studio at his death, were several portraits, of which those of the Duke of Medina Celi and Giovanni Andrea Doria were the most interesting. A beautiful head of a woman, at Bowood, painted by El Mudo—and said to be that of Doña Maria Pacheco, wife of Padilla, the ill-fated leader of the malcontents of Toledo in 1522,—is a gem, even in the collection of Lord Lansdowne; brown Castile never produced a lovelier face or a more delicately painted head; but as a portrait it must be either ideal or a copy, since the brave lady died two years before the painter's birth. His own portrait, painted in a striking forcible style by himself, formed part of the

---

[1] *Handbook* [1845], p. 813 [3rd edition, 1855, p. 755].

Castilian plunder of Marshal Soult,[1] who likewise carried off from the Escorial his picture of Abraham and the Angels.[2] Of his few pictures on this side the Pyrenees, the "Holy Family," in the private gallery of the King of Holland,[3] also deserves notice; the Virgin and Babe are seated near a column, and St. Joseph appears behind; and the whole composition is full of grace and Venetian richness of colour. The saints and apostles who figure in eight of the side altars of the Escorial, his last works, are excellent examples of his style. Their grand and simple forms and noble heads, and their draperies falling in broad masses of rich warm colour, are worthy of the majestic temple which they adorn. Lope de Vega, in the Laurel de Apolo, laments the death of El Mudo, whom he lauds as the Spanish artist best able to cope with Italian rivals. Of his works he says,—

"Ningun rostro pintó que fuese mudo"—

"No countenance he painted that was dumb."

---

[1] [No. 4 of the sale catalogue of the Soult collection. Now in the author's collection at Keir. It was exhibited at the Art Treasures Exhibition in Manchester in 1857, No. 216.] In the *Revue de Paris*, tom. xxiii. p. 215, M. Thoré thus describes this portrait of El Mudo: "Cette figure a une ire effrayante et comme une puissance magnétique; il semble que le muet cherche à parler; c'est une nature primitive et rude qu'on ne peut regarder longtemps en face, et qui, sans exaggeration, vous force à baisser les yeux."

[2] Id. p. 214. See supra, p. 304.

[3] [Sold in 1850.—Ed.]

a thought which he also expanded into this epigram:—

"No quiso el cielo que hablase,
Porque con mi entendimiento
Diese mayor sentimiento
Á las cosas que pintase
Y tanta vida les dí
Con el pincel singular
Que como no pude hablar
Hice que hablasen por mí."

Speech heaven denied to him whose dumbness threw
A deeper sense and charm o'er all he drew;
And, mute himself, his breathing pencil lent
Canvas a voice, than mine more eloquent.

Luis de Carbajal was born at Toledo in 1534, and was uterine brother of Juan Bautista Monegro, a sculptor of some repute. He studied painting in the school of Juan de Villoldo, whom he may have accompanied as a boy to Madrid, when that master was employed in the Bishop of Plasencia's chapel in the church of S. Andres.[1] At least he early removed to the capital, and there acquired some eminence in his art and the post of painter to the King, in which capacity the first picture he is recorded to have executed was a "Magdalene," finished in 1570, for the cloister of the Infirmary at the Escorial. On the death of El Mudo, Carbajal and Sanchez Coello were appointed to complete the

[1] Supra, chap. iii. p. 169.

series of pictures for the side altars of the church, of which seven were accordingly painted by Carbajal, who has imitated, with some success, the grand manner of the dumb master. He painted several other easel pictures for the monastery, and likewise some frescoes in the great cloister, where so many famous Italians came to display their artistic powers. He afterwards passed some time at Toledo, where he painted several pictures with Blas del Prado, for the church of the Minim Fathers; and where he also left in the winter chapter-room of the Cathedral the portrait of Archbishop Don Bartolomé Carranza de Miranda. This portrait was probably executed before the prelate's incarceration in 1559, or at least before his removal to Rome in 1566. The sad and anxious face deserves notice as the likeness of a man whose cause divided the Council of Trent, agitated the whole Spanish realm, and rang through Catholic Europe; who remarkably exemplified in his own person the contradictions of the human heart and the vicissitudes of human fortune; who, when a simple professor at Valladolid, sold his library to feed the poor, and was reckoned a model of charity and meekness, and yet, as a royal confessor, sitting at the ear of Mary Tudor, sent many a martyr to the flames at Smithfield; who, becoming Primate of Spain, spent his last eighteen years in the prisons of the Inquisition, on a charge, amongst others, of having preached before the court of England the heresy of Philip Melancthon; and who was finally buried in a Roman convent, by the order of the Pontiff who had condemned him, beneath an epitaph which declared him to have been a man "illustrious in lineage, life, eloquence, alms-deeds, and doctrine."[1] The date of Carbajal's death is unknown, but he must have lived to a good old age, for we find him, so late in the next reign as 1613, at work with other artists on certain ceilings at the Pardo.

Blas del Prado was likewise a Toledan, and one of the ablest artists who ever, to use the stately words of Don Juan de Butron,[2] "imbibed genius from the gilded waters of the Tagus." The date of his birth is very uncertain; and Palomino and Cean Bermudez differ in their statements by nearly fifty years, for the former asserts that he was born in 1497 and died in 1557, whilst the latter proves, from documents in the Cathedral archives at Toledo, that he was alive near the close of the century. He was probably born about 1540; the chapter

---

[1] The life of this unfortunate archbishop was written by Pedro Salazar de Miranda. An able sketch of it, with an abstract of his celebrated cause (which filled twenty-four folio volumes, each containing from 1000 to 1200 leaves, of the records of the Inquisition), may be found in Llorente, *Inquisicion de España*, tom. vi. p. 65 to p. 216. His portrait, engraved by Barcelon, may be found amongst the *Retratos de los Españoles Ilustres*, folio, Madrid, 1791, a work printed in the royal press, and of some value, which would have been greatly enhanced had the names of the painters been appended to the portraits.

[2] *Discursos Apologéticos*, p. 122.

employed him in 1586, and named him its second painter in 1591. His principal works were the pictures that he painted in 1591, with Carbajal, for the Minims at Toledo; a large altar-piece, representing St. Blas and other personages, for the chapel of that saint in the Cathedral, besides some smaller pictures; a "Holy Family" for the sumptuous Jeronymite house at Guadalupe; and some paintings in the churches and convents at Madrid, amongst which was a "Descent from the Cross" in the church of S. Pedro, which has been praised by Cumberland.[1]

In 1593, the Emperor of Morocco applied to Philip II. for the loan of a painter, as Pedro the Cruel some ages before had borrowed the plasterers of the Sultan of Granada.[2] The Catholic King returned answer that they had in Spain two sorts of painters—the ordinary and the excellent,—and desired to know which his infidel brother preferred. "Kings should always have the best," replied the haughty Moor; and the Spaniard accordingly sent Blas del Prado to Fez.[3] There he painted various works for the palace, and a portrait of the African monarch's daughter, to the great satisfaction of her father, who, though an indifferent Mussulman, was a generous prince, for, having kept the artist in his

---

[1] *Anecdotes*, i. p. 126.   [2] Supra, chap. ii., p. 85.
[3] Lope de Vega; *Memorial Informativo* appended to Carducho's *Diálogos*, p. 165.

service for several years, he finally sent him away with many rich gifts. Returning to Castile with considerable wealth, Blas del Prado indulged himself in a traveller's whim of wearing the Moorish dress, and eating in the Oriental fashion, reclining amongst cushions. Pacheco, who may have known him either at Toledo or when he passed through Seville on his way to Barbary, relates that he painted fruit-pieces with great truth and taste. He died probably about 1600. The Academy of S. Ferdinand at Madrid possesses a fine work by him, of which the subject is the "Virgin and Infant Saviour" seated amongst clouds, which seem to hang round the upper part of a brick tower, whilst a woman in nun's weeds and a man in a black dress are kneeling in prayer beneath. The features of Mary are somewhat too Toledan and coarse; but the adorers and a lovely child between them are fine subjects finely treated, with very careful execution, and a rich though sober colouring. A still finer picture by Blas del Prado hangs in the Queen of Spain's gallery,[1] representing the "Virgin, Babe, and St. Joseph" enthroned, attended by St. John and St. Ildefonso, and adored by Alonso de Villegas, the historian of the Calendar, by whom the painting was probably given to some shrine. The Virgin

[1] [*Catalogo de los cuadros del Museo del Prado de Madrid*, sexta edición, 1889, No. 944.]

here shows nothing of the Gothic blood of Castile; her features are of Italian delicacy, and her pure brow and eyes, bent kindly on the suppliant, might have been painted by Andrea del Sarto, delighting in downcast eyelids. The head of St. Joseph is Rafaelesque, and the drawing and tone of the whole composition displays a knowledge of the best models. The portrait of the black-robed chaplain[1] — with his harsh face full of lines and wrinkles, and his stiff hands pressed rigidly palm to palm—is very characteristic of the tedious writer whose pen dwells with most complacency on those thoughts and deeds of holy men that most tend to mar the beauty of holiness. The following inscription in white letters at the bottom of the picture — B. MARIE IOANNI EVANGELISTE ET ILDEFONSO BLAS DEL PRADO PICTORE M. ALFONSVS DE VILLEGAS PATRONIS D. ANO 1539— seems to have been traced long after it had left the easel. As Villegas was not born till 1533, it is probable that the date ought to be 1589.

Juan Pantoja de la Cruz was born at Madrid in 1551. He studied painting in the school of Alonso Sanchez Coello, and soon became sufficiently distinguished to obtain the posts of painter to the King and gentleman of the chamber (*ayuda de cámara*). Palomino, who possessed the original

---

[1] This priest's portrait, engraved by Ballester, in the *Españoles Ilustres*, seems to be taken from this picture.

sketches of the noble monuments of Charles V. and Philip II., in the church of the Escorial, says[1] that these were executed for Pompeyo Leoni by Pantoja. Oil-paintings of these monuments, likewise by him, existed at the Escorial in the time of Cean Bermudez, and are there still. Whilst Sanchez Coello lived, Pantoja seems to have shared the royal favour with him, and after his death to have enjoyed it in still fuller measure. He made many portraits of Philip II. and his family, most of which have perished in the fires of the palaces. The National Museum at Madrid possesses a fine example of his powers in the portrait of Isabella of the Peace,[2] whose dark hair, large brilliant black eyes, and rich complexion, afford an agreeable relief to the monotonous grey eyes and pale cheeks of the house of Austria. The head is full of beauty and life; the dress of black velvet, though closed to the throat, is becoming, the hoop or "*guardainfante*" of the Castilian court, introduced in the Emperor's reign, not having as yet expanded into its full amplitude; a small ruff encircles the neck, and the robe is garnished with a profusion of gold chains and jewellery, all admirably designed and painted. Unless there is some

---

[1] Palomino, tom. iii. p. 413.
[2] (*Catalogo* 1889, No. 924. The author's suggestion that it is a copy of an earlier picture is adopted by Don Pedro de Madrazo, the compiler of the *Catalogo Descriptivo é Historico*, 1872 (p. 505).—ED.]

mistake in the date of the painter's birth, this portrait was probably copied from one by his master, as Queen Isabella died in 1568, when Pantoja was only seventeen years of age. He must often, however, have seen her on public occasions, and perhaps may have noted her sweet smiles in some of her visits to the studio of Sanchez Coello. Of his many portraits of her lord, one only is to be found in the Queen of Spain's gallery. But that one[1] is well worthy of note, for it shows how the crowned monk of the Escorial looked when on the brink of the grave. In Pantoja's worn, sickly, sour old man, with lack-lustre restless eyes, protruding under-lip, and

"—— pallid cheekes and ashe hew,
In which sad Death his portraiture had writ,"[2]

wearing a rusty sugar-loaf hat, and holding in his hand a common brown rosary, we see the last stage of the sumptuous prince whose youthful bearing has been made immortal by the pencil of Titian. About the same time, or perhaps a little earlier, Pantoja painted for the convent of St. Mary,[3] at Naxera, the portrait of Ruy Perez de Ribera, which was esteemed one of his best, and those of the Princess of Brazil and the Empress Mary, for the

---

[1] *Catálogo*, No. 277 [edition of 1889, No. 931].
[2] Spenser's *Daphnaida*, lines 302-3.
[3] I inquired for it there, but without success. The convent is in ruins.

royal barefooted nuns of Madrid, amongst whom these royal ladies ended their days. He also pourtrayed Francisco de Salinas, the famous blind musical professor of Salamanca, and author of a Latin treatise on music, who enjoyed the favour of the Duke of Alba and the poetical praises of Fray Luis de Leon.[1] This portrait, which represents Salinas playing on an organ, has been engraved by Esteve.[2]

On the accession of Philip III., Pantoja retained his post and favour at court. In 1603 he executed, by the King's order, for the chapel-royal of the Treasury, two large compositions representing the Nativities of the Virgin and Our Lord, into which he introduced the portraits of many members of the royal family. In the former, St. Anne is dimly seen reclining in a state bed with crimson hangings; in the foreground stands a graceful damsel bathing the new-born babe. In the latter, the Virgin has the features of Queen Margaret, and the Austrian lip and hanging cheek may be detected in several of the surrounding shepherds and peasant girls. Both pictures are signed JVAN PANTOJA DE LA +, 1603; they are now in the royal gallery at Madrid.[3] Pantoja afterwards painted a portrait of Philip III. on horseback, which was sent to

---

[1] See his fine Oda V., *Obras*, 8vo, Madrid, 1816, tom. vi. p. 15.
[2] Amongst the *Españoles Ilustres*.
[3] [*Catálogo*, 1843, Nos. 175 and 181, edition 1872, Nos. 933 and 934].

CH. V.

Florence as the model for the noble equestrian statue in bronze begun by Giovanni di Bologna, the Flemish sculptor, and finished, after his death, by his scholar, Pietro Tacca. The statue of Henry IV. of France, torn from its pedestal on the Pont Neuf at Paris and melted down in the great Revolution, was likewise commenced by Bologna and completed by Tacca, and the horse was said closely to resemble the pacing steed which the Castilian King still bestrides in the garden of the royal Casa del Campo, near Madrid, where the work was placed, in 1616, by Antonio Guidi, Tacca's nephew.[1] The date of Pantoja's death is uncertain, but it must have taken place in or before 1609,[2] for Lope de Vega, in his "Jerusalem Conquistada," Canto xix., published in that year, laments him and some other painters in these lines—

"Al pie de un lauro tres sepulcros veo
En cuyo bronce perdurable escucho;
Apeles yace aqui, Zeuxis, Cleoneo,
Juan de la Cruz, Caravajal, Carducho,
Murieron ya. Qué funebre trofeo
Muerte cruel!"

Style and works.

Besides his portraits and other works painted for the royal family, Pantoja de la Cruz executed

---

[1] Ponz, tom. vi. pp. 141, 142.
[2] Palomino and Cean Bermudez say 1610, an error for the correction of which I am indebted to the *Cartas Españolas* for August 9th, 1832, p. 160.

various altar-pieces for churches and religious houses. His style much resembles that of his master, Sanchez Coello, and is more remarkable for care and finish than for force and freedom; his drawing is good, and his colouring rich and pleasing. The portrait of Queen Margaret in the royal collection at Madrid,[1] which is probably one of his latest, is certainly one of his best pictures, being executed in a bolder and broader manner than is usual with him. Of his skill in painting animals an anecdote has been preserved by Francisco Velez de Arciniega, a writer on medicine and natural history.[2] One of the King's fowlers having caught a fine eagle, of the bearded kind, in the royal chase near the Pardo, his Majesty commanded Pantoja to paint it, which he did so effectively, that the sitter, getting loose, flew at the canvas and tore it to shreds with his beak and talons, and the work had to be done over again. The bird, which was of a reddish black colour, was afterwards kept in the hospital of Anton-Martin, at Madrid, where Arciniega often saw him, and admired "his grave and composed manner of gazing, which showed no little grandeur and authority."

---

[1] *Catálogo* [1843], No. 222 [edition of 1889, No. 926].
[2] *Historia de los Animales mas recibidos en el uso de la Medecina*, por Francisco Velez de Arciniega, Boticario, 4to, Madrid, 1613.

Other court artists.

Teodosio Mingot and Gerónimo Cabrera.

Such were the chief Spanish artists who flourished under the patronage of Philip II. There are still a few who deserve a passing notice, although their works have rarely survived. Teodosio Mingot, a Catalonian, and Gerónimo Cabrera, painted certain frescoes in the Queen's apartments at the Pardo about 1570. According to Palomino, Mingot studied in Italy, and likewise worked with Becerra in the Alcazar of Madrid; he died in 1590, aged thirty-nine.

Diego de Urbina.

Diego de Urbina was a native of Madrid, and one of the King's painters; he may perhaps have been the scholar of Sanchez Coello, whom he assisted in painting the triumphal arches for the entrance of Queen Anna into the capital in 1570. In 1572 he painted for the royal monastery of Santa Cruz six pictures on subjects taken from the history of the Virgin and Our blessed Lord, and on the finding of the true cross by the Empress Helena, and he designed the retablo in which they were placed. The paintings, though defective in drawing, displayed some power of colouring; the sculpture was in the grand style of Becerra. The chapter of Burgos employed him, with Gregorio Martinez, to paint and gild for their Cathedral the retablo of the high altar, a sumptuous work, which was completed in 1594, and brought the artists the sum of 11,000 ducats.

Antonio Segura.

Antonio Segura was a painter and architect, employed in 1580 to carve a retablo for the Jeronymites of San Yuste, and to copy for it Titian's "Glory," then removed to the Escorial. He accomplished his task so much to the King's satisfaction, as to be named master of the works at the Alcazar of Madrid, and at the Pardo, under Francisco de Mora, a post which he held till his death in 1605. Rodrigo de Holanda became painter to Philip II. in 1591, with an allowance of 100 ducats, which, in consideration of his good services, was continued to him by Philip III., in 1599, when paralysis had deprived him of the use of his limbs. In 1593 Juan Gomez was named as one of the royal painters, with the like salary. For the church of the Escorial he painted, from a design by Tibaldi, a large picture of St. Ursula and her virgins, a pleasing work, which replaced an unsatisfactory composition on the same subject by Cambiaso; he also retouched Zuccaro's "Annunciation" and "St. Jerome;" and he painted a good original picture, representing "Our Lord, Mary Magdalene, and St. John," for the Carmelite friars of Segovia. He died in 1597, leaving a widow, Francisca, sister to the architect Mora, and seven children. To the first the King gave a pension of 100 ducats, and one of the latter, Juan Gomez de Mora, succeeded his uncle as master of the royal works.

Esteban Jordan was a painter and sculptor in the

Painters of illuminations. Fray Andres de Leon.

royal service; his best work was a high altar, carved for the Benedictines of Monserrate.

The art of illumination was carried to high perfection at the Escorial; and Fray Andres de Leon, under whose direction it was practised there, was one of the most skilful painters of miniature in Spain. He had learned somewhat of the use of the pencil from Fray Cristobal de Truxillo, an indifferent master, in the Jeronymite monastery of Mejorada, whence he was translated in 1568 to the Escorial. There he distinguished himself by the beauty and splendour of his illuminative drawings—especially in the "Liber Capitularius"—which were sometimes taken for the works of the Italian Clovio. He likewise painted some little pictures which hung in the chamber of Relics. Fray Julian Fuente del Saz was his scholar, and little inferior to him in skill. Fray Martin de Palencia was a Benedictine monk of the convent of San Millan at Suso. Between 1570 and 1580 he resided for some time at Avila and Madrid, where he was employed by Philip II. in illuminating various books and parchments for the Escorial, and received an annual salary of 100 ducats, raised to 150 during his stay in the capital. Few artists ever excelled him in the richness of his embellishments and the beauty of his dainty devices, of which he left many valuable specimens in a precious volume of "Prayers for

Processions," written on vellum, and long preserved by the Benedictines of Suso.

In this sumptuous reign the embroiderers took rank among artists. That nothing might be wanting to the splendour of the Escorial, the King established in the convent a school of embroidery under the direction of Fray Lorenzo de Monserrate and Diego Rutiner, where exquisite needlework for vestments and altar-cloths was wrought from the designs of Tibaldi and other great painters.

Meanwhile the Castilian artists of the Church kept pace, in numbers and skill, with those of the Court. Nicolas de Vergara, the elder, was one of the chief artists of Toledo at the accession of Philip II. From his profound knowledge of drawing, the grandeur of his figures, and his refined taste in ornament, he is supposed to have studied at Florence or Rome. The chapter of Toledo chose him for their painter and sculptor in 1542, and many of the windows of the Cathedral were painted by him or under his direction. He was likewise engaged with Berruguete in superintending the embellishments of the tomb of Cardinal Ximenes at Alcalá de Henares. For the Cathedral-cloister, at Toledo, he made sketches for certain frescoes representing scenes in the infernal regions, which, however, were never executed; and he designed the rich silver urn, made by the goldsmith Merino, for the precious remains of St. Eugenius. He died at Toledo, in 1574, and the painted windows of the Cathedral, which he left incomplete, were finished by his sons and scholars, Nicolas and Juan, in 1580. Nicolas de Vergara, the younger, had been appointed, in 1573, sculptor to the chapter; and three years afterwards was named master of works to the Cathedral. For the choir he executed, in bronze and iron, the beautiful lateral lecterns; and he designed the new Sagrario, or chapel of the Host, which was finished in the next reign by Monegro. He seems to have been a man of ready and elegant fancy in all matters of sculpture and architecture, both great and small; for we find him designing, in 1573, the bronze ornaments for the choir-books of the Escorial, and in 1575 a church for the Bernardine nuns at Toledo; giving a plan, in 1590, of a sumptuous ark of silver to enshrine the bones of S$^{ta.}$ Leocadia, and, in 1595, of a chapel to contain the Host and the relics of the rich Jeronymites at Guadalupe. He died at Toledo, in 1606, greatly lamented by his friends and the lovers of art.

Luis de Velasco was a painter of considerable eminence, although he has had the misfortune to have escaped the notice of Palomino and Ponz, who have not only omitted all mention of his name, but have even attributed his works to Blas del Prado. He was living at Toledo in 1564, and in 1581 he was chosen painter to the chapter. His best works were an "Incarnation of the Saviour," hung over a door in the cloister; and three pictures in an altar, likewise in the cloister, representing "The Virgin and Babe attended by Saints and Angels, and adored by an Armed Knight"—a noble and beautiful work —"St. Damian," and "St. Cosmo." These three paintings were executed in 1585, by order of the Archbishop, Cardinal Quiroga, by whom Velasco was paid 419,788 maravedis for his labour. He likewise painted, in 1594, the portrait of that prelate, and in 1599, that of Archbishop Garcia de Loaysa, for the winter chapter-room. In his drawing and colouring Velasco displayed considerable acquaintance with antique sculpture and with the works of the best Italian painters. He died in 1606, leaving a son, who became painter to Philip III.

Isaac de Helle was a painter in the employ of the chapter of Toledo, and by the orders of that body executed, in 1568, certain paintings for the cloister of the Cathedral. In the sacristy there likewise hung a picture, painted by him on panel, representing the Bishop, St. Nicasius, sick in bed, visited by another saint or apostle. It was so good that it sometimes passed for the work of Berruguete, and displayed something of the bold manner of Michael Angelo.

Domenico Theotocopuli, painter, sculptor, and

CII. V.
Domenico Theotocopuli, "El Greco."

architect, more familiarly known as "the Greek "— *El Griego*, or *El Greco*—holds a high place amongst the worthies of Toledo. Contemporary with him there were two other Greek artists in Spain, Pedro Serafin, a painter at Barcelona, and Nicolas de la Torre, a Candiote painter of illuminations, employed at the Escorial, each of whom was sometimes called El Griego. Of his early history nothing has been preserved, except the tradition that he studied in the school of Titian. Hence it is probable that he was born at Venice, of one of the Greek families who had taken refuge beneath St. Mark's wing from the sword of the Turk at the fall of Constantinople. He was born, says Palomino, in 1548; and it is possible that he may have been the son of a certain Domenico dalle Greche, who engraved, in 1549, a drawing of Titian's, representing "Pharaoh and his host overthrown in the Red Sea;"[1] or he may have been a native of Corfu or one of the Greek islands, like his contemporary and fellow-painter, Antonio Vassilacchi; for, not unmindful of his race and language, he frequently inscribed his name in the Greek character on works painted in Castile. The

Works at Toledo.

first authentic notice of his life that remains to us is that he was residing in Toledo in 1577, when he

---

[1] The plate is inscribed "In Venetia, p. Domenico dalle Greche, dipintore Venetiano, MDXLIX." See Weigel's *Kunst Catalog*. Sechste Abtheilung, No. 7371, Leipsig, 1844.

DOMENICO THEOTOCOPULI

began, for the Cathedral, his great picture of "The Parting of Our Lord's Raiment," a work, still adorning the sacristy, on which he was employed for ten years, and which Cumberland thought worthy of the pencil of Titian.[1] The august figure of the Saviour, arrayed in a red robe, occupies the centre of the canvas; the head with its long dark locks is superb, and the noble and beautiful countenance seems to mourn for the madness of them who "knew not what they did;" His right arm is folded on His bosom, seemingly unconscious of the rope, which encircles His wrist, and is violently dragged downwards by two executioners in front. Around and behind Him appears a throng of priests and warriors, amongst whom the Greek himself figures as the Centurion in black armour. He has likewise painted his beautiful daughter—distinguished by the white drapery on her head—as one of the three Maries in the foreground; at least, if her portrait in the Louvre[2] be authentic. In drawing and composition this picture is truly admirable; and the colouring is, on the whole, rich and effective, although it is here and there laid on in that spotted, streaky manner which afterwards became the great and prominent defect of El Greco's style. He likewise carved the retablo, in which this picture once hung;

---

[1] *Anecdotes*, vol. i. p. 158.   [2] [See infra, p. 338, and note 2.]

but, on the sacristy being rebuilt, it was removed, and the present marble retablo was erected in its place. For the painting he was paid by the chapter 119,000, and for the sculpture 200,600 maravedis. In the sacristy of the Hospital of St. John Baptist there hangs a small copy of the "Parting of the Raiment," or more probably a repetition by the master, or the original sketch, for it differs from the picture at the Cathedral in the colour of some of the draperies; it is in a very ruinous condition, and will soon be mere rags and dust.

Paints "St. Maurice" for the Escorial. Whilst thus engaged in the service of the Cathedral, El Greco received the royal commands to paint, for one of the altars of the Escorial church, a picture on the subject of St. Maurice and his Christian legion, who feared God rather than the Emperor Maximian, and preferred death to idolatry. Unluckily for the artist, it seems that his friends had been in the habit of commending his works by declaring that they might pass for those of Titian—a praise which by no means satisfied the Greek's ambitious soul, and only prompted him to invent a style altogether new, and peculiar to himself. Proceeding on this principle, he addressed himself to the martyrdom of the pious soldiery with great diligence, and presently produced a picture, from an artistic point of view, little less extravagant and atrocious than the massacre which it recorded. The one must have disturbed the established ideas and opinions of the artists assembled at the Escorial almost as rudely as the other troubled the repose of the secluded Valais. Dry, hard, and harsh in colouring, the painting was full of strange and distracting flashes of light, utterly destructive of unity and breadth; nor did the admirable heads occurring here and there do much to counteract its general disagreeable effect. The King was greatly disappointed when he saw it; he ordered the stipulated price, of which the amount has not been recorded, to be paid, but would not permit the picture to be hung in the church. It was therefore degraded to a more obscure part of the building, and placed in the chapel of the college. El Greco does not appear to have been in very flourishing circumstances when he began to work for his royal patron; for an order is extant, addressed by Philip II. to the Prior of the Escorial, and dated the 25th of April 1580, authorising that dignitary to allow him a little money that he might provide himself with materials, and to furnish him with some of the finer colours, especially "ultra-marine."[1] Had he but adhered to his Titianesque style, he might have obtained the post of King's painter, and found

Produces a disagreeable picture,

which displeases the King.

---

[1] *Arquitectos*, tom. iii. p. 349, where the order is given at full length.

employment for life, and a rich harvest of fame, at the Escorial.

The ill success of his experiment seems, for a time at least, to have led El Greco back to his earlier and better paths; for in 1584 he painted, by order of Cardinal-Archbishop Quiroga, a large picture, "The Burial of the Count of Orgaz," which is justly esteemed his masterpiece, and which the prelate presented to the Toledan church of Santo Tomé, where it still remains.[1] The artist, or lover of art, who has once beheld it, will never, as he rambles among the winding streets of the ancient city, pass the pretty brick belfry of that church—full of horse-shoe niches and Moorish reticulations — without turning aside to gaze upon its superb picture once more. It hangs to your left, on the wall opposite to the high altar. Gonzalo Ruiz, Count of Orgaz—head of a house famous in romance—rebuilt the fabric of the church, and was in all respects so religious and gracious a grandee, that when he was buried in 1323 within these very walls, St. Stephen and St. Augustine came down from heaven,

---

[1] A notice of Santo Tomé and its picture is one of the very few deficiencies in the *Handbook* [1845].* The picture is indeed noticed (in p. 771), but it is erroneously stated to be in the Museo Nacional, at Madrid. Mr. Borrow remarks of the "Entierro," "could it be purchased, it would be cheap at £5,000." *Bible in Spain*, 12mo, London, 1844, p. 214.

* [The omission and mistake were rectified in the third edition, 1855, in which (at p. 781) an account of the picture and its correct locality is given.—ED.]

and laid his body in the tomb with their own holy hands, an incident which forms the subject of the picture. St. Stephen is represented as a dark-haired youth of noble countenance, and St. Augustine as a hoary old man wearing a mitre, both of them arrayed in rich pontifical vestments of golden tissue, embroidered with coloured figures, and at the bottom of St. Stephen's robe a large piece of work representing his martyrdom. They support the dead count in their arms, and gently lower him into the grave, shrouded, like a baron of Roslin, "in his iron panoply." Nothing can be finer than the execution and the contrast of these three heads; never was the image of the peaceful death of "the just man" more happily conveyed than in the placid face and powerless form of the warrior; nor did Giorgione or Titian ever excel the splendid colouring of his black armour, rich with gold damascening. To the right of the picture, behind St. Stephen, kneels a fair boy in a dark dress, perhaps the son of the count. He is looking out of the picture, and pointing with his left hand to a white rose embroidered on St. Stephen's sleeve; out of his right pocket peeps the corner of a white handkerchief, on which the Greek has inscribed his name in Greek characters; beyond rises the stately form of a grey friar; to the left, near St. Augustine, stands a priest in an alb, looking upwards, and farther to the left two priests in gorgeous vestments, holding, the one a book, and the other a taper. Behind this principal group appear the noble company of mourners, hidalgos and old Christians, all, with olive faces and beards of formal cut, looking on with true Castilian gravity and phlegm, as if the transaction were an every-day occurrence. The chief mourner, whose delicate hands and lace ruffles appear on each side of St. Stephen's head, wears on his breast the red cross of Santiago, and a knight of the same order stands behind St. Augustine. As they are mostly portraits of noted personages, perhaps some of the originals did actually stand a few years later, with the like awe in their hearts and calm on their cheeks, in the royal presence-chamber, when the news came to Court that the proud Armada of Spain had been vanquished by the galleys of Howard, and cast away on the rocks of the Hebrides. The upper part of the picture represents a different scene, in a far inferior style—the soul of Gonzalo entering the heavenly mansion. Here El Greco's desire of avoiding all resemblance to Titian again proved too strong for his taste; Our Lord sits enthroned amongst clouds flat and sharp as the pasteboard clouds of the stage; and, somewhat lower, the Virgin, at whose feet kneels the emancipated spirit, in the form of a naked man, of a livid hue, and of a size so disproportionate to the heavenly host around him, that he might be mistaken for some ungainly Goliath of Gath, or vanquished gyaunt of romance. For this picture—the finest at Toledo, and, notwithstanding its faults, one of the noblest productions of the Castilian pencil—the painter was paid 2,000 crowns by the Archbishop. The story on which it is founded is told in the inscription on a black marble slab, let into the wall beneath it—an inscription which is printed on next page, because I believe it has never been printed elsewhere.[1]

In the collection of the Academy of St. Ferdinand, at Madrid, there is a small repetition, perhaps the original sketch, of the "Burial of Orgaz," admirably painted, and perhaps more pleasing than the great picture, inasmuch as a great part of the celestial and defective portion is wanting.

El Greco was, when he pleased, an admirable painter of portraits. He was eminently successful, in 1609, in taking the likeness of the poet, Fray Feliz Hortensio Palavicino, who rewarded him with a laudatory sonnet,[2] wherein he was compared to

---

[1] I find no mention of either picture or story in the *Descripcion de la imperial ciudad de Toledo*, por el Doctor Francisco de Pisa, fol., Toledo, 1617, nor in the *Historia de la imperial noblissima inclita y esclarecida ciudad de Toledo*, por Don Pedro de Roias, Conde de Mora. 2 tom., fol., Madrid, 1654-63; nor in Florez, *España Sagrada*, tom. v. and vi., 8vo, Madrid, 1763-73. The whole story, with the inscription, will be found in P. de Rojas' *Discursos illustres Históricos i Genealogicos*, 4to, Madrid, 1636, fol. 145-150.

[2] The lover of encomiastic verses may find it in Palomino, tom. iii. p. 428.

CH. V.

Inscription beneath El Greco's "Entierro del Conde de Orgaz."

DIVIS BENEFICIS ET PIETATE S.

TAMETSI PROPERAS SISTE PAVLVLVM VIATOR ET ANTIQVAM VRBIS NOSTRÆ
HISTORIAM PAVCIS ACCIPE.
D. GONSALVS RVIZ A TOLETO ORGAZI OPPIDI DOMINVS CASTELLE MAIOR NO
TARIVS INTER CÆTERA SVÆ PIETATIS MONVMENTA THOMÆ APOSTOLI QVAM
VIDES ÆDEM VBI SE TESTAMENTO IVSSIT CONDI. OLIM ANGVSTAM ET MALESAR
TAM LAXIORI SPATIO PECVNIA SVA INSTAVRANDAM CVRAVIT AVDITIS MVLTIS
CVM ARGENTEIS TVM AVREIS DONARIIS DVM EVM IVMARE SACERDOTES PARANT
ECCE RES ADMIRANDA ET INSOLITA DIVVS STEPHANVS ET AGVSTINVS COELO DE
LAPSI PROPRIIS MANIBVS HEC SEPELIERVNT QVÆ CAVSA HOS DIVOS IMPVLERIT QVONIAM
LONGVM EST AVGVSTINIANOS SODALES. NON LONGA EST VIA SI VACAT. ROGA OBIIT
ANN. CH MCCCXII. COELESTIVM GRATVM ANIMVM AVDISTI. AVDI IAM MORTALIVM IN
CONSTANTIAM. ECCLESIÆ HVIVS CVRIONI ET MINISTRIS TVM ETIAM PAROCHIÆ PAVPERI
BVS. ARIETES II GALLINAS XVI VINI VTRES II LIGNORVM VECTVRAS II NVMOS QVOS NOSTRI
MORA PETINOS VOCANT DCCC. AB ORGAZIIS QVOT ANNIS PERCIPIENDOS IDEM GONZALVS TEST
AMENTO LEGAVIT ILLI OB TEMPORIS DIVTVRNITATEM REM OBSCVRAM FORE SPERANTES CVM DVOBVS
AB HINC ANNIS PIVM PENDERE TRIBVTVM RECVSARENT. PINCIANI CONVENTVS SENTENTIA CONVICTI SVNT ANNI
CH MDLXX AVDREA NONIO MATRITANO HVIVS TEMPLI CVRIONE STRENVÆ DEFENDENTE ET PETRO RVI
Z DVRON OECONOMO.

Prometheus. In the hospital of St. John Baptist at Toledo, he has finely pourtrayed the mild features of Cardinal Tavera, which he must have copied from the work of some older artist. At Illescas, a town lying on the weary plain midway between Madrid and Toledo, in the spacious church of the Hospital of Charity, where El Greco was architect and sculptor, he has left a good altar-piece representing "S. Ildefonso," a venerable man in a dark pontifical habit, writing at a table covered with red velvet—for which some worshipful Toledan canon may have served as a model. In the Royal Gallery at Madrid there are many of his portraits, most of them good, especially one [1]—a dark, handsome man in armour, with a curious chain of gold and tri-colour silk round his neck—which Velazquez never excelled; and that of the President Rodrigo Vazquez,[2] the inexorable old man who stood by whilst his fallen rival, Antonio Perez, was tortured to the confessing point.[3]

A fine full-length portrait of Vincentio Anastagi, in a steel cuirass, green velvet breeches, and white

---

[1] It occurs amongst his works, which are to be found between Nos. 1134 and 1154 of the *Catálogo* 1843 [edition of 1889, Nos. 238 to 247 und 2124, where his pictures are classed as belonging, not to the Spanish, but to the Italian school.]

[2] *Catálogo*, No. 1134 [edition of 1889, No. 241].

[3] For an account of this striking historical scene, see Bermudez de Castro, *Ant. Perez*, p. 151.

hose, one of the stout Knights of St. John who kept the outpost of Christendom against the Turk with the Grand Master Giovanni di Valetta, is probably the best specimen of his pencil in England. It adorns the rich collection of William Coningham, Esq. On a pedestal near the warrior is the following inscription :—

FRÁ VINCENTIO ANASTAGI, DOPPÒ ESSERE STATO GOVERNATORE DELLA CITTA VECCIA DI MALTA, ET AVER COMANDATO NELL' ASSEDIO DELLA MED$^{MA.}$ ISOLA AD UNA DELLA DUE COMPAGNIE DE' CAVALLI CHE DENTRO SI TROVARONO ET AD UNA COMPAGNIA DE FANTI COMANDO PIV VOLTE AD ALTRE COMPAGNIE DI FANTARIA FÙ SARGENTE MAGGIOR DELLA MARCA, FÙ HONORATO IN PIV VOLTE DAL GRAN MASTRO DI TRE COMMEND^{E}, E MORI IN MALTA CAP^{NO} DELLA CAP^{NA} DELLE GALERE L'ANNO 1586 E DELL' ETA SUA 55.

His delineation of his own fine Hellenic features in the Louvre,[1] from which our engraving is taken, is a very pleasing portrait. The portrait of his daughter[2] is one of the purest gems of that collection, and would be a gem even in the Royal Gallery of Spain. She is painted in the prime of life and loveliness; her dark eyes and rich complexion are

---

[1] Galerie Espagnole, No. 260 [now at Keir].
[2] Id., No. 259 [bought by Sir William Stirling-Maxwell, Bart., and now at Keir. Exhibited at Art Treasures Exhibition, Manchester, 1857, No. 234.—ED.].

finely set off by the white-furred mantle drawn over her head; and her countenance, in depicting which her fond father has put forth all his skill, is one of the most beautiful that death ever dimmed, and that the pencil ever rescued from the grave. As this fair maiden figures in the great Toledan altarpiece, painted between 1577 and 1587, it is probable that her portrait was executed not long after the latter year. In the Royal Gallery of Naples there is a portrait (bust size) of Giulio Clorso, a grave old man, with an illuminated missal in his hand, ascribed to El Greco—an excellent work, but more probably by an artist of Venice.

El Greco has been justly described as an artist who alternated between reason and delirium, and displayed his great genius only at lucid intervals.[1] There is probably no other painter who has left so many admirable and so many execrable performances. Strange to say, in his case, the critics cannot fix the epoch when his "early bad manner" gave way to his "good middle-style," or when his pencil lost the charms of its prime; for he painted well and ill by turns throughout his whole career. The disagreeable "St. Maurice" was executed between the times when his two best works were commenced. The fine portraits of Tavera and

---

[1] *Arquitectos.* tom. iii. p. 138.

Palavicina were painted in or about 1609, which is also the date of his delightful "Holy Family" and his offensive "Baptism of Christ" at the Toledan Hospital of St. John Baptist. In the latter picture, the narrow draperies, and the gleams of light, thin and sharp as Toledo sword-blades, produce effects not less unpleasing than difficult to be described intelligibly to those who are unacquainted with the Greek's style. He might have painted it, by the fitful flashes of lightning, on a midsummer night, from models dressed only in floating ribands. In the Louvre [1] we find near his excellent portraits,[2] an "Adoration of the Shepherds," in his most extravagant style, in which the lights on reddish draperies and dark clouds are expressed by green streaks of so unhappy a tint, that those harmless objects resemble masses of bruised and discoloured flesh. Yet the perpetrator of these enormities sometimes painted heads that stood out from the canvas with the sober strength of Velazquez's, and coloured figures and draperies with a splendour rivalling Titian.[3] With all his faults El Greco was

---

[1] [The Louis-Philippe collection was sold by auction in 1853.—ED.]

[2] [That of Pompeyo Leoni, No. 21 of the Louis-Philippe sale catalogue, was bought by Sir William Stirling-Maxwell, Bart., and is now at Keir. It was exhibited at the Art Treasures Exhibition in Manchester, 1857, No. 518.—ED.]

[3] Amongst the other "things of Spain," well and wittily treated of by the lively M. Théophile Gautier, are the works of El Greco. "Pour donner à sa peinture," says he, "l'apparence d'être faite avec une grande

a favourite artist in Spain, and his pictures were highly valued. For the church of Bayona, a village in the province of Segovia, he executed a series of paintings on the life of Mary Magdalene, which were refused, about the close of the seventeenth century, to Cardinal Puertocarrero, although his Eminence offered to buy them for 5,000 crowns, and replace them with pictures by Luca Giordano, the famous and fashionable court artist of the day.[1]

Theotocopuli was much engaged as sculptor and architect. At Madrid he designed, in 1590, the church of the college of Doña Maria de Arragon, and carved the "abominable"[2] retablo of the high altar; at Illescas he built, about 1600, two churches, that of the Hospital of Charity, still existing, with its good classical altar, and that of the Franciscan friars, with the marble tombs and effigies of the Hinojosas, its founders, now demolished; at Toledo, he gave the plan of the city hall, a solid plain building of two storeys, resting on Doric pillars and flanked with towers; he carved, in 1609, the retablos for the church of the St. John Baptist's

---

fierté de touche, il jette çà et là des coups de brosse d'une pétulance et d'une brutalité incroyables, des lueurs minces et acérées qui traversent les ombres comme des lames de sabre; tout cela n'empêche pas le Greco d'être un grand peintre; . . . dans tout cela règnent une énergie dépravée, une puissance maladive, qui trahissent le grand peintre, et le fou de génie." *Voyage en Espagne*, pp. 43, 189.

[1] Palomino, tom. iii. p. 426.
[2] *Arquitectos*, tom. iii. p. 138.

Palavicina were painted in or about 1609, which is also the date of his delightful "Holy Family" and his offensive "Baptism of Christ" at the Toledan Hospital of St. John Baptist. In the latter picture, the narrow draperies, and the gleams of light, thin and sharp as Toledo sword-blades, produce effects not less unpleasing than difficult to be described intelligibly to those who are unacquainted with the Greek's style. He might have painted it, by the fitful flashes of lightning, on a midsummer night, from models dressed only in floating ribands. In the Louvre[1] we find near his excellent portraits,[2] an "Adoration of the Shepherds," in his most extravagant style, in which the lights on reddish draperies and dark clouds are expressed by green streaks of so unhappy a tint, that those harmless objects resemble masses of bruised and discoloured flesh. Yet the perpetrator of these enormities sometimes painted heads that stood out from the canvas with the sober strength of Velazquez's, and coloured figures and draperies with a splendour rivalling Titian.[3] With all his faults El Greco was

---

[1] [The Louis-Philippe collection was sold by auction in 1853.—ED.]
[2] [That of Pompeyo Leoni, No. 21 of the Louis-Philippe sale catalogue, was bought by Sir William Stirling-Maxwell, Bart., and is now at Keir. It was exhibited at the Art Treasures Exhibition in Manchester, 1857, No. 518.—ED.]
[3] Amongst the other "things of Spain," well and wittily treated of by the lively M. Théophile Gautier, are the works of El Greco. "Pour donner à sa peinture," says he, "l'apparence d'être faite avec une grande

a favourite artist in Spain, and his pictures were highly valued. For the church of Bayona, a village in the province of Segovia, he executed a series of paintings on the life of Mary Magdalene, which were refused, about the close of the seventeenth century, to Cardinal Puertocarrero, although his Eminence offered to buy them for 5,000 crowns, and replace them with pictures by Luca Giordano, the famous and fashionable court artist of the day.[1]

Theotocopuli was much engaged as sculptor and architect. At Madrid he designed, in 1590, the church of the college of Doña Maria de Arragon, and carved the "abominable"[2] retablo of the high altar; at Illescas he built, about 1600, two churches, that of the Hospital of Charity, still existing, with its good classical altar, and that of the Franciscan friars, with the marble tombs and effigies of the Hinojosas, its founders, now demolished; at Toledo, he gave the plan of the city hall, a solid plain building of two storeys, resting on Doric pillars and flanked with towers; he carved, in 1609, the retablos for the church of the St. John Baptist's

Works of sculpture and architecture.

---

fierté de touche, il jette çà et là des coups de brosse d'une pétulance et d'une brutalité incroyables, des lueurs minces et acérées qui traversent les ombres comme des lames de sabre ; tout cela n'empêche pas le Greco d'être un grand peintre ; . . . dans tout cela règnent une énergie dépravée, une puissance maladive, qui trahissent le grand peintre, et le fou de génie." *Voyage en Espagne*, pp. 43, 189.

[1] Palomino, tom. iii. p. 426.
[2] *Arquitectos*, tom. iii. p. 138.

Hospital; and, in 1611, he erected in the Cathedral, by order of the chapter, the catafalque, or temporary monument for the celebration of funeral solemnities for Margaret of Austria, Queen of Philip III.

Few artists were ever more unweariedly industrious than El Greco, even in his old age. Never idle for a moment, he must have not a little astonished, by his indomitable energy, the slow and otiose Toledans amongst whom he lived. Pacheco, who visited him in 1611, relates that he showed him a large closet filled with the plaster models of his various sculptures, and a chamber full of the sketches of all his pictures. In the course of their talk, El Greco declared his opinion that colouring was a more difficult part of the painter's art than drawing, and that Michael Angelo, "though a good professor, knew nothing of painting." Besides uttering these heresies, to the horror of the Sevillian, he explained and defended his own harsh and spotty style, avowing that it was his practice to retouch a picture till each mass of colour was distinct and separate from the rest, and asserting that it gave strength and character to the whole.[1] But in spite of his eccentric style and opinions, the school of Theotocopuli produced Maino, Tristan, and Orrente, who rank amongst the best Castilian painters. He

---

[1] Pacheco, p. 242.

was a man of wit and some learning, and is said by Pacheco to have written on the three arts which he professed. His brother artists were perhaps more benefitted, however, by his legal than by his literary efforts; for he successfully resisted, in 1600, a tax attempted to be levied upon his works at Illescas, and obtained from the Council of State a decree against its exaction. Living till the reign of Philip IV., he saw the veteran painters of Castile vanquished at Court by a stripling from Andalusia; and he died at Toledo in 1625, to the general sorrow of the city, and was buried in the church of S. Bartolomé. His friend, the poet Luis de Gongora, celebrated his memory in the following fantastic sonnet, perhaps intended to be inscribed on his tomb:—

Sonnet by Gongora.

> Esta en forma elegante ¡ó peregrino!
>   De pórfido luciente dura llave,
>   El pincel niega al mundo mas suave,
>   Que dió espíritu al leño, vida al lino.
> Su nombre, aun de mayor aliento digno
>   Que en los clarines de la fama cabe,
>   El campo ilustra de ese mármol grave:
>   Venéralo, y prosigue tu camino.
> Yace el Griego: heredó naturaleza
>   Arte, y el arte estudio, iris colores
>   Febo luces, sino sombras Morfeo.
> Tanta urna, á pesar de su dureza,
>   Lagrimas beba y quantos suda olores
>   Corteza funeral de árbol sabeo.

> Stranger! beneath this polish'd porphyry stone,
>   Lock'd from the world, the sweetest pencil lies

to arouse them for midnight mass, and matins, and to number the hours of their quiet recreation. Notwithstanding these secular employments, he paid strict obedience to the severe rule of his order, and, after having filled for many years the office of procurator to the convent, he died there, in 1627, full of days and honour.

Josef Martinez flourished at Valladolid towards the end of the century, and painted so nearly in the style of the Florentine masters, that it is probable that he studied in their city. For the chapel of the Annunciation in the convent of St. Augustin, he executed various pictures representing events in the life of the Virgin, and also the fresco decorations and the designs of the rich tiles (*azulejos*) which adorned the walls. This fine chapel was finished in 1598, and destroyed by the French Imperial troops. One of the pictures—that of the "Annunciation"—was alone saved from the wreck, and is now in the Museum of Valladolid;[1] in the lower part of the canvas the Blessed Mary is seen receiving the salutation and message of the angel; above, the heavens open, the dove descends, and the Eternal Father is seen, with outstretched arms, as if in the act of benediction, and attended by angels; throughout, the drawing is good, the draperies

---

[1] In the great hall; see *Compendio Histórico de Valladolid*, p. 47.

finely managed, and the colouring rich and effective; the picture is signed, with true Spanish abbreviation, **MRÑEZ** The same artist also painted some good pictures and altar-pieces for the chapel of Christ in the convent of Bernardine nuns.

Gregorio Martinez was another painter of good reputation at Valladolid, and was employed, in 1594, by the chapter of Burgos to gild the high altar of that Cathedral.[1] Cean Bermudez once saw a small picture on copper, signed with this master's name, representing the Virgin and some saints, and coloured in a style resembling that of Venice.

Burgos possessed two painters, Juan de Aneda and Juan de Cea, whose names have been preserved by a few pictures, painted for the Cathedral of that city, about 1565.

Catalonia produced in this reign a few artists whose names have survived, although their works have, for the most part, perished or been forgotten. In the Cathedral of Tarragona, in 1563, Pedro Pablo, and Pedro Serafin, a Greek, painted the doors of the great organ; the outside displaying a composition on the subject of the "Annunciation of the Virgin," and the inside of the leaves displaying the "Nativity" and "Resurrection" of the Saviour The artists received for their labour 300 Catalonian

---

[1] Supra, p. 322.

pounds, and were employed by the chapter in various other works. Pedro Guitart executed six pictures in oil for the high altar of the church of San Pedro, at Reus, in 1576; and Isaac Hermes, in 1587, the paintings of the high altar and other works in the Cathedral of Tarragona.

Luis Pascual Gaudin, born in 1556, at Villafranca, in Catalonia, took the Carthusian vow in the Chartreuse of Scala Dei, in 1595, whither he probably carried with him a considerable knowledge of painting, which he there found leisure to improve. Many chambers of that monastery were adorned with his works; in one of the Sacristies hung a set of "Evangelists," and in another a series of "Apostles;" the refectory had two large compositions of "Our Saviour washing the Disciples' feet," and of His "Prayer in the Garden;" and many more of his pictures were to be found in the chapter-room. Pacheco says that he painted largely for the Grand Chartreuse, the original retreat of St. Bruno, but it does not appear whether the artist himself visited the wild solitudes of Lorraine. He seems, however, to have travelled to Seville, where he was a guest at the Chartreuse, and painted for that sumptuous convent a series of works on the life of the Virgin. In these compositions the Blessed Mary appeared without any veil, and attired in a Venetian robe with "sleeves as large as wheels" and fancifully decorated with coloured ribands—a dress, in the opinion of the purist Pacheco, "altogether unbecoming the gravity and grandeur of Our Sovereign Lady." Notwithstanding this breach of etiquette in costume, Cean Bermudez considered that these pictures established the skill, if not the orthodoxy, of Gaudin; who likewise painted, for the Sevillian Carthusians, the life of their patron saint, in a series of compositions, supposed to be a repetition of those executed for the Grand Chartreuse. After quitting Seville he visited another of the great foundations of his order, that of Portacœli, near Valencia, where he painted a "Last Supper" for the refectory, and various other works. In his own convent at Scala Dei he held the office of vicar, and he died there in 1621, leaving behind him many pictures, and a high reputation as a painter, a divine, and a saint. In the conventual record he was noticed as—"Vir quidem picturæ arte præclarus, theologia præclarior, virtuteque (patrum qui cum eo vixerunt testimonio) præclarissimus."

Of Castilian sculpture in this reign, Valladolid must be considered the principal seat, as being the residence of Juan de Juni, the best sculptor of Spain. Although his works obtained for him a high reputation, and many of the finest of them still exist, the notices of his life are few and contradictory. Palomino asserts that he was a native of

Flanders;[1] Cean Bermudez supposes, from his name, that he was an Italian. Both of them relate that he had so distinguished himself at Rome, as an architect, that he was chosen by Don Pedro Alvarez de Acosta, Bishop of Oporto, to build the episcopal palace in that city; that the same prelate, when translated to Osma, employed him, in 1556, as a sculptor in the Cathedral there; and that he died at Valladolid, in the reign of Philip III. Acosta was raised to the See of Oporto in 1507, and Philip III. ascended the throne in 1598, so that this account makes the life and labours of the artist extend over nearly a century.

The researches of Bosarte[2] have been more recent and accurate. He explains that the term Fleming in the reign of Charles V. was applied not only to natives of the Low Countries, but also to such Castilians as followed the Court, and enjoyed the favour of the dominant Flemish party. He sought diligently, though in vain, for a signature of Juni; and in the absence of such proof, conceives that that name may have been a corruption of some Latinised form of Juan or Joanes. Cean Bermudez, however, afterwards found, at Valladolid, Juni's signature attached to a contract, where the surname was written as above, without any accent on the

---
[1] Palomino, tom. iii. p. 416.
[2] *Viaje*, p. 163.

final *i*—whence he infers that it was a name native to Castile.¹ Bosarte was unable to discover any record of the artist's visit to Oporto, nor any mention in the local histories of his labours there. The earliest notice of Juni's existence that rewarded his research, is contained in a document which he prints, and from which it appears that Juan de Juni, being an inhabitant of Valladolid, acquired, in 1545, a considerable piece of building ground on the Campo Grande of that city, belonging to Don Hernando Niño de Castro, and lying near the monastery of the Holy Ghost, on perpetual lease, at the yearly rent of 3,000 maravedis.

In the same year, Juni began one of his most important works—the high altar of the Church of Our Lady "de la Antigua," at Valladolid. The price agreed on was 2,400 ducats. But after the agreement had been made, and the work begun, a rival sculptor, one Francisco de Giralte, offered to do it for 100 ducats less. Out of this offer arose a lawsuit, which lasted five years, and ended in Juni's rebating 104 ducats of his price — thus sacrificing his fair profits, as he himself declared— in order, it is supposed, to prevent his plans and drawings from falling into the hands of Giralte. A new agreement was therefore drawn up in

Works at Valladolid. Altar in church of "Nuestra Señora de la Antigua."

---

¹ Cean Bermudez, *Los Arquitectos*, tom. ii. p. 69.

August 1551, and the artist's wife, Doña Anna Aguirre, gave security over her dowry that the conditions should be fulfilled. The altar was of great size, being fifty feet high and thirty wide, and provided with concealed staircases for the convenience of lighting it up. It was carved of wood, the master executing the large statues with his own hands; and when finished it gave so much satisfaction to the parish, that Juni was paid 2,500 ducats for his labours.

For the church of "the Anguishes" he carved an excellent "Mater Dolorosa" in Sorian pine. This Virgin was seated on the ground, her head half turned away, and looking with tearful eyes to heaven. Her dress consisted of a crimson robe and blue mantle, and a yellow cloth on her head, which half concealed her brow. In her right hand she held some small iron knives, which the devotion of succeeding times changed into long swords of silver. Hence she was called "Our Lady of the Knives" (*de los Cuchillos*). Bosarte[1] speaks with rapture of the fine design and draperies of this statue, and of the sublime expression of the head, on which it was impossible to look without emotion. The sculptor seemed to have been inspired by the noble lament of Jeremiah for the desolate daughter of Zion, "who

---

[1] *Viaje*, p. 174.

sitteth solitary; she that was great among the nations; who weepeth sore in the night, and whose tears are on her cheeks; she hath none to comfort her; all that honour her despise her; yea, she sigheth and turneth backwards." This superb image narrowly escaped being violated by a pious and wealthy Count of Ribadavia—a peculiar votary of the Lady of Sorrows—who many times wished to robe her statue in costly stuffs, and was with difficulty induced to content himself with the ordinary and cheaper acts of devotion.

For the convent of the Franciscans, Juni executed a "St. Anthony of Padua with the Infant Saviour;" and for the Franciscan nuns of St. Isabel a "St. Francis of Asisi adoring a Crucifix." The parish church of Santiago likewise boasted one of his finest works—a magificent composition of many figures as large as life, representing the "Adoration of the Magian Kings." In this altar-piece Bosarte[1] especially praises the head of the Virgin, "which," he says, "had it been of bronze or marble, and dug out of an excavation, would have passed for a relic of the finest times of Greek art." He notices also the haughty and life-like form of the Moorish Prince, and remarks that some of the attendants wear caps so like those met with in the works of Michael

[1] *Viaje*, p. 180.

Angelo, that it would seem that Juni had studied the sculptures of that master.

In 1556, Juni designed and executed the carvings of the altar on the Trascoro[1] of the Cathedral of Osma, by order of Bishop Acosta. These noble sculptures, which still exist, represent scenes taken from the life and passion of Our Blessed Lord. The munificent prelate, who presented them to the church, died in 1563, and lies buried at Aranda de Duero, beneath a stately monument, sculptured by Juni.

In 1557, Juni was employed to erect a retablo in the church of St. Mary, at Medina de Rioseco, with sculptures representing the conception and birth of the Virgin, for which purpose Alvaro de Benavente had bequeathed 450 ducats.[2] The contract subscribed by Juni, and preserved by Cean Bermudez, is most prolix and precise; it fixes the subjects of the bas-relief in each compartment, as "St. Joachim upbraided in the Temple, at Jerusalem, for his wife's barrenness, by the high priest, Issachar;" "The Angel appearing to St. Joachim in his sheepfold;" and "The Presentation of the long-hoped-for babe, in the Temple, by St. Joachim and St. Anne;"—it stipulates that the material shall be the

---

[1] The Trascoro is the back part of the high wall which, in most Spanish Cathedrals, closes the end of the choir.
[2] *Los Arquitectos*, &c., tom. ii. p. 222

"best wood of Soria, dry, and with few knots;" and it binds the artist to carve, gild, and paint the whole retablo to the satisfaction of the legatees. The work appears to have been completed with great success—the sculptures were bold and spirited, and the architectural decorations rich, various, and pleasing. It was placed in the chapel of the Beneventes; and there Juni likewise painted some frescoes—representing "The Creation," "The Fall," "The Expulsion of Adam and Eve from Paradise," and other sacred subjects. He also sculptured some sepulchral urns and statues in marble—and designed the other architectural ornaments, and the rich iron railing of the same chapel.

In 1571, he finished, for the Cathedral of Segovia, a retablo, which contained a "Descent from the Cross,"—a composition of many figures, and full of power and grace. In 1583, he executed a number of sculptures for the high altar of the church of Santoyo—taken from the histories of Our Lady and St. John Baptist—amongst which was placed, in a prominent position, a statue of the Baptist, carved by Alonso Berruguete. The Franciscans of Valladolid possessed, in the chapel of their convent, a large composition in clay, representing "The Entombment of Our Lord," now in the Museum,[1] and

---

[1] *Compendio Histórico*, p. 76.

CH. V. esteemed one of the best and latest of his works. Amongst its many and various figures, those of Nicodemus and Joseph of Arimathea were remarkable for their spirit—the one being a model of ideal beauty, and the other seeming the portrait of some venerable friend, or father of the convent. This "Entombment" was finished in 1586; after which year the name of Juni ceases to occur in conventual records or tradition. It is therefore probable that he soon afterwards went to his rest—perhaps beneath the shadow of some stately altar, rich with the monuments of his genius.

Family. By his wife, Doña Anna de Aguirre, Juni left a daughter, Anna Maria, who seems to have been either an only child, or the only one of his children who survived him. She married, first, Juan de Muniategui, and, secondly, Benito Chamoso, with the latter of whom she for some time inhabited her father's house in Valladolid. Being sold, perhaps after Doña Anna Maria's death, this house became by a singular chance, in 1616, the dwelling of Juni's ablest successor in art at Valladolid—the sculptor Gregorio Hernandez.

Style and merits. Although the scanty memorials of Juni's life are altogether silent as to his early history, the evidence of his style goes far to prove that he had studied his art on the banks of the Arno, and was learned in all the wisdom of the Florentine sculptors. Perhaps no modern sculptor has ever so nearly resembled or approached Michael Angelo in genius; like him, he wielded a fearless and furious chisel, and delighted to dare every difficulty of attitude; and he loved to body forth energy and strong emotion rather than softness and repose. His grand imposing forms, and heads full of fire, vividly recall those of the great Florentine, and leave little doubt that the Spaniard had lingered beneath the dome of the Medici Chapel, gazing on the wonderful effigies it enshrines, that he had studied the terrible Moses, and imbued his mind with the stern beauty of the "Pietà," of the Vatican. There occur here and there in his compositions saintly figures, in broadly-flowing draperies, that might have been carved out of the Sistine frescoes, and weeping matrons—on whose dim and wasted features the lines of beauty still linger—that seem borrowed from those wondrous "weird women," the Parcæ of the Pitti palace. This strong and fiery manner may have been adopted by Juni in opposition to that of Berruguete, who affected the calmer and more classical graces, and whom it was his ambition to equal or excel. It sometimes, however, gives to his works an air of violence and exaggeration. His colouring is usually sombre, and sometimes heavy and leaden; the sculpture, as well as the painting of the Castiles, eschewing those splendid and glow-ing hues, in which the statuary and canvases of Andalusia rejoice.

Rafael de Leon was a sculptor, famous in Castile during this reign, of whom nothing is known but that he was an artist of reputation at Toledo, and for some crime or misfortune was forced to take refuge in the Bernardine convent at Valdeiglesias, in 1561. The abbot received him kindly, and employed him to carve the stalls and canopies of the choir. This work—which was reckoned one of the finest of the kind in Spain—was not completed till 1571, and for his ten years' labours the sculptor received 24,921 reals of plate, and a gratuity of 300 ducats.[1] These stalls were carved in oak or walnut, and designed in the Italian, or "cinque-cento" style. The back of each stall was adorned with a bas-relief on some subject taken from Holy Writ; on the divisions between the seats stood exquisite figures of Jewish prophets, or saints of the order of St. Bernard; and above all, a range of Caryatides supported a massive overhanging cornice, profusely enriched with masks and cupids, satyrs and cherubs, urns, monsters, and garlands of fruit and flowers. The Bernardine monks, therefore, chanted their solemn litanies to Our Lord and the Virgin in a choir most pantheistically adorned, where Judaism

---

[1] Taking 8 reals of plate at 39 pence, and the ducat at 53 pence sterling, these sums are worth £602. 4s., and £66, 5s. respectively.

strove with the classical mythology, and the fables of the Calendar were blended with the truths of the New Testament; but the effect was grand, and the execution of infinite delicacy. These celebrated carvings were removed at the suppression of the monastery, and are now in the University of Madrid, where they are to adorn the great hall, but where they will probably show with far less majesty than in their native choir.[1]

Pedro Arbulo Marguvete is supposed to have been a scholar of Berruguete, and lived at San Domingo de la Calzada, a town lying amongst the bleak hills to the north-east of Burgos. A few leagues farther north, there is a village on the banks of the Ebro, called San Ascensio, for the parish church of which he carved the retablo of the high altar. It was simple and classical in design, the lower part being of the Ionic order, and the upper part of the Corinthian. Between the columns, and in various niches, were bas-reliefs and statues, displaying great care and science in the anatomy, and much power in the composition. On this work, and the stalls of the choir, the artist spent six years; and he was paid for his labour 7,387 ducats, in 1575.

---

[1] Widdrington's *Spain and the Spaniards*, in 1843, vol. i. p. 36. These agreeable volumes are the work of Captain Cook, already quoted, who has changed his name since the publication of his *Sketches in Spain*.

Miguel de Ancheta studied sculpture at Florence and Rome, and afterwards practised it at his native city of Pamplona. For the church of Tafalla, a neighbouring town, he executed a rich retablo; a "St. George slaying the Dragon," in alabaster for a public hall at Zaragoza; and a fine "Assumption of the Virgin," for the high altar of the Cathedral of Burgos. His most important work was the stalls of the choir in Pamplona Cathedral, which were carved in English oak, and were considered the finest in Navarre. Dying before this choir was quite finished, he was buried in the Cathedral cloister, where this pithy epitaph marks his place of rest:—

AQUÍ YACE ANCHETA
ELQUE SUS OBRAS NO ALABÓ
NI LAS AGENAS DESPRECIÓ.

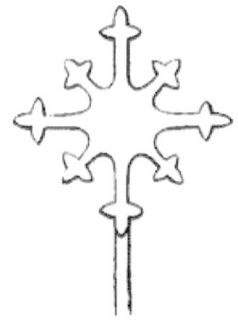

www.ingramcontent.com/pod-product-compliance
Lightning Source LLC
Chambersburg PA
CBHW022109290426
44112CB00008B/605